PRAISE FOR *SPEAKING*

D0591906

"Months after the most historic protests in our lifetimes, we continue ... front the same stubborn inequities, crises, and catastrophes. This stubborn continuity compels us to reevaluate our common assumptions about the nature of the problem. It compels us to renew our political commitments to change but not necessarily in the same ways that we have before. Most of all, the ongoing suffering and despair in our societies compel us to think anew and creatively, sometimes drawing on the historical, for effective ways that ordinary people have confronted the powerful. It compels us to be radical by grabbing hold at the root of our problem—a neoliberal, capitalist world order built on human suffering and abject inequality.

David Palumbo-Liu's *Speaking Out of Place* is a deeply moral and utterly human meditation on the nature of our despair and the means by which it can be transformed. Most of all, he argues that what is missing is our sense of place, belonging, and mutuality that, when intact, showcases our connection and potential for solidarity in our shared struggle for a humane and just world. Here is the exact book we need for the troubled historical moment through which we are living." —**Keeanga-Yamahtta Taylor**, author of *From #BlackLivesMatter to Black Liberation*

"In the face of accelerating fascism and a planet on fire, David Palumbo-Liu provides a road map for finding our political voices by speaking "out of place." This is an urgent call to seize the moment before it's too late." —**Roxanne Dunbar-Ortiz**, author of *Not "A Nation of Immigrants," Settler-Colonialism, White Supremacy, and a History of Erasure and Exclusion*

"It's not enough to be against the rising tide of authoritarianism and climate chaos. David Palumbo-Liu examines how only through "a positive obsession with justice" and a collective willingness to learn to speak a new language and remake our places do we have a chance at saving the planet and building the world we all need." —**Nick Estes**, author of *Our History Is the Future: Standing Rock Versus the Dakota Access Pipeline, and the Long Tradition of Indigenous Resistance*

"David Palumbo-Liu's *Speaking Out of Place* is a wake-up call to the twin dangers of fascism and a no-less cruel and ecocidal neoliberalism. Brilliant, clear-eyed, wide-ranging, and erudite without being esoteric, this book is a vital assault on the repressive amnesia that obliterates the memory of even our most recent struggles. Palumbo-Liu reminds us that we already have all that we need to reimagine our societies and ourselves, to re-forge the solidarity necessary to get us through such catastrophic times, to make this planet a place where voices clamor outside of the violent control of capital, loudly and freely, alive." —**Ben Ehrenreich**, author of *Desert Notebooks: A Road Map for the End of Time* and *The Way to the Spring: Life and Death in Palestine*

"*Speaking Out of Place* is a radical and original reassessment of democratic deliberation and political transformation. Instead of treating 'free speech' in simplistic terms, Palumbo-Liu examines the triad of voice, place, and space. This holistic analysis helps us understand who gets heard, where, and why. True democracy, Palumbo-Liu shows, is a raucous polyphony, a chorus emanating from specific communities and contexts and struggles that reverberates widely, unsettling and challenging those accustomed to controlling the terms of the debate." —**Astra Taylor**, author of *Remake the World: Essays, Reflections, Rebellions*

"David Palumbo-Liu's most recent work is a clarion call, an incisive commentary on our times, and an impressive work of passion and moral clarity. Focusing on forms of contemporary oppression and new social movements, Palumbo-Liu insists upon the centrality of voice and place to the most pressing issues of our time. His writing draws on social and po-litical theory, poetry, activist writing, to show us that the ideologies that still clutch us have as their primary concern "the individual" as economic actor and "the market" and its profit-driven values—a poor way to define the public sphere. In contrast, he allies with those who are generating the value of human and humane interdependence, of commonly shared goods, and of social and economic equality, so often brutally dismissed as fairy tales. But in this work we see how homelessness, displacement, internment, violence, and exploitation are each countered by emergent and intensifying social movements that move beyond national borders to the ideal of a planetary alliance. As an activist and a scholar, Palumbo-Liu shows us what vigilance means in these times. This book takes us through the wretched landscape of our world to the ideals of social trans-formation, calling for a place, the planet, where collective passions can bring about a true and radical democracy." —**Judith Butler**, author of *The Force of Nonviolence: An Ethico-Political Bind*

"Fearless, timely, and necessary. In this bracing, multivalent analysis of our troubled political culture, David Palumbo-Liu offers us a clarion call to action. Reading it, I feel emboldened, encouraged, and powerfully amplified." —**Ruth Ozeki**, author of Booker finalist *A Tale for the Time Being*

"In *Speaking Out of Place* David Palumbo-Liu has brought to the fore the type of text that is rare in our current culture. There is a sort of transversal vector in play that brings with it the unexpected and at the same time the familiar. It is a gem. I loved reading it." —**Saskia Sassen**, author of *Expulsions: Brutality and Complexity in the Global Economy*

"David Palumbo-Liu gives us hope for a world on fire. Digging deep into our common humanity, he urges us to speak, to organize and to fight for justice wherever we live, and to stand down reaction wherever it resides. From Palestine to the Amazon, Palumbo-Liu reminds us to take back the planet that belongs to us, to love ourselves and each other."—**Bill V. Mullen**, author of *James Baldwin: Living in Fire*

"David Palumbo-Liu masterfully paints a global picture of the daunting challenges to our very survival. Rather than use the weight of that challenge to terrify us into action or to crush our hope, he pieces together the most quotidian stories of courage and resistance to show us that revolution is latent within us and that the technologies of our salvation are ones that we have long known and fiercely protected. *Speaking Out of a Place* is profoundly humane, self-aware in its humility, and generous in its thoughtful offerings. Palumbo-Liu reminds us that the horizon before us is not an end but an opportunity for new beginnings." —**Noura Erakat**, author of *Justice for Some: Law and the Question of Palestine*

"The historical and contemporary stories in *Speaking Out of Place* are as instructive as they are inspiring. Palumbo-Liu gives us a global landscape of many dimensions, pulling us into the infinite number of spaces we can disrupt, reshape, and build when we find the courage to insert our "unauthorized" voices. The activists in this book, both well-known and not, speak in words, in dance, in pictures, in food, and even in silence. Read this, and raise your voice." —**Rinku Sen**, author of *The Accidental American: Immigration and Citizenship in the Age of Globalization*

Speaking Out of Place

Getting Our Political Voices Back

DAVID PALUMBO-LIU

Haymarket Books
Chicago, Illinois

Published in 2021 by
Haymarket Books
P.O. Box 180165
Chicago, IL 60618
773-583-7884
www.haymarketbooks.org
info@haymarketbooks.org

ISBN: 978-1-64259-585-7

Distributed to the trade in the US through Consortium Book Sales and
Distribution (www.cbsd.com) and internationally through Ingram Publisher
Services International (www.ingramcontent.com).

This book was published with the generous support of Lannan Foundation and
Wallace Action Fund.

Special discounts are available for bulk purchases by organizations and institutions. Please email orders@haymarketbooks.org for more information.

Cover design by Matt Avery.

Printed in Canada.

Library of Congress Cataloging-in-Publication data is available.

CONTENTS

To all those finding their voices and working for a more just world

INTRODUCTION

> One of the first steps toward creating an enlarged concept of our humanity is to develop an enlarged concept of our relation as human beings to politics.
>
> —James and Grace Lee Boggs, *Revolution and Evolution in the Twentieth Century*[1]

Though written in 1974, the Boggs' prescription above is more pertinent today than ever, as the world confronts unprecedented challenges that threaten both democracy and the planet. During the Trump presidency, the United States experienced what was without doubt its closest brush yet with flat-out fascism. While the country has always had a fascist tendency, never before had fascism gripped the entire governmental apparatus or enjoyed the backing of nearly half the voting public. But the ascent of fascism is not limited to the United States; around the world we see the rise of fascism and ethno-nationalism, and the dominance of neoliberal policies. We must understand this political trend if we are to reconceptualize our relationship to politics and to other human beings.

One way we have lost a sense of being together and of being potent political actors is through the delegation to others of our responsibilities—we have given them our voice. And the people to whom we have given our voice are some of the most irresponsible on earth. By the same token, we have become used to thinking we have no right to have an opinion that does not register on the very limited menu of possibilities that has been set before us. We have also lost a sense that we have a right to determine the nature of our relationship to place, on multiple scales—from our homes and neighborhoods, to our towns and cities, to our countries, to the international sphere, and to the planet. Somehow we have accepted that we depend not on each other, but on the very few people who rule us. We need to shift the focus back to the people, and care wisely for our precarious world—because our leaders have proven themselves both uninterested in the most pressing needs of the planet and incapable of imagining what we need to do.

To begin to meet the challenge set by James and Grace Lee Boggs, I turn to three key words: "voice," "place," and "space." By "voice" I mean not just our actual voices, but all means of human expression, including putting one's body on the line. I use "voice" to name a political, ethical, and moral instrument for affecting change. By "place" I mean more than physical places—like the streets of our neighborhoods—but also those elements of place that form our sense of belonging. Therefore, when those involved with the struggle for social justice occupy the streets and use our voices, we can imagine *belonging with others*—those who are also protesting in streets across the globe. In this sense, we are in the same place, and we are filling it with the same voice.

Taking the ideas of "voice" and "place" together, we are often told that we are "speaking out of place," or that we "don't know our place." When that happens, we are being chastised and silenced. The message of this book is that we need to both challenge such an accusation—that we have overstepped the proper boundaries—and to reclaim the "place" of speaking, by inventing our own places from which to speak. Finally, and in a closely related way, I use "space" to refer to people's ability to symbolically "fill" actual places with meaning. Often this meaning is subversive or forbidden; think, for example, of professional football players "taking a knee" at a stadium, a place supposedly "out of bounds" for political activism. Much to the chagrin of people who wish to "escape from politics," these activist-athletes make this shared place into their "space," their arena for staging protest. We can and should be doing so in other places as well: we must revise our notion of what constitutes political activism and make every public space an anti-fascist, anti-racist, and pro-democratic one. To do this we must disabuse ourselves of a sense that has always been cultivated by people in power—that "ordinary citizens" are unqualified and unable to speak on issues that deeply affect their lives, and that they must defer to experts, pundits, and those in power. These "ordinary" people include most especially young people, people of color, and the poor. This book is meant to help us all reimagine and reinvigorate ourselves, our capacities, our sense of politics and of solidarity—because we are going to need each other.

It does not matter that Donald Trump was defeated in his 2020 bid for a second term as president, and those who would believe we are past this dark stage of our history are mistaken for at least three reasons. First, during his presidency Trump systematically filled the courts with reactionary judges and purged career officers in every branch of government, replacing them with loyalists. Whether he is president or not, these individuals are ideologically like-minded, and they are not going anywhere. All that remains to be seen is how long it will take before these reactionary forces regroup. The second reason it is foolhardy to celebrate Trump's defeat is that the sentiments and ideologies that gave rise to his presidency in the first place did not come from someplace outside the United States. Nor are they going anywhere, except, perhaps, underground for a while. They will simply be looking for a new host. Finally, we must bear in mind Joe Biden's 2020 campaign promise to Wall Street: "Nothing is going to change." By that he meant that the norms of the market would be reinstated once he took over the presidency from the chaotic and destabilizing rantings of Donald Trump—the same investments of energy, capital, and resources would circulate to benefit the same oligarchs. Here I make the case that instead of pinning our hopes on one or another charismatic political leader, we should summon the energy and strength we unearthed in our opposition to Trump and all that he stood for, and use it to create and embody a different sense of how to live and strive for social, economic, and political justice. To do so would bring about a different kind of political life than the one centrists and rightists want us to settle for. This would mean regaining our own voices instead of letting others speak for us—the dangers of which history has amply demonstrated.

Two developments in particular helped push Donald Trump out of office. One was the COVID-19 pandemic. The pandemic reached into all of our lives and touched us in all sorts of ways—for more than a half million individuals and their loved ones in the United States alone, in the most profound way possible. Had Trump had any capacity or will to act as a humane and competent leader, many of those lives would not have been lost, and both the short- and long-term damage of the pandemic could have been better contained. His incompetence and narcissism resulted in massive death and destruction, in ways that cannot be blamed on the virus alone.

While the pandemic was a force of nature, the second development that helped topple Trump was brought about by masses of people drawn together by outrage and disgust over the brutal murders of Black people at the hands of the police, or in some cases, self-appointed vigilantes operating with nearly the same impunity. The world was shown in real time the torture and asphyxiation of George Floyd as he begged for his life, and the subsequent spectacle as police tear-gassed, beat, kicked, and clubbed peaceful demonstrators protesting his killing and, more broadly, the long history of police brutality against Black people. These protests were made up of people of all skin tones, young and old. This massive moral army convened spontaneously; demonstrations occurred in every state in the Union, in cities, suburbs, and rural places. And these protests spread globally, as people marched both in solidarity with US demonstrators and in protest against the racist brutality of state actors in their nations.

While these mass demonstrations erupted out of pure moral outrage, such outrage cannot be sustained forever; indeed, it eventually subsided among the battered survivors of those four years of Trumpism—which saw constant attacks on civil liberties, human rights, freedom of the press, women, minorities, the environment, and international relations. While we might take comfort in the return to "normalcy" with Biden's election, we must never forget that for most of America, the pre-Trump "normal" was terrible. Widespread racism, poverty, burgeoning health costs, and other sources of suffering are not gone and can easily be used by opportunistic politicians to launch new campaigns of bigotry.

Thus, between the precarity of our devastated planet and a political system that lies in tatters, we stand at a decisive point in history. We can either backslide into the status quo, or we can learn from the lessons of the Trump era, as well as those learned during previous times of grave injustice, hate, and destruction, and transform the very idea of "normal life." In this book, I argue that to do this we must continue the righteous momentum of the anti-Trump protests and embrace it, teach it, and embody it in our everyday lives. We need to demonstrate a better way of living together, for the sake of each other and others to come, and for the sake of the planet. Two things are certain: we will not have another chance, and it will take all of us. The pandemic and the global collective action against police and state brutality have exposed entrenched systemic weaknesses and inequities that are supported by ideologies of hatred and greed. Those ideologies are not free-floating abstractions, but things people take on board in all sorts of ways—if not actively, then by letting others persuade them of their legitimacy. This book is an argument for decolonizing our minds and modeling, in our words and actions, a set of values that is humane and just. But first, I need to set the stage.

Today's Historical Moment

During the 2016 presidential campaign, I was alarmed by the way Trump claimed to speak for others, and the ways his supporters had gladly given over their voices to him. He had clearly tapped into a set of beliefs that they had felt unable to express openly. Trump was voicing those hateful, bigoted, and stupid things, day after day, night after night, and seemingly across all media platforms, appearing on mainstream talk shows, across platforms and web forums of the so-called alt-right, and even on progressive sites—not to mention Facebook, Twitter, and other social media. The amplification of his voice became such that one could neither escape it nor the flood of commentary that came in the wake of every speech, every press conference, indeed every utterance and every tweet. In the face of this overwhelming flood, my question became: What about other voices? The liberal and the conservative media had their pundits, their go-to sources on Wall Street, inside the Beltway, in think tanks, and in the academy, and they were all caught up in the mode of simply responding to Trump. The "opinions" they amplified were cherry-picked, tailor-made to create a conventional frame around an entirely unconventional phenomenon. Trump continued to dominate every news cycle, using lies and distortions to create chaos and uncertainty, stir fears, and breed animosity.

Nevertheless, the progressive Left began to push its way into the public eye, buoyed by the election of Alexandria Ocasio-Cortez to New York's fourteenth congressional district in 2018, along with Ilhan Omar in Minnesota, Ayanna Pressley in Massachusetts, and Rashida Tlaib in Michigan. Their newfound influence came in tandem with the

exponential growth of the Democratic Socialists of America (DSA), followed by the momentous surge of Bernie Sanders's second presidential
campaign in 2020, in which Sanders gained more support than any other candidacy except Biden, who benefited from the full support of the
mainstream media and of the Democratic National Committee (DNC).
It became patently clear that Sanders's diagnoses of the catastrophes that
had been unleashed since Trump took office had gained widespread cred-
ibility. By late March 2020 it had come down to this, as scholar-activist
Keeanga-Yamahtta Taylor wrote in an article for *The New Yorker*, aptly
titled "Reality Has Endorsed Bernie Sanders":

> The argument for resuming a viable social-welfare state is about not
> only attending to the immediate needs of tens of millions of people but
> also re-establishing social connectivity, collective responsibility, and a
> sense of common purpose, if not common wealth. In an unrelenting
> and unemotional way, COVID-19 is demonstrating the vastness of
> our human connection and mutuality. Our collectivity must be borne
> out in public policies that repair the friable welfare infrastructure that
> threatens to collapse beneath our social weight.[2]

Socialist sensibilities and materialist understandings of everyday life became part of popular political discourse exactly because they were validat-
ed by the absence of anything vaguely resembling concern for the public
good. Perhaps most importantly, socialism was the preferred political
understanding of rising numbers of young people who were coming of
age during two recessions, immense environmental degradation, and persistent police killings of Black and brown men, women, and non-binary
people. Socialism resonated with them, and many older people as well,
as the logical response to a prevailing disillusionment with the conventional political parties, both of which are deeply entrenched in, and speak
the language of, neoliberalism. Departing from the tendency to fixate on
Democrats and Republicans, critical theorist Nancy Fraser identifies the
new hegemonic forces, more precisely, as two different brands of neoliberalism: reactionary and progressive. Neither of the two is able or willing
to address the failure of political democracy: "Since both are in bed with
global finance, neither can challenge financialization, de-industrialization,
or corporate globalization. Neither can redress declining living standards,
ballooning debt, climate change, 'care deficits,' or intolerable stresses on

community life. To reinstall either of these blocks in power is to ensure not just a continuation but an intensification of the current crisis."[3]

The moral bankruptcy of both major political parties is indexed by the fact that support for socialism never stopped growing, even in the face of ridicule and derision from liberals and conservatives, and either neglect or distortion from the media. As Bhaskar Sunkara, founding editor of *Jacobin* magazine, noted:

> Even after being subjected to three years of attacks from both the Right and corporate Democrats, Bernie Sanders is among the most popular politicians in the United States. His central demands—a universal jobs program and single-payer health insurance—both enjoy substantial support among voters. Polls show that 52 percent want a jobs guarantee nationwide, with an even higher favorability in poor states like Mississippi (72 percent). Medicare for All could be just as popular a platform plank: in April 2018 support for the measure crept above 50 percent.[4]

And a year later, facing an audience on *Fox News*, Sanders's comments on the need for economic justice drew applause:

> When an audience member asked him about why he calls himself a democratic socialist, he didn't shy away from the term: "Democratic socialism to me is creating a government, and an economy, and a society that works for all rather than just the top 1%." He denounced absurd inequalities and said that human beings were entitled to basic rights of health and education, things that shouldn't be privileges, the result of accidents of birth. And an audience that we've been told hated socialism, and feared government, applauded.[5]

A Gallup poll taken a month later in May of 2019 showed that 43 percent of those surveyed said some form of socialism would be good for the country. Taken in the context of American politics since the 1950s, this is a remarkable figure.[6]

Despite a slew of early primary victories, the Sanders campaign faltered, for a number of reasons. The fact that he stood in stark contrast to every other Democratic candidate, along with his early front-runner status, meant that the other candidates not only ganged up on him, but also brought with them the support of the Democratic establishment. He was called a "radical," red-baited for his praise for the advances in Cuban society due to Fidel Castro's reforms, and in the end, Democrats sought refuge in the remainder and reminder of the Obama era: Joe Biden. Also instrumental in tamping down the surge of Bernie Sanders was the on-slaught of the pandemic, which ended the rallies to which Sanders was drawing huge numbers, as well as the news coverage they brought. It also made people afraid to go to the polls, and the polls themselves proved to be problem-ridden. Compounded by the effects of voter suppression and gerrymandering, the resulting storm was enough to swamp Sanders's presidential bid.[7]

Nonetheless, as Sanders repeatedly said during the campaign, it wasn't about him; it was about "us." The urgency of that message became even more pronounced in the days and weeks after he suspended his campaign. If outrage over economic inequality and the lack of affordable health care were the issues at that propelled him, and socialism, forward, the catastrophe of the pandemic and the murder of George Floyd in Minneapolis on May 25, 2020, illuminated even more intensely and broadly the failures of the government to attend to the needs of the people. In response to these events, we saw masses of people acting in solidarity and caring for each other in heroic and profound manners.

By May 2020, the United States had nearly the greatest number of deaths per capita—about 30 per 100,000 people.[8] And by June, the country, which has 4 percent of the world's population, accounted for 25 percent of cases. As one journalist put it, "The world [was] putting America in quarantine."[9] Trump had finally met a foe he could not hoodwink—after all, he and his incompetent allies were unable to contain nature. Nevertheless, despite the spread of mass illness and death, Trump tried to force people back to work in order to calm the tumbling stock markets, since he was ostensibly elected on the promise that he would make the economy "great." With forty million people out of work, Trump's top economic advisor, Kevin Hassett, spoke about the masses of working people with a revealing air of instrumentality: "Our capital stock hasn't been destroyed—our human capital stock is ready to get back to work, and so there are lots of reasons to believe that we can get going way faster than we have in previous crises."[10] As many were quick to point out, "capital stock" is common parlance among economists; nevertheless, in an address to the broad public, the term was a clear expression of Hassett's and Trump's view of workers as mere automatons. Ultimately, it was the ill and the dead who paid the price of Trump's tactics of delay, ignorance, and mendacity.[11]

All too soon, as an already-frayed safety net failed and corpses piled up, the economy buckled. Whole industries virtually collapsed (hotels and airlines, in particular), and at one time a barrel of oil carried a negative value. These crises shone a light on long-standing structures of income inequality and state violence; on a corrupt, dysfunctional federal government; and on lethal racism. And because the pandemic was caused by viruses transmitted from nonhuman animals to humans, it underscored the degradation of the environment and the devastating effects of climate change, which continues to bring about the forced migration of animals outside of their endemic habitats, along with the melting of permafrost that unleashes ancient deposits of greenhouse gases, as well as bacteria long believed extinct. As the famed primatologist and conservationist Jane Goodall told the French press:

> It is our disregard for nature and our disrespect of the animals we should share the planet with that has caused this pandemic, that was predicted long ago. Because as we destroy, let's say the forest, the different species of animals in the forest are forced into a proximity and therefore diseases are being passed from one animal to another, and that second animal is then most likely to infect humans as it is forced into closer contact with humans. It's also the animals who are hunted for food, sold in markets in Africa or in the meat market for wild animals in Asia, especially China, and our intensive farms where we cruelly crowd together billions of animals around the world. These are the conditions that create an opportunity for the viruses to jump from animals across the species barrier to humans.[12]

As early as 2014, journalists had warned of "zombie diseases of climate change":

> The newly active permafrost is packed with old *stuff*: dead plants, dead animals, mosses buried and reburied by dust and snow. This matter, long protected from decomposition by the cold, is finally rotting, and releasing gases into the atmosphere that could quicken the rate of global warming. This matter is also full of pathogens: bacteria and viruses long immobilized by the frost. Many of these pathogens may be able to survive a gentle thaw—and if they do, researchers warn, they could re-infect humanity.[13]

In the face of the ruthlessness of both the virus and the capitalist system of extraction and exploitation, people suddenly became aware of a basic fact of life: we are all interdependent. In the words of Margaret Levi, director

of the Center for Advanced Study in the Behavioral Sciences at Stanford
University:

> We are in a community of fate that COVID-19 has created. Our desti-
> nies are now clearly entwined as we join together to fight this virus and
> protect ourselves and our societies. The pandemic makes us aware of
> our reliance on and obligations to a wide network extending beyond
> family, friends, and neighbors to all those who contribute to our health
> care, supply chains, education of our children, etc. Even the invisible
> workers are becoming visible: the grocery clerks, the cleaners, the san-
> itation personnel who make it possible to survive and thrive. Such a
> community of fate can cut across polarization and become the basis of
> mobilization for the policies to promote flourishing.[14]

In this sense, the virus made a distinctly political point about capitalism's
indifference to human suffering, for it made plain its role in the creation
and exacerbation of suffering. It also revealed, for all to see, the bankruptcy
of the neoliberal notion of the individual as the only real unit of value. The
onslaught of death, alienation, and hopelessness that spared no national
space threw into relief the fact that the system was entirely dysfunctional.
It was in that context that the need for a radically different way of life and
politics became vividly clear. As a cochair of the Detroit chapter of the
Democratic Socialists of America remarked: "People are really starting to
just look around and say, 'Man, capitalism isn't working.' . . . If the markets can't even produce hand sanitizer or toilet paper or masks during a
plague—what good is this system?"[15] And as the world was reeling under
the devastation caused by the pandemic, the murders of Ahmaud Arbery,
George Floyd, Tony McDade, Breonna Taylor, and countless others before
them in the United States joined the pandemic in the public consciousness.
The quick succession of the killings, and in the case of Arbery and Floyd,
their explicit premeditation by white civilians and a white policeman, supported by three other cops, immediately brought forth the still-vivid memories of other murders of Black men, women, and non-binary people. Since
August 2014 we had seen the killings of Michael Brown, Trayvon Martin,
Eric Garner, Dontre Hamilton, John Crawford III, Ezell Ford, Dante Parker,
Tanisha Anderson, Akai Gurley, Tamir Rice, Rumain Brisbon, Jerame Reid,
Tony Robinson, Eric Harris, Walter Scott, Freddie Gray, Sandra Bland, and
many, many others. All of them were unarmed.[16]

In the face of this immense grief and anger, tens of thousands of people marched under the banner of #BlackLivesMatter. In the same manner that a new understanding emerged that the "economy" was dependent on the lives and bodies of workers who Trump was more than happy to sacrifice, now more and more people realized that the "peace" enjoyed by most of the white population was bought at the expense of Black lives. Crucially, people began to understand both of these issues in political terms. They were beginning to connect the dots. An informal multiracial, multigenerational coalition emerged across the country as masses of people donned masks and marched, the urgency of their protest only intensified by the fact that it was taking place in the midst of the pandemic. Indeed, a politicized "community of care" developed among protesters and health care professionals and others—all in support of life, dignity, and justice.[17] In response, Trump called on police and the military to put down what he and others called "Antifa" and "Marxist" "riots." Throughout Trump's presidency, such terms had been a frequent trope; he even borrowed a false news report from an alt-right media site and slapped the label of "Antifa agitator" on a 75-year-old white male pacifist who was brutally attacked by the police, suffering serious head injuries.[18] The branding of all opposition as "Antifa" activism counts on a basic and willful distortion of anti-fascist work. It also obscures the obvious question: What, at this precise historical moment, would warrant alarm over fascism, and resistance to it?

Politics at a Crossroads

At this point, I want to stop and take stock of the different strands of political affiliations and commitments that these crises brought to the fore. Only after giving at least a brief account of the different ideological leanings that were at play in 2020 can we tackle the idea of political "voice" and understand well the stakes of the struggle to shift attitudes toward political engagement. While each of these ideologies, tendencies, and affiliations were certainly present on the American landscape well before the Trump presidency, there can be no doubt that his ascension to the White House—along with his control over the Senate and the Department of Justice, and placement of ultraconservative justices on the Supreme Court—facilitated the convergence of fascist, white supremacist, alt-right, and evangelical forces. Trump instilled an overwhelming

sense of fear in the minds of members of Congress, encouraged lawless-
ness within the Department of Justice and the police, and stoked racism,
sexism, anti-Semitism, and Islamophobia like no other leader before him.
Indeed, as soon as Donald Trump had emerged as a candidate for the
presidency, people had commented on his "fascist" ideas and persona. In
the course of his term, he did nothing to prove them wrong—in fact,
everything he did seemed calculated to embody fascism.

Fascism is commonly understood as taking form in the consolidation
of political and financial elites, the destruction of democracy, the scape-
goating and elimination of certain populations, and the creation of a cult
of authoritarianism, characterized by faith in a "strong man" figure who
promises to bring a civilization back from the brink of extinction and
restore it to its former glory. Its hallmarks are violence, force, disinfor-
mation, and attacks on journalists, intellectuals, and others who might
threaten the leader's monopoly on "the truth," or "the facts."[19]

Impatient with exercises in discovering what counts as pure "fascism,"
the Italian polymath Umberto Eco opted to focus on something broader,
what he called "ur-fascism." According to Eco, among its tendencies are
the following:

> Ur-Fascism grows up and seeks for consensus by exploiting and exac-
> erbating the natural fear of difference. The first appeal of a fascist or
> prematurely fascist movement is an appeal against the intruders. Thus
> Ur-Fascism is racist by definition. . . . Ur-Fascism derives from individ-
> ual or social frustration. That is why one of the most typical features
> of the historical fascism was the appeal to a frustrated middle class, a
> class suffering from an economic crisis or feelings of political humil-
> iation, and frightened by the pressure of lower social groups. . . . To
> people who feel deprived of a clear social identity, Ur-Fascism says that
> their only privilege is the most common one, to be born in the same
> country. This is the origin of nationalism. Besides, the only ones who
> can provide an identity to the nation are its enemies. Thus at the root
> of the Ur-Fascist psychology there is the obsession with a plot, possibly
> an international one. The followers must feel besieged.[20]

Indeed, the "fear of difference" was a mainstay of Trump's rhetoric, as
seen in his persistent attacks on difference in nearly all its forms—in
terms of race, national origin, gender and sexuality, and perspective.

Crucially, besides launching this war on difference, he furthered
a long-standing conservative war against the checks and balances of

government. Trump put people in power who declared that the president had absolute power, that he could "do whatever he wants."[21] The fact that Trump was impeached by the House, with vast amounts of evidence, did not prevent what seemed a foregone conclusion—that he would be exonerated in the Republican Senate. Senate leader Mitch McConnell declared, even before the Senate hearings began, that there would be no impeachment in the Senate, and that his colleagues would be working in close consultation with the president's lawyers. *Fox News* proclaimed, "McConnell told Fox News Thursday night that he will coordinate the defense of President Trump in any impeachment trial with White House lawyers and proclaimed that there was 'zero chance' the president would be removed from office."[22] Only someone feeling completely in power could make such a pronouncement, in violation of the very oath all senators take to hear a case dispassionately.

Fascism thrived in the ascension of white supremacism, with Trump naming as one of his top advisors Stephen Miller—a man who would soon facilitate terrorist acts against immigrants, creating concentration camps at the US–Mexico border where refugees from Central America and Mexico were held, summarily stripped of their rights.[23] As historian Alexandra Minna Stern noted:

> According to white nationalists, the foremost tactics for forging a white ethno-state are the forced and incentivized removals of non-white peoples, through repatriation and deportation, the revocation of birthright citizenship, ideally retroactively, as well as the annulment of naturalization of those lacking "good character." One especially horrific conceit of the proposed white ethno-state is the purging of non-white children, given that they embody America's multiracial future and portend the coming of "white genocide."[24]

Aiding and abetting such racist attacks was the evangelical Right—indeed, the group that formed Trump's most loyal base. Here, too, Trump put people like Mike Pompeo in positions of enormous power. As secretary of state, Pompeo made no secret of his loyalties and his Christian Right agenda. One of the first signs of his frontal attack on international relations was seen when he convened of a panel on "unalienable rights," which sought to replace normative international human rights conventions and protocols with a unilateral "American" one. Reacting to this with shock and dismay, a coalition of organizations—including Robert F. Kennedy Human Rights, the Center for Health and Gender Equity, the Council for Global Equality, and the Global Justice Center—filed a suit against Pompeo and the State Department, stating that Pompeo's panel was "stacked with members who have staked out positions hostile to LGBTQ and reproductive rights . . . holding closed door meetings to conduct significant Commission business outside of the public's view and scrutiny, including efforts to redefine human rights terminology and commitments" and was "failing to provide adequate notice of meetings and to release key documents to the public." Mark Bromley, chair of the Council for Global Equality, stated, "Secretary Pompeo often argues that the modern proliferation of human rights claims cheapens the currency of human rights but it is this illegal Commission, with its warped use of religious freedom and natural law to deny rights, that cheapens the very notion of religious freedom and our country's proud tradition of standing up for the rights of those who are most vulnerable."[25] Indeed, Donald Trump's foreign policy was deeply informed by both the evangelical Right and by his own messianic delusions. During his April 2019 state visit to the UK, the *Guardian* reported: "Over an ensuing half-hour rant, Trump trucked in antisemitic tropes, insulted the Danish prime minister, insisted he wasn't racist, bragged about the performance of his former Apprentice reality show, denied starting a trade war with China, praised Vladimir Putin and told reporters that he, Trump, was the 'Chosen One'—all within hours of referring to himself as the 'King of Israel.'"[26]

A draft of the report of the commission claims that the primary tradition "that formed the American spirit" was "Protestant Christianity . . . infused with the beautiful Biblical teachings that every human being is imbued with dignity and bears responsibilities toward fellow human beings, because each is made in the image of God." It goes on to say that "[f]oremost among the unalienable rights that government is established to secure . . . are property rights and religious liberty." It is hard to square "religious liberty" with the declaration that the fundamental basis of the "American spirit" is "Protestant Christianity," especially as Pompeo, here as elsewhere, has made no secret of the extremist, evangelical version of Christianity that he not only endorses, but uses in policy making. Likewise, his emphasis on property rights is skewed toward a very capacious view of that idea—from Confederate statues to so called "stand your ground" laws to gated communities and corporate "property" of all sorts. The draft itself reads like a political campaign and features a large color photo of Pompeo on the second page. If there was any doubt about who might be Trump's successor in a bid for an extreme Right evangelical candidate, Pompeo made his intentions clear.[27] The episode that will go down in history as the epitome of Trump's racism, fascism, and indebtedness to the evangelical Right came on June 2, 2020, in Washington, DC, when he ordered the police and National Guard to beat peaceful protesters and fire tear gas at them so that the street could be cleared for his surprise march to St. John's Episcopal Church, where he stood in front of the church for a few minutes, held up a Bible (upside down), had his photo taken, and then left.[28]

Upon witnessing the attack and the photo-op, Bishop Mariann Edgar Budde of the Episcopal Diocese of Washington voiced her outrage:

> The President did not pray when he came to St. John's, nor . . . did he acknowledge the agony of our country right now. . . . And in particular, that of the people of color in our nation . . . who are rightfully demanding an end to 400 years of systemic racism and white supremacy in our country. And I just want the world to know, that we in the diocese of Washington, following Jesus and his way of love . . . we distance ourselves from the incendiary language of this President. . . . We align ourselves with those seeking justice for the death of George Floyd and countless others. . . . And I just can't believe what my eyes have seen."[29]

Trump's treatment of the streets as "war zones" that had to be "dominated" reached new depths in late July, when he sent unidentified troops in camouflage clothing, helmets, and gas masks, into Portland, Oregon. These troops were in fact members of the Border Patrol Tactical Unit (BORTAC), an elite group comparable to the Navy SEALs. According to reporter Ed Pilkington, "Bortac agents are trained for Swat-style raids on organized gangs smuggling immigrants or drugs across the US border. They have been deployed in Iraq and Afghanistan, as well as in many Latin American countries."[30] The fact that they were, for all intents and purposes, indistinguishable from alt-right groups like the Proud Boys and Patriot Prayer meant that their presence and provocations heightened tensions in what were largely peaceful demonstrations for Black lives and democracy. These forces began wantonly attacking protesters and non-protesters alike, dragging them into unmarked vehicles and interrogating them without charge. The *Guardian* rightly named this "made-for-TV fascism";

just as when Trump had "cleared" the streets for his Bible photo-op, the ex–reality TV host had designed the Portland offensive to play to his base across the mediascape.[31]

While it is critical to name fascism for what it is, it would be a huge mistake to then expect moderate Republicans or Democrats to be vastly more pro-democracy. Liberals find it easy to place the blame for Trump entirely on Republicans, and to assume a superior position when it comes to issues of injustice and economic destruction. But, as historian and sociologist Harvey Kaye puts it:

> Republicans have had no monopoly on subverting democracy and the rights of working people. When and where were workers and environmental activists heard when the Clinton administration negotiated NAFTA [North American Free Trade Agreement] and the Obama administration negotiated the now derailed TPP [Trans-Pacific Partnership] which Obama saw as central to his "legacy"? When and where were the American people brought into the conversation when the Obama White House negotiated the Affordable Care Act with Big Pharma and the health insurance industry, accepting concessions that would come home to haunt the early successes of the act? And let's not forget that it was not only Senate Republicans who voted for the Bush administration's USA Patriot Act in 2001, a law that's critically threatened the privacy of US citizens. Only one Democratic senator dissented, Wisconsin's Russell Feingold. We have had nothing less than 40 years of creeping authoritarianism.[32]

Since 1980, and increasingly since the election of Bill Clinton, the country has been run less by Democrats or Republicans and more by a neoliberal elite that has in many ways remained perfectly comfortable with a brand of neofascism. And this is true not only of the United States but also of many other dominant nation-states. In 2018, French sociologist Éric Fassin offered a broader picture of the phenomena Kaye noted above:

> How can we make sense jointly of these two simultaneous phenomena— the rise of the far right, in Europe and elsewhere, and the authoritarian evolution of neoliberal regimes? On the one hand, we have white supremacy and political xenophobia, from Donald Trump to Viktor Orbán or Matteo Salvini. On the other, what can be called "democratic coups." Remember Greece? . . . the "democratic" variation of the coup requires "banks, not tanks." The same applies to Brazil, from Dilma to Lula: a military coup was not needed; parliamentary votes and judicial decisions do the job. . . .

[T]here is nothing incompatible between neoliberal policies and far-right politics: the EU has now accepted far-right governments. . . . The EU thus subcontracts the handling of the refugee crisis to Erdoğan's Turkey and to Libya's mafia-like coastguards. Again, France is no exception, especially when it comes to migrants. It is true that Macron applauded when Trump, under pressure from all sides, decided to drop his policy of separating undocumented aliens from their children; but the consequence is that the US will follow the example of France: children sent with their parents to detention centers.[33]

In fact, as far back as 1935, the Marxist playwright Bertolt Brecht had argued that "fascism is the true face of capitalism." He pointed out that "democracy" can cover over the real violence of fascism:

Democracy still serves in these countries to achieve the results for which violence is needed in others, namely, to guarantee private ownership of the means of production. The private monopoly of factories, mines, and land creates barbarous conditions everywhere, but in some places these conditions do not so forcibly strike the eye. Barbarism strikes the eye only when it happens that monopoly can be protected only by open violence.[34]

What we found, then, in Trump's willingness to let the violence of the pandemic and the violence of the state fall upon common people, was an extraordinary moment—one in which the operations of neoliberal capitalism and fascist racism were laid bare with a vengeance. The greatest mistake we could make would be to let that exposure be covered up and forgotten. It would be as if the sun finally shone brightly on evil, and we shielded our eyes from it. The dominance of neoliberalism has a stake in the erosion of democracy's possibilities, and if we avert our eyes from its less visible operations, we will lose it. One of the most hopeful signs that more and more people were now actually *looking* for political and social alternatives to the vacuous and moribund "norm" came with the 2018 election of a socialist to the US Congress.

It was precisely the remarkable success of Alexandria Ocasio-Cortez that the neoliberal wing of the Democratic Party found alarming. Alarming because an openly and proudly socialist candidate had not only emerged outside the dominant political machine, had not only won elected office, displacing its preferred candidate, but, most importantly, because she did not then fall into line with the DNC, but rather continued precisely the same political trajectory that had brought her to office. And her words hit home within a burgeoning socialist base.[35] Ocasio-Cortez's election, and that of Omar, Pressley, and Tlaib, added significantly to the idea that Bernie Sanders had instilled in the American psyche—democratic social-ism was not "radical" in the ways both the Republicans and Democrats were saying it was; that is, it was not "extreme." Rather, socialism was radical in the true sense of the word. As the storied scholar-activist Angela Davis puts it: "'Radical' simply means 'grasping things at the root.'"

In order to convert sporadic, event-based, eruptive energy into a sustained movement, it is essential that we break down the "experts as leaders" mentality, along with the pundit-dependent and celebrity-driven model of charismatic political life, the fixation with the two-party system, and indeed with electoral politics as a whole. In their place, we must as-semble a broad coalition of people from all walks of life to work together, empowering themselves to make a set of common demands for fairness, equality, and justice. And to do this we must regain our radical social and political identities, and our voice.

Voice and Place

> There's really no such thing as the "voiceless." There are only the deliberately silenced, or the preferably unheard.
>
> —Arundhati Roy

Above I mentioned Trump's "visit" to St. John's Episcopal Church in June 2020. I return to this point because it provides exactly the negative im-age of what I am arguing for in this book. Trump used state power to violently displace people from their rightful place, and at the same time to silence their voices. He broke up the public common ground and the freedom to speak, so that his monotonous image could take their place. What I am arguing for is precisely the opposite: we need to reclaim public space and shout over the repressive speech of the powerful. Make no mis-take—Donald Trump is simply the latest in a long line of anti-democratic, authoritarian figures whose modus operandi is precisely the same, and there are plenty still to carry on his work.

We need to remember that the very term "fascism" comes from *fasces*, a bundle of wooden rods surrounding and supporting an axe handle, from which the head of the axe protrudes. It was a symbol designating a Roman magistrate, signifying the concentration of power, and it was also a real object carried on the magistrate's left shoulder. In the twentieth century, the symbol was reanimated by Italian fascists. This image of concentration of power in the state, and the suppression of other voices, gives us a basic model against which to pose democracy, and the democratization of voice. It is a battle between those with voice and those without it, characterizing one of the basic confrontations of all politics. Again, it is a *radical* political moment. To make good on this moment will require that we understand both our power and our obligation to award rights to others, instead of merely counting on states or governments to do so. We are so used to thinking of rights as someone else's responsibility that we have forgotten a crucial feature of democracy: we, the masses, have the capacity to envision what the state cannot, or will not, see in terms of rights. To fight fascism thus first requires that we demystify, and then dismantle, the *fasces*.

To further illuminate this issue, I turn to the German-born humanist thinker Hannah Arendt and her famous phrase "the right to have rights," which comes from her 1951 essay "The Decline of the Nation-State and the End of the Rights of Man."[36] Of particular importance here is the passage where Arendt shows how and why nation-states are imperfect vehicles for the granting of rights: at a certain point in history, there occurred "the transformation of the state from an instrument of the law into an instrument of the nation." By that she means we see the emergence of ethno-nationalism: "The nation had conquered the state, national interest had priority over law long before Hitler could pronounce 'right is what is good for the German people.'"[37] And this is precisely the dangerous place in which we find ourselves, with Trump's proud adoption of the label of "nationalist," and indeed the proliferation of nationalist regimes all over the world. This power grab relies on a paradigm that narrows the scope of rights dramatically and makes them the property of only some of the people. The nation-state then leverages one group against the other.

Thus, when it comes to a model for human rights, we need to look somewhere other than nations, which Arendt claims have become ethno-nations that distribute rights unequally and with prejudice. So who else can we rely on to perceive a need for rights, and to work to grant them as justice requires? Looking at her own age, Arendt sees some hope in a new burgeoning human capacity, one "in which 'humanity' has in effect assumed the role formerly ascribed to nature or history." What she means by this is that instead of thinking only "nature" or some abstract force called "history" can endow rights, "in this context . . . the right to have rights, or the right of every individual to being to humanity, should be guaranteed by humanity itself."[38] This might well be taken as Arendt's prescription that humanity reconceptualize its relationship to politics, as James and Grace Lee Boggs would suggest much later.

That might seem like the end of her argument—a challenge to "humanity" to take on the project of not only creating, but also of guaranteeing universal human rights, independent of any bestowments that might issue forth from states or formal international bodies such as the United Nations. But there is a missing connection that we need to look at carefully—for "humanity," in order to perform this urgent task, requires a specific "place in the world": "The fundamental deprivation of human rights is manifested first and above all in the deprivation of a place in the world which makes opinions significant and actions effective." It is this "place in the world" that refugees and stateless people no longer have.[39] In the chapters that follow, I will argue that in today's world, the erosion of the right to have rights is due to something else besides the lack of a nation to which one belongs—a loss that can nevertheless be attributed to the fact that more and more people find themselves in a situation not unlike the stateless people whose condition prompted Arendt to compose her essay in the first place. Today we find ourselves lacking a political voice that is necessarily "significant" or "effective," at the same time we lack a "place" where our opinions count.

We should use this idea of a "place in the world which makes opinions significant" to describe the condition under which we can begin to fulfill the mission of creating rights. We are thus obliged to *create that place on our own*, a common place, so to speak, where we grant each other and ourselves at once the capacity to utter significant things. Simply put, our voices can be heard and recognized as such because we, in entering this conversation, are predisposed to hear and, critically, to listen broadly and with a mind toward fighting the very real effects of fascism and neoliberalism. But this is just the first step. The second step, which relies on the first, is to create worlds that are open to others, places of justice. That can entail breaking the hold some people have on some places, places they fashion such that they reverberate with their voices alone; it can also entail creating different places altogether. In either case it involves action, and action alongside others. In the case of the false image of Trump in front of St. John's, this means aligning ourselves with the protesters he drove away, and it means shifting our view from the figure of a "leader" to a view of ourselves occupying the public streets.

Now, what does this exclusion look like, and what does it have to do with "voice"? How have we been trained to ignore the voices of others? And, how have we submitted to a condition in which we are deprived of a place in the world where our opinions are significant? In other writings Arendt calls up Aristotle's use of the term *aneu logon* (without words) to describe those who have the faculty of speech but are excluded from political membership; therefore, no matter what they say, their utterances are not recognized as speech but heard as mere noise. In this case, he is referring to groups located outside the *polis*—enslaved people and barbarians. Under this political condition, the sounds produced by their "voices" are the equivalent of noise produced by animals.[40]

The French political philosopher Jacques Rancière refers to the same ancient concept, to which he adds an important political element. Instead of a "decisive opposition" between those who have speech and those who do not, Rancière sees a continual struggle over where one is located on that sociopolitical map. For him, this struggle over where one fits in the dyad of voice/voiceless is at the heart of politics: "Political activity is whatever shifts a body from a place assigned to it or changes a place's destination. It makes visible what had no business being seen and makes heard a discourse where once there was only place for noise; it makes understood as discourse what was once only heard as noise."[41] When Rancière talks about making something visible what has "no business being seen," and making a discourse heard where "once there was only place for noise," this is what I have been calling "speaking out of place": we entitle ourselves to appear in public as people with voices that must be reckoned with. We do not unquestioningly accept the policing of place and the muzzling of voices. We dare speak unpopular things, and we do not bow before "experts" or "opinion makers" in the form of elected officials. We voice our own opinions outside the vocabulary of pundits; we invent a political discourse that speaks to real needs and real desires that will not be contained. And we do so as members of a community that cares seriously for others, in the sense that they are our equals. This means all members of the community need to contribute to the struggle against the extinction of our speech.

Of course, in considering Rancière's assertion, one is immediately confronted with a seeming impossibility: if one has no *logos*, no speech, how does one do all this? How can one even put forward an argument? How can one shift one's body from one place to another, especially if one is oneself *without* speech—how can one possibly better one's situation? Here is the place where the imagination, the creative capacity, and a revitalized political will are all necessary to redesign political space and one's place in it. Rancière seems to point to a solution to this riddle when he refers to a story found in the writings of the Roman historian Livy. In particular, he focuses on an event that took place at the end of the war with the Volscians, as the plebians were in retreat over the Aventine Hill.

The Aventine Hill is the southernmost of Rome's Seven Hills. As one history tells it, the Aventine Hill "was first populated in the seventh century BC by refugees of cities that had been conquered by Rome. From 494 BC on it became a preferred residential area for plebeians, the common working class. In 456 BC a law even assigned the area to the working class." That is to say, its "speechless" population was made up of conquered foreigners, barbarians, and the working class—the dregs of Roman society. The scene was set for a famous confrontation between the plebians and the patricians. Rancière writes: "The position of the intransigent patricians is straightforward: there is no place for discussion with the plebs for the simple reason that plebs do not speak. They do not speak because they are beings without a name, deprived of logos—meaning, of symbolic enrollment in the city. . . . Whoever is nameless *cannot* speak."[42]

However, instead of retreating into silence and defeat, the plebs not only fight back, but do so in an unprecedented and immensely creative manner:

> Faced with this, what do the plebs gathered on the Aventine do? They
> do not set up a fortified camp on the manner of the Scythian slaves.

> They do what would have been unthinkable for the latter: they establish another order, another partition of the perceptible, by constituting themselves not as warriors equal to other warriors but as speaking beings sharing the same properties as those who deny them these. They thereby execute a series of speech acts that mimic those of the patricians: they pronounce imprecations and apotheoses; they delegate one of their number to go and consult their oracles; they give themselves representatives by rebaptizing them. In a word, they conduct themselves like beings with names.[43]

That is, they do not fight; they do not try to argue. How can they, when their words can only be heard as noise? Instead, they demonstrate through their actions that they are just as capable of acting like citizens as citizens themselves: in that interval of time and space they have invented for themselves, they act equal and think of themselves as equal. They present evidence of their capacities. Here is the crucial point: they are not merely "imitating" the citizens. Their act shows more than slavish imitation—it shows creative, collective, and communal resistance. It talks back from a place where they are not authorized to be, a place they have invented for themselves outside the imaginative capacities of the state.

The plebs have taken on the guise of patricians; they have asked to be recognized not as "themselves" but what they aspire to be—equal. They have proven their capacity to act exactly as patricians do: they have set up a parallel sociopolitical order that has all the markings of a patrician order but it bears the unmistakable sign of self-invention. After all, the only thing the citizens have done is to occupy a privileged space into which they were born. The plebs show their superior imaginations and their greater political will, bent not toward conservatism but toward progress.

The plebs made things happen that they were not supposed to be able to happen. They *brought something new into the world*—a new relation between those with voices and those without. Of course, they were not victorious in any immediate sense. But they entered a political historical record and showed that the necessary relation between those who have and those who have not is neither eternal nor natural. It can be changed. In that way, their legacy remains at the core of progressive activism today. As Mark and Paul Engler say, "If there is a common trait in the most prominent movements of the past century—whether they involve efforts to end child labor, redefined the role of women in political life, or bring down an apartheid regime, it is that they took up causes that established power brokers regarded as sure losers and won them by creating possibilities that had not previously existed."[44]

Preexisting and deeply entrenched political apathy, bigotry, and intellectual self-doubt worked together to allow Trump and Trumpism. This apathy and doubt will take some time to combat effectively because they stem from real and credible material causes, rooted in an especially spirit-depleting form of capitalism. Neoliberalism professes the sacred value of the individual even as it does its best to erode and exploit people's capacities to act and think critically and to act together. The deleterious effects of the long run of neoliberal chicanery are multiple, and they eat at the heart of any chance to change the course of history, even in small and incremental ways. We have to break free from the station in life to which we have been assigned, and which we have too often accepted as if it were inevitable, and intrude into the world of privilege, of political equality.

This is not at all impossible—in the past, people have used their energy, imagination, and sheer willpower to create powerful moments that lead to others. They have tapped into an as-yet-unexhausted reserve of moral righteousness, ethical humanism, and political imagination. And they have done so collectively and lent each other the strength necessary to shine a light in the darkness. They have shown us it is possible to trust our own instincts about justice, fairness, and what is decent and right—and thus laid the groundwork for us to start building and earning the trust of others. Today's efforts combine many of the fundamental values and beliefs of previous activism with the new knowledge and insights of younger activists. And this is happening at the most critical time imaginable—a moment when the social, cultural, and political battles from the 1960s on seem on the verge of defeat by a neoliberalism that emerged in the 1980s and whose dominance has continued well into the twenty-first century.

Celebrating and Growing Political Activism in the Twenty-First Century

The voices, places, and spaces in this book are imbricated with the legacy of political activism in which I myself was a participant. I cut my political teeth just after the US free speech and civil rights movements and was baptized as an activist in the year sociologist Immanuel Wallerstein called the "year of global revolution"—1968. In that era the idea of "liberation" was first and foremost in people's minds, but liberation took many forms. Emerging from the anti-imperialist wars of national liberation and decolonization, the term was applied to feminist, queer, and other kinds of liberation, as well as to anti-racist and Indigenous struggles. Environmental rights, housing rights, voting rights, and expanding civil rights were also at the fore. While it can and should be argued that so many of these aspirations were smothered and tamed by liberal compromises and deal cutting, many important gains were made.

But even if one is skeptical about what the '60s and '70s accomplished, the very fact that many, many people were *talking* about things—in abrasive, unauthorized ways—was significant. An overall progressive attitude that confronted powerful institutions seemed to prevail: pollution was real and it was bad, and racism, bigotry, and sexism were negative, beyond debate. Many of us believed this progressive direction was a product of social evolution, of conviction.

Most important, people *talked back* to established authorities. We accused them of lying, of hiding the truth, of spouting falsehoods. We were constantly told by those forces that we did not know what we were talking about—that we were speaking out of place. But history has proven that in many key instances, we certainly did know something we were not supposed to know. The leak of the Pentagon Papers—classified documents that revealed the true extent of the United States' secret military campaigns in Vietnam, Cambodia, and Laos, and the falsehoods that the Pentagon had spread in the media to maintain support for the war—is probably the best-known example of this. Whistleblower Daniel Ellsberg's courageous act occupies most of the historical memory of that event, but what is largely forgotten is the fact that people *read* the news reports with a particular kind of interest, acuity, urgency, and intelligence, and we read them *together*, in conversation and debate. The case had been made, long before the papers were leaked, that the US government was dishonest and secretive; the Pentagon Papers simply confirmed, with myriad evidence, how right the people's instincts had been. Despite the fact that voices of protest had been shut down and delegitimated by military experts and mainstream politicians, self-appointed "patriots," and devious pundits, those in the anti-war movement intuited that something in the official Pentagon messaging was suspect. And remember, this was before the days of the internet. Data and information were much less available. But the critical capacity and political will to doubt—and to devote tremendous energy to offering alternate narratives and explanations to those promulgated by Washington—was vibrant and shared among many.

Through a slow but steady process of grinding down, more and more people seem to have become convinced that it is no longer their place to speak about certain things, including many of the most important aspects of their lives, while there has also been a growing dearth of healthy skepticism of received "truths." It is crucial to understand that this loss of confidence has not been due to a lack of spirit or the capacity for conviction. Rather, it is in large part the result of changes in material history. Such changes are not random or accidental; they are both the indirect and direct result of a political strategy most blatantly owned by the Republican Party—a strategy meant to keep people immiserated and at the same time utterly cynical about their ability to change their situation. But many in the Democratic Party are complicit with this, too, and all too often their appetite for political power has resulted in them becoming bed partners with their supposed adversaries. As poverty, debt, and precarity have come to haunt most households in the United States, people have come either to accept the dominant narrative—that they themselves are to blame for their situation, for their failure to follow the dictates of austerity or to work enough hours (or jobs)—or else to rail blindly against "government" or "the rich."

Most dangerously, people have been told they are speaking out of place when they dare to venture into the "world of politics." What seemed to have been nearly lost (and this is again part of the right-wing calculation) is the capacity and will to seriously inquire into the ways structural and systemic violence has become embedded in our institutions—in politics, finance, our workplaces, our schools—and how that violence has dulled our senses of who we rightfully are and what we can, and should, rightfully say. In sum, we are in a state of planned political silencing—an internalization of the messaging of those in power.

But the pandemic and George Floyd rebellion reanimated something that had been tamped down and out of sight—an explosion of political energy. We had seen several signs of the spirit of protest, including the #MeToo movement against sexual abuse and harassment, the movement for gun control led by high schoolers in Parkland, Florida, the growth of a global climate change movement and the Sunrise Network, #BlackLivesMatter and the Movement for Black Lives, as well as the international Boycott, Divestment, and Sanctions movement for Palestinian rights. And as I noted above, the convergence of the pandemic and the murder of George Floyd brought the failures of neoliberalism and the systemic anti-Black violence of the state into full view, prompting masses of people to take to the streets in ways they previously had not. Most importantly, people were beginning to connect the dots. They saw the connection between the National Rifle Association, the alt-right, and the police; they saw the connection between transnational corporations, the government, and climate change, between the toxic masculinity expressed in sexual violence and the cover-up of that violence. It became harder and harder to dismiss these connections as the product of conspiracy theories, precisely because the evidence was no long hidden from view—people saw with their own eyes the racist murders of Black people, the bodies stored in refrigerator trucks in New York because the morgues were overfilled. And they saw the government both deny that things were that bad, and then unleash brutal repression on those who said differently.

But people kept protesting. And remarkably, the idea that Black lives matter became a matter of common belief. A Rasmussen poll taken in June 2020 showed that 62 percent of respondents viewed #BlackLivesMatter favorably—an astonishing figure, given that in 2015, 52 percent polled felt #BLM was not interested in equal justice, and 78 percent said "all lives matter," while only 11 percent said "Black lives matter." As recently as January 2020, Americans had been more optimistic about race relations in this country than they had been in years.[45] This is striking evidence that we are experiencing a dramatic shift in public consciousness in terms of the issues targeted by public protest. But it is not clear how this consciousness will be sustained. We are in a pivotal moment, when we must understand how voices have been silenced, democracy threatened, and the world imperiled. We must also come to see that by looking at fundamental operations that serve to invalidate voices, we create the opportunity both to reclaim our own, and, importantly, to reinvent the idea of speaking out as urgent in the current moment and beyond. Only by getting back in touch with our right, ability, and obligation to continue to speak out can we move forward, rather than regress into the neoliberal norms of hyper-individualism, the market, and the destruction of life.

I think of "voice" like an instrument that we must repair, polish, and make useful for the new world in which we live. In this spirit, the chapters to come will look at historical moments when people have invented new ways of speaking up politically that expose the mechanisms that maintain silence and quietude. Following in their footsteps, and building upon what they began, we must break out of the containers that keep us sealed into individual spaces, that decry collective work, and that tell us that we do not know "enough"—as if that were true, and even if it were so, as if it were a permanent state over which we had no agency. It means an energetic rejection of all attempts to convince us that we are speaking "out of place" when we claim and put into action the very idea of democracy.

Reclaiming the Space of Democracy

Previously, I introduced the story of the plebians' act of defiance on the Aventine Hill. I showed how Jacques Rancière uses that historical event to discuss the ways Roman citizens were thought to have voices that produced significant language, while the sounds coming out of the mouths of noncitizens were regarded simply as noise. Throughout his work, Rancière uses the French word *partager* to describe this kind of division that creates difference between people, according them unequal rights. Rancière's translators commonly treat "partition" as an English equivalent, and Rancière's well-known phrase, *partage du sensible* is thus rendered "partition of the sensible." It is fairly clear how this translation would work in the case of the Aventine Hill: we find there the division, the "partition," of citizen and noncitizen, human voice and nonhuman sound. But it's more complicated than that. Because *partager* also means "to share." Think of one of the most holy and mundane acts—taking a loaf of bread and tearing off a piece to give to someone else.

Rancière perpetually plays off this double meaning to symbolize the constant work of politics. For him, "[w]hat really deserves the name of politics is the cluster of perceptions and practices that shape this common world. Politics is first of all a way of framing, among sensory data, a specific sphere of experience. It is a partition of the sensible, of the visible and the sayable, which allows (or does not allow) some specific data to appear; which allows or does not allow some specific subjects to designate them and speak about them."[46] There is thus a tremendous tension between what is sharable and what is not—and, similarly, who is included in, or excluded from, political life.

In this regard, in a true democracy, there is an open and constant debate over what and who is to be included in the "sensible," which aligns precisely with Rancière's insistence that we recognize both the repressive nature of "partition" as well as its role in historical change, political flux, and the constant struggle to achieve true democracy. Democracy is a living thing that changes as social life changes; for example, we can think of gay rights as an "identity" that emerges via debate, deliberation, and struggle. The permanent assignment of groups into those with voice and those without it runs exactly counter to fundamental notions of democracy: "Democracy is more than a social state. It is a specific partition of the sensible, a specific regime of speaking whose effect is to *upset any steady relationship between manners of speaking, manners of doing and manners of being.*"[47]

In a very similar vein, political scientist Wendy Brown's discussion of democracy shows how "partition" works to set up certain groups as rulers, and others as not, and how the achievement of a true democracy requires a broad and expansive *sharing* of power among the people.

> *Demos/kratia.* The people rule. Democracy signifies the aspiration that the people, and not something else, order and regulate their common life through ruling themselves together. Conversely, democracy negates the legitimacy of rule by a part of the people, rather than the whole—for example, only those with property, wealth, education, or expertise—or by any external principle, such as power, gods, violence, truth, technology, or nationalism, even as the people may decide that one or more of these ought to guide, even determine, their shared existence.[48]

In this respect, we can see one important facet of neoliberalism's antidemocratic nature, which confers power to a specific set of human beings endowed with wealth and influence.

Yet the notion that economic "being" is the essential character of human life, and that wealth and material affluence are indices of a person's

value (and right to participate in a democracy), is not unique to neoliberalism. We must remember that in 1965, Martin Luther King Jr. made
a very similar diagnosis, and a specific prescription with regard to the
devastation of the body and the mind that capitalism had wrought by that
time in history. Looking at the American scene in the mid-1960s, King
declared: "We must rapidly begin to shift from a 'thing-oriented' society to a 'person-oriented' society. When machines and computers, profit
motives and property rights are considered more important than people,
the giant triplets of racism, materialism, and militarism are incapable of
being conquered. . . . Call it democracy, or call it democratic socialism,
but there must be a better distribution of wealth within this country for
all God's children."[49]

The condition King deplored only worsened as neoliberalism gained
a foothold in the 1980s, largely because it took over both the Republican
and the Democratic Parties, which were similarly tethered to capitalist
extraction and exploitation. Both had a role in intensifying the message
of individualism and destroying movements for collective rights, such
as labor unions. Canadian American writer and filmmaker Astra Taylor
describes this operation lucidly:

> Capitalism was born of enclosure, a process that ripped people from
> their land and communities and made them dependent on the market.
> The resulting individualism, taken to its extreme, erodes the very idea
> of the people. Instead of being a demos, a collectivity asserting our po-
> litical sovereignty and deciding how to live together, we are left on our
> own—liberated or isolated depending on how you see it—searching
> for a path to the top, even if we have to climb over others to get there.[50]

As terrible as neoliberalism is in terms of its antagonistic relationship to
democracy and any sense of collective responsibility and obligation, we
must not forget that the Trump years made things exponentially worse.
To the ruthless logic of neoliberalism, Trump added a universe of gaslighting. Nothing that anybody said but himself and his loyalists held
any truth—everything but him and his was "fake." Nearly every public
speech Trump made was converted into a rally or a transactional spectacle: for example, in March 2020, during a press briefing on the pandemic,
he gave the stage over to his corporate sponsors for free advertising.[51]
Trump's rallies became known both for Trump's off-script rantings, for
the explosions of laughter over his jokes, and the cheers at every punch

line. The tightly framed shots, the carefully choreographed staging of speakers, and Trump's inherent ability to appeal to the worst instincts of his base presented a powerful media moment that was repeated constantly, establishing a depressing image of permanent political power based on a consensus of congealed hatred. But a single instance punctured that bubble, at least momentarily, and in that interval a very powerful antidote was released.

On September 7, 2018, an unlikely individual gained national, if not international, recognition, simply by making a few facial gestures. The unknown young man, referred to as "Plaid Shirt Guy," (later identified as Tyler Linfesty, a Billings West High School senior) stood behind Trump during a speech at a rally on Montana. Within a few minutes, the Guy had captured worldwide media attention. What did he do, what did he say? Very, very little. When one looked at Trump, the Guy was completely unremarkable and barely noticeable—he was simply one of the bit players in the chorus behind Trump, positioned directly over Trump's right shoulder. It's hard to tell if he even knew he was framed in the cameras aimed at Trump. This young man was dressed simply in a plaid shirt, with a Democratic Socialists of America button on his chest coming in and out of sight. He remained pretty expressionless throughout the speech, but every once in a while, when Trump would utter some lie or nonsense, Plaid Shirt Guy would raise his eyebrows, frown in puzzlement, or mouth a single word: "What?" He was soon removed by a Trump staffer who had seen what he was doing and replaced with a Trump supporter.

But what exactly had he done that was so disruptive? How could one, *silent*, nearly motionless person, break through the din of the crowd and the amplified voice of the president of the United States? In an interview with CNN, Linfesty said his reactions were "actual, honest" reactions to the Trump's remarks, adding, "I was not trying to protest." [52]

As it turned out, Plaid Shirt Guy gave voice to millions of people who were watching Trump and feeling the same surges of doubt, puzzlement, incredulity. Viral video of the Guy provided a huge boost to the spirits of those who were baffled and depressed by the robotic enthusiasm of the Trump crowd, who mindlessly cheered even the most ludicrous statements. The Guy broke the spell of irreality and, for a few key moments, completely took over the rally. And Trump's handlers knew it; if the crowd in the auditorium was oblivious to what was happening, Trump's people knew the Guy would reach millions of viewers worldwide.

It is by simply standing up, calling out lies, and serving as a token of another reality that each of us can speak out of place, and add to one of the most important political tasks there is: to show that another kind of reality exists, aside from authoritarian illusions promulgated by the voices of fascists. By 2018, too many had sunk into a feeling of power-lessness; we had sensed that Trump and his people had cowed nearly everyone and everything, and that the entire state was now under his thumb. All this despite the fact that polls regularly showed that six out of ten Americans disapproved of Trump and wanted him gone. What Plaid Shirt Guy did, simply by reacting spontaneously, was to unblock public outrage. Two years later, in September 2019, Alex Kack, an activist in Arizona, similarly drew attention at a City Council meeting in Tuscon. As Kack describes it:

> Two anti-immigration activists created an uproar. During the meeting, they began to yell and wave their signs around while one filmed the commotion on her phone. It was obvious that they had missed the en-tire point: that this was just a formality and the requirements to get the measure on the ballot had been met. Some people fled the awkward-ness, others booed and tried to yell over them, one man clutched his banjo, and I just sat there and laughed. In the past 48 hours, I've gained over 50,000 Twitter followers, received praise, been called all sorts of names and even got to see myself on Stephen Colbert. It's been surreal to say the least, and it's all because I did something simple and natural. I just laughed.[53]

Now, I am certainly not making the argument that all we need to do is to laugh, as individuals (although it certainly can't hurt). What I am saying is that laughter often results from the release of tension that has built up for some time—a feeling of outrage that has been kept bottled up. Sometimes this is out of discretion, sometimes out of a sense of despair and hopelessness. What both these instances show is that in these very different occasions, the emperor's new clothes were shown to be an illu-sion. Feelings of hopelessness were put on hold, as one was relieved to see that one was not alone in feeling disgust and outrage at Trump's stupidity and bigotry, and disbelief that Trump seemed to still have a hold on so many. What these episodes showed was that one could break into the mainstream mediascape and call its assumptions into question. And just one month after Kack drew national attention for his laugh, hundreds of people stood up at Major League Baseball's World Series and, in response to the announcement that the president was in attendance, began shouting, "Lock him up!"[54] We had reclaimed a media moment traditionally exploited by every president, transforming it into a public referendum.

For another example, consider the restaurants, which are within their rights to refuse service to people who are disturbing other customers, that refused service to various Trump aides—aides who were responsible for any number of heinous and cruel policies. The *Washington Post* and other media chastised the restaurant owners, saying that they had let their politics interfere with these people's rights to privacy. But Mari Uyehara, writing in *GQ*, had another recommendation: "blacklist every last one of them": "The David Axelrods of the world believe that immigrants and their sympathizers should be forced to cook for, serve, and clean up after their very own abusers in silence. Their outrage lies with protecting the comforts and ease of the powerful, while accepting that the vicious dehumanization of most vulnerable among us is somehow politics as usual." She continued: "Richard Hass, the President of the Council on Foreign Relations, who made the most revolting claim, commenting on MSNBC's Morning Joe that Sanders's ejection 'violates the spirit of the Civil Rights Act of 1964.' Hass believes that our press secretary's suffering in not finishing her free cheese plate is on the same moral plane as black Americans, in the Jim Crow era, getting murdered, beaten and attacked by police dogs for seeking equal rights."[55] This contrast is yet another illustration of this book's focus: the occupation of places for different purposes and different publics. When Hass attempted to equate the systematic deprivation of rights to Black people as an entire race to the very limited and idiosyncratic act of a restaurant manager's denial of service to a group of political functionaries, the absurdity of the comparison shined a light on both anti-Black racism and white privilege. We had a battle for symbolic space, and, fortified by the historical truth, anti-racist voices prevailed, just as the silent protest of Plaid Shirt Guy exposed the madness of Trump's rantings.

Many other such examples can be found outside the borders of the United States. Consider the case of Otpor (Resistance), a Serbian student-led group formed in 1998 in protest against the autocratic reign of Slobodan Milošević. The group's tactics were extremely shrewd, well thought-out, and creative. They started with very small acts, just to prove to people that such acts could actually *take place*. Numbering in the hundreds, those small acts changed the public landscape onto a political canvas. The most notable, eye-catching, and humorous happened at an opening ceremony for a new bridge:

> When authorities in the city of Novi Sad tried to surround their post-war reconstruction efforts with official pomp—even though the new bridge the government constructed over the Danube River amounted to little more than a temporary pontoon—activists responded by ceremoniously building their own toy bridge over a pond in one of the city's central parks. The stunt left authorities with two bad options: look cartoonishly repressive by arresting people for playing around with a Styrofoam prop, or let Otpor continue to mock the regime.[56]

Like Plaid Shirt Guy and the restaurant manager who refused service, the activists in Serbia reframed the moment, reinvented place, and showed truth where authorities tried to obscure it.

Each of these acts of disbelief, defiance, and outrage points to the perseverance of moral clarity. That clarity allows us to see through the hallucinatory haze of gaslighting politicians and pundits, and help others to do so as well. It shows we each have within us a political voice that is healthy and capable to speak in multiple ways—in humor, in rage, in empathy, and in courage. In the chapters that follow, we will see other examples of how people have used their imagination, creativity, moral intuition, and sense of ethics and justice to speak out of place, disrupting what appear to be hermetically sealed spaces and reclaiming them for democracy.

Chapter 1 begins by delving deeper into the idea that politics largely involves the debate about whose voice counts, and in what situations. This chapter inaugurates our effort to see "place" thorough different eyes—to see the world around us as open to our voices, our energies, and our struggles. This is where we make difference. Through this lens, we'll look at the history of sports arenas as places of politics, despite claims to the contrary, and how they set the stage for the Colin Kaepernick protests and events that followed. We'll then turn to various moments of occupation and protest, and draw out the idea of protests as both planned and "eruptive." While both of course are essential, it is the latter kind that need to be more fully understood, because they point both to underlying understandings that have been repressed and to a particular kind of political voice that demands to be sustained. The chapter concludes with examples of popular takeovers of public spaces that the state has refused to protect and make safe.

With that foundation in place, the remaining chapters turn to an examination of our places of habitation, of work, of human relationships, and of our relationships to other forms of life and the planet itself. We'll begin to open our eyes both to the partitioning of place by forces of exploitation and extraction, and to people's efforts to imagine and establish vibrant and just relationships outside those miserable and alienated circuits of capital. Chapter 2 is specifically concerned with issues of land, space, and territory, and the kinds of voices that speak back from and across places of precarity and loss at the scale of neighborhoods and cities. The central conceptual element here is the Marxist thinker Henri Lefebvre's notion of the "right to the city"—people's prerogative to create, nurture, and endow with meaning their own surroundings, outside of the limited blueprint of capitalism and labor. I discuss the phenomenas of rent, displacement, and eviction, and show the importance for democracy of a sense of belonging and a sense of home. As with the other chapters, I end this one with examples of eruptive voices and actions that break through the partitioning of place and map out a different, more humane, set of relationships.

Chapter 3 expands the scale of place, voice, and home, turning to global borders and the effects of neoliberalism on laborers, immigrants, and refugees. I show how "place" in this context involves camps, specialized zones, and other mechanisms for the management of the ebb and flow of labor across borders, going on to explain how people have invented ways to circumnavigate these borders and create spaces of possibility and hope.

On a similarly planetary scale, chapter 4 applies these frames to issues of environmental justice, including the most urgent problem of our time—climate change. I examine the importance of Indigenous belief systems that show us the way out of an environmentalism still tethered to capitalism, and present readings of a set of literary narratives to show how art might provide us the very images we need to think of a planetary future. I ask the questions: What responsibilities do we have to the planet, if we think of not only a home for the "human family," but for life itself? And what kind of politics will this require? Throughout, I make the argument that we have precious little time left to change tack—that the "success" of capitalism in transforming everything into a resource for commodification, and everyone into a worker/consumer, leaving only the tiniest fraction of human beings with astronomically disproportionate wealth and power, is destroying the planetary home and human community.

CHAPTER 1

SPEAKING OUT OF PLACE

The year 2019 saw an eruption of protests around the world, each in response to profound social, political, economic, and environmental crises. As remarkable as the coincidence of these historical events was the fact that each one seemed to be predicated on similar crises. In a year-end "dossier," the Tricontinental Institute for Social Research observed that the world "oscillates between crises and protests":

> We live in a time of protests: no country is immune from demonstra-
> tions that flood the streets and make demands upon structures that
> are deaf to the needs and aspirations of the people. Millions of people
> experience the pain and indignity of unemployment and cuts in State
> spending on education, health, poverty alleviation, and elderly care.
> The slogans are in different languages, but the meaning is the same: we
> refuse, we resist, we will not tolerate the plague of austerity.[1]

In September 2019, journalist Ben Ehrenreich noted the geographic diversity of these protests: "In the last 12 weeks, protests have spanned five
continents—most of the planet—from wealthy London and Hong Kong
to hungry Tegucigalpa and Khartoum. They are so geographically disparate and apparently heterogeneous in cause and composition that I have
not yet seen any serious attempt to view them as a unified phenomenon."
Ehrenreich made just such an attempt, asserting that much, if not all of
this discontent, could be blamed on neoliberalism, which he described as

> a globally applicable method for preserving the current overwhelming
> imbalance of power. It works microcosmically on a municipal level—
> think decaying public transit systems with an apparently bottomless
> budget for racist fare enforcement, while billionaires hop in helicopters
> from rooftop to rooftop—and macrocosmically on a planetary scale,

in which national elites collude with multinational corporations and
international financial institutions to keep labor cheap and wealth and
resources confined into established channels.[2]

This book follows a similar trajectory in its analysis—from the level of
towns and cities, and upward to the planetary scale. In each case we will
be attending to the local, global, and planetary damage neoliberal and
capitalist ideologies have wrought. Both ideologies drive the same message: of primary interest is the "individual," which is regarded solely as an
economic actor, and the "market," which is thought of as a global system
of exchange and profit making. Ideas on human and humane interdependence and shared welfare have been deemed mere fairy tales. Neoliberalism
dismisses any notions of nonmarket value and humane interdependence;
capitalism's goals are to extract and exploit both nature and human resources for the good of a tiny portion of humanity. What the people who
filled the streets were protesting was both the ground-level injuries to
everyday life and the global harm that they witnessed with their own eyes
and experienced with their own bodies. We now find ourselves at a pivotal
moment in history, where the all-encompassing, self-interested values of
neoliberalism, the exclusionary mandates of ethno-nationalism, and the
rapacious logic of late capitalism have facilitated the spread of pandemics
and the degradation of the environment.

Instead of seeing an ethos of the common good, we see immense
wealth and power concentrated in the hands of a tiny number people,
with those who do the labor getting less and less.[3] Currently, the top
1 percent owns as much as the entire middle class and continues to accu-
mulate tremendous wealth, undeterred by the COVID-19 pandemic; it is
even finding ways to make money off it.[4] When whistleblowers pointed
out Amazon's dangerous and exploitative work conditions during the
pandemic, Bezos fired them.[5] As Veena Dubal, a legal scholar and labor
activist, told me: "Amazon, through its various subsidiaries, leverages
every imaginable exploitative labor practice to minimize overhead and
risk. They use independent contracting, subcontracting, piece-pay, and
grinding automated quota systems to ensure that workers who produce
value for the company have to work long and hard, for as little as possible.
And in many instances, especially in the context of contracting and subcontracting, the workers also have to bear all the legal risk, without any

basic safety net protections. Not all of these practices are legal, but that does not stop this company."[6] Indeed, when even the frail protections of laws and constitutions are shredded, the situation becomes nearly impossible. Thankfully, in global protests against police violence and racism, for the environment and the health of the planet, and in support of other struggles for liberation, we find sure signs that the human will for justice is far from depleted. But to fully realize our power, we must first disabuse ourselves of the constraints that have been placed on our ability to see our capacity to effect change.

We need to imagine and invent a new sense of the "place" from which we speak—one that urges us to take possession of, and to speak from, a place that we claim for ourselves as legitimate, as real, as vibrant, and most importantly, as politically necessary. When we do this, we are using our voices in places that have been thought of as unauthorized, illegitimate, bereft of value, anarchistic, and unruly.

For example, since 2016, when football quarterback Colin Kaepernick first took a knee in protest against police brutality aimed at Black bodies, the world has looked at sporting arenas differently. That is an immense achievement, and an unsettling one to many who feel that stadiums should be reserved for pleasure and entertainment only. But the so-called politicization of entertainment spaces is hardly new, nor is it the result only of dissent; as we will examine in detail momentarily, for many decades the National Football League's owners have determined the ways football stadiums are used to promote militarism and patriotism. By taking a knee, players opposed such an exploitation of the playing field, demanding that their presence there be viewed not simply as paid labor. Thus, these battles over what can take place in these spaces of public congregation reveal the power relations that exist not so far beneath the surface of a supposedly "politics-free" space. And the debate over the use of place forces these historical contradictions to the surface in very powerful ways.

In 2017, in response to the protests launched by Colin Kaepernick, then–Houston Texans owner Bob McNair was alleged to have told his fellow owners, "We can't have the inmates running the prison," and from the other side of the line of management and ownership, LeBron James publicly called out the slave-owner mentality of NFL owners.[7] Such disputes have the potential to serve as revelatory political moments that open new ways of seeing not only specific places, like the football field, but also larger areas of public life.

Indeed, these acts of protest in places believed to be politically neutral do something that street demonstrations do not always do. Take the example we saw in the introduction of the restaurant owners who refused service to Donald Trump's racist advisors—the very people who were instrumental in thinking up and implementing inhumane immigration policies that affected, among many others, restaurant workers. This form of political protest was not supposed to "take place," given that such a refusal of service conjures a political memory of Black people being refused a place in US eateries, and the lunch counter protests that followed. But when restaurant owners refused to serve powerful Washington figures, they completely inverted the historical model: when people speak out of place, the tables are turned, and even more so when customers, and a media audience of millions, applaud the act. That is to say, when acts of protest erupt in unexpected places, carried out by unlikely people, an opening for political activism and participation bursts forth, breaking the placid surface of managed life. They show the power of an imagination that rebels against the assignment of certain people to certain places, and the relations of power that reside in those assignments. Rich and influential customers are not supposed to be turned away, but in these cases the restaurant managers were acting in solidarity with their coworkers. And Black protestors taking a place at lunch counters and on buses—places they were not supposed to be—were challenging the given order of things, showing that the universe would not explode if they disrupted it by demonstrating their willingness to prove the wrongness of the given order of segregation. Each of the instances that follows serves as an example of people stepping out of their assigned roles and filling supposedly neutral, "apolitical" spaces with the political content of their choice. Each of these instances also shows people tapping into a political power they might not have thought they had—and when this happens, they model something for others to do as well.

A key word here is "unauthorized." According to the *Oxford English Dictionary*, the word "authorize" means "to give official permission for or formal approval to (an action, undertaking, etc.); to approve, sanction." But another, older definition gives us something more to work with:

"To vouch for the truth or reality of; to attest." In this sense, battles over authority can thus be read as battles over the truth, over reality, and, most importantly, over a vision for a reality to come. "Unauthorized" in this sense means to vouch for the truth or the reality of something without being given permission to do so. It is time to act in unauthorized manner—to raise our voices, informed both by a determination not to unquestioningly accept our conventional roles and by a radical imagination that recognizes the necessity of justice—of life over death. This is "speaking out of place" in ways that redefine what that place is, and it has important implications for the issue of protests on the playing field, and our understanding of their history.

Taking the Field

Despite the claims of sports "purists" who decry Kaepernick's decision to take a knee rather than stand during the playing of the national anthem, American sports arenas have never been apolitical spaces, and one of the myths about athletes—that they have little authority to speak about anything besides sports—is likewise untrue. In one particular instance, one of the most famous athletes of the day was formally *asked* to make a political statement. In 1949, the House Un-American Activities Committee (HUAC) asked baseball star and public celebrity Jackie Robinson to testify as part of its hearings on suspected Communist activities. It was their hope that Robinson would condemn a speech that Paul Robeson had recently delivered in Paris at the Soviet-sponsored World Peace Conference.

Not only was he a world-famous singer, actor, and political activist; Robeson was also an accomplished athlete—honored as an All-America football player while at Rutgers University. In contrast to Robeson, who was criticized by the Right for his work against racial, economic, and political injustice, Robinson was regarded as the "good" Black athlete and public figure. One of the conditions to which Robinson agreed in signing a contract with the Brooklyn Dodgers in 1947—thereby becoming the first Black man to play in the major league in the modern era—was that he kept silent on and off the field, regardless of what kinds of racist insults were hurled at him. He was explicitly *unauthorized* to speak, for the sake of what the owner and manager of the Dodgers, Branch Rickey, called "the great experiment" of professional baseball's racial integration.

Besides his status as a sports celebrity, there was another reason HUAC chose Robinson to serve as a counterexample to Robeson: Robinson was an army veteran and a devoted Christian who was on record as opposing Communism—thus he seemed to be the perfect Black athlete to repudiate Robeson's sympathies with anti-racist, anti-fascist, and anti-imperialist movements. What HUAC had not counted on was that Robinson had also experienced racism in some of its worst forms. In 1944, while stationed at Fort Hood, Texas, he had refused to move to the back of the bus when ordered to do so by the white bus driver—that is, he had refused to show that he "knew his place." For that act of defiance, Robinson had been charged with insubordination and conduct unbecoming of an officer. Ultimately, he was found not guilty of all charges.

Given his recognition of racism in the United States, and the fact that, like Robeson, he had acted against that racism, what was the Dodgers second baseman going to say during his appearance? Would he condemn Robeson, or take his side? Doing the former would consolidate his "good Black" status in the eyes of the white American public; doing the latter would likely erase both his hero status and his career. In the end, he chose neither. Instead, in his testimony before HUAC, Robinson did something extraordinary—he reclaimed that congressional space as his by using the bulk of his time to denounce American racism:

> White people must realize that the more a Negro hates Communism because it opposes democracy, the more he is going to hate any other influence that kills off democracy in this country—and that goes for racial discrimination in the Army, and segregation on trains and buses, and job discrimination because of religious beliefs or color or place of birth. . . . And one other thing the American public ought to understand, if we are to make progress in this matter: The fact that it is a Communist who denounces injustice in the courts, police brutality, and lynching when it happens doesn't change the truth of his charges. . . . Negroes were stirred up long before there was a Communist Party, and they'll stay stirred up long after the party has disappeared—unless Jim Crow has disappeared by then as well.

As journalist Johnny Smith notes, "more than 40 years before Kaepernick started the 'take a knee' movement, Robinson wrote in his autobiography, *I Never Had It Made*, 'I cannot stand and sing the anthem. I cannot salute the flag; I know that I am a black man in a white world.'"[8]

Jackie Robinson did not refuse to appear. But when he did, he delivered words that were not supposed to be uttered. He created an off-script moment that was never imagined to have been able to occur—he spoke out of place, in his own voice. HUAC knew then, as everyone else knows now, just how influential sports figures are in the American imagination. The episode helps us understand why in the eyes of some, athletes need to be silenced, or only authorized to speak on message. For when they go off-script, important things can happen. Along with the "race barrier," Robinson broke the political speech barrier, too, and started a tradition that connects to the Kaepernick protests. But between Robinson's 1949 testimony and the 2016 protests of Kaepernick and other professional athletes in support of #BlackLivesMatter, the world witnessed one of the most important acts of "speaking out of place" ever to occur on an athletic field. It happened during the 1968 Olympic Games in Mexico City. Among other things, it is significant because the protest was conceived as an indictment of both American racism and the violation of international human rights. Two Black athletes, John Carlos and Tommie Smith, used the Olympic podium to make an international statement whose impact reverberates to this day.

The 1968 Olympics

As we will see, the actions of Smith and Carlos were roundly condemned as entirely out of place, inappropriate, and a terrible instance of politics contaminating the purity of the games, which were supposed to exist in an ideal world of sports competition, divorced from both financial and political interests. Yet an explosive 1999 article in the *New York Times* reported the discovery of documents that prove that not only politics but also dirty money have been present in the Olympics from as far back as the mid-1930s. Remarkably, the International Olympic Committee member implicated in that scandal, an American named Avery Brundage, also led the IOC in 1968.

The *Times* article presented evidence that Brundage, perhaps with help from the Belgian count Henri de Baillet-Latour, was involved in setting up illegal payments from the fascist German government via the German Olympic Committee: "Brundage's papers at the University of Illinois include a 1938 letter from the president of the German Olympic Committee assuring him that his Chicago construction company's bid to help build the German Embassy in Washington had been accepted."[9] The *Times* also discovered a letter from another IOC member, addressed to Brundage, which read: "It is too bad that the American Jews are so active and cause us so much trouble. It is impossible for our German friends to carry on the expensive preparations for the Olympic Games if all this unrest prevails." So any talk about the "purity" of the Olympics can be set aside, given the rotten foundation of this early event, not to mention the dozens which have followed. Indeed, since the games' inception, politics and money have been at their very center—in this case, fascist politics and money.

It was this mixture of support for authoritarian violence and the unrestrained hunt for high-performance commercial dollars that set the stage for the 1968 Olympics, as mass student demonstrations exploded in Mexico City, disrupting the IOC's carefully laid plans. In fact, the committee was complicit in the state's now-infamous massacre of hundreds of student protestors: "To clean up the city for visitors and a huge television audience, demonstrating Mexican students were machine-gunned, their blood scrubbed from the stone streets and information about their deaths suppressed for many years. No Olympic official lodged a protest."[10]

While the IOC was focused on profit, the national and international political context for protest by Black athletes revolved around anti-racism and human rights. Carlos, who, together with Smith, raised a black-gloved fist and bowed his head for human rights, described the long, difficult, and meticulous planning behind the protest. It was not just a general sense of racial injustice that could be seen in urban decay and violence, anti-Black racism, police repression, and the war in Vietnam that had sparked the protest, but also the fact that in February 1968 Brundage, now president of the IOC, had readmitted apartheid South Africa to the committee. Carlos's thought was "[I]f South Africa was in, we were out." Dr. Martin Luther King Jr. had also met with several athletes and convinced them that an Olympic boycott would have "global reach."[11]

As the games grew near, two things happened that threw the momentum for the boycott off track. First was the earth-shaking event of King's assassination in April. The second was the capitulation of the IOC to re-ban South Africa (remarkably, Brundage was outvoted). Yet the protests that sprang up across the nation in reaction to King's assassination, as well as the massive student demonstrations in Mexico City against the games, led Carlos and Smith to continue with plans to protest. As Carlos himself notes:

> In the first week of October, 1968, just a few short days before the opening of the games, there was a river of young blood in the Mexican streets. Hundreds of students from the state university were massacred by the state military in Mexico City's Tlatelolco Square. Apparently the students had been protesting nonviolently all year and the confrontations with the police had been mild. But now the Olympics were coming up and students had started using slogans incorporating the Olympics, asking how their country could have money for the games while the people went hungry. Well, someone snapped somewhere, because on government orders, the troops and their military leaders stopped such talk in as extreme a way as possible, cornering the students in the public square and butchering them like hogs, all in the name of making Mexico City "presentable" for an international audience. . . . To the great shame of the Olympic movement, all that bloodshed and death was never mentioned once during the games. . . . I believe that they, not Tommie and me, are the true Olympic martyrs, and they must never be forgotten. We discussed it on the plane going down there because for us, this was more than just talk. They were in the original drafts of our statement in Mexico City.[12]

The murder of protesters and bystanders was a bloody and punitive reclamation of space by the state and a silencing of popular voices—not only those of the injured and killed, but also those who would now be afraid to speak. Rather than view the massacre as distinct from the situation of Black Americans, Carlos and Smith saw it as of a piece with the violence they had witnessed in their own country, and the racism that had existed for centuries before them:

> It wasn't just about Vietnam, Dr. King's assassination, the murders of the Mexican students, or this media tag about some Age of Aquarius "Revolt of the Black Athlete." It was about everything that led up to 1968. It was about the stories my father told me about fighting in the First World War. It was about the terrible things he was asked to do for a freedom he was denied when he returned home.[13]

This story about Carlos's father should remind us of serviceman Jackie Robinson's rude awakening to American racism—his act of protest against being told to sit at the back of the bus, even while in military uniform.

After their raised-fist protest, Carlos and Smith got support from both likely and unlikely sources. The anchor of the women's gold-medal-winning sprint relay team, Wyomia Tyus, dedicated their relay win to Smith and Carlos. And even the Harvard crew team issued a statement: "We—as individuals—have been concerned about the place of the black man in American society in their struggle for equal rights. As members of the US Olympic team, each of us has come to feel a moral commitment to support our black teammates in their efforts to dramatize the injustices and inequities which permeate our society."[14] Thus, Carlos and Smith's act of speaking out and taking over place in turn led others to join them and expand the protest—Carlos and Smith's moral courage turned them into leaders, and turned people who might not have done anything at all into public allies, proving once again that one should not underestimate the power of speaking out of place.

The blowback against Carlos and Smith was immediate and vicious. After Brundage exerted pressure on the United States Olympic Committee, the pair were expelled from the games for violating "basic standards of good manners and sportsmanship." Nevertheless, when the official film of the games was released, footage of the demonstration was included. Brundage had written in vain to the Mexico 1968 organizing chief, Pedro Ramírez Vázquez, in an effort to censor the images: "It was very disturbing to have you confirm rumors about the use of pictures of the nasty demonstration against the United States flag by negroes in the official film of the Games of the XIX Olympiad . . . it had nothing to do with sport, it was a shameful abuse of hospitality and has no more place in the film than the gunfire at Tlatelolco."[15] One of the ugliest attacks in the American media came from sportscaster Brent Musburger, who declared, "Perhaps it's time 20-year-old athletes quit passing themselves off as social philosophers," referring to the duo as "black-skinned stormtroopers."[16] (A half century later, protesting Black athletes were referred to by another epithet—"sons of bitches"—by none other than the president of the United States.)[17] Once again, Musburger's slur used the rhetoric of Black youth not knowing their place—they were there to entertain, and nothing else, and certainly not to think either philosophically or politically. Of course, Carlos, Smith, and history have all proven Musburger wrong.

We must remember that the raised-fist protest was, after all, not merely a protest against the racism and imperialism of the United States, nor was it solely a sign of support for Black Power—it was also meant to draw attention to struggles for international human rights. The third runner on the awards stand, a white Australian sprinter named Peter Norman, acted in solidarity by wearing a button of the pro-boycott Olympic Project for Human Rights. For that, he too was excoriated. In Carlos's words:

> The press treated him terribly: he was the white man who stood with those two aboriginal devils, John Carlos and Tommie Smith. . . . He merely wore a button supporting human rights and said, "I believe in supporting humanity in every way that we can to make this a better world." He was shut out of the Australian track and field world . . . even though he was the most accomplished sprinter in that country's history.[18]

It was only posthumously, in 2012, that Norman received an apology from the Australian Parliament. In a recent talk, Carlos brought up the subject of Kaepernick's protests during the national anthem. He drew numerous parallels between his and Kaepernick's cases. Indeed, and reaching back to Robinson's comments quoted above, there is a true continuity of Black athletic protest, running in tandem with the persistence of anti-Black racism.

While this ethos of protest is often beneath the surface, as I will discuss in detail below, it can take a particular convergence of historical events to make these voices erupt, and a message to take fire. That is what we saw in 1968, and in the #BlackLivesMatter protests of early 2000s. One person behind the 1968 Olympic protests was a professor at the University of California, Berkeley, named Harry Edwards. In a recent interview, he drew connections between 1968 and 2008:

> It was always clear there were ongoing waves of athletic activism, framed up by historical developments of the moment. Whether abject segregation with Jack Johnson, Jesse Owens and Joe Lewis; whether an effort to desegregate with Jackie Robinson, Larry Doby, Kenny Washington and Chuck Cooper; whether the Black Power Movement, which instituted a new frame of reference beyond the Civil Rights and desegregation effort. We're now in a fourth wave that was framed up by the Black Lives Matter movement. . . . African American athletes are still black in America, you still risk everything, including your life. It takes a tremendous amount of courage to make a statement when

people say: "play the sport, entertain me, sit down, shut up." . . . It is not
that we haven't made progress; we obviously have. It is just that there
are no final victories because the dynamics of the developments at the
interface of sports, race and society continue to evolve and change.[19]

It is no coincidence that in 1968, the same year that the black-gloved
protest took place at the Olympic Games, the NFL determined that when
"The Star-Spangled Banner" was played, players were supposed to line up
facing the flag, helmet tucked under their left arm and right hand placed
over their heart. In that tumultuous social, cultural, and political year, the
world was filled with a sense that the personal was political. In one case,
as the anthem played, a 26-year-old linebacker for the St. Louis Cardinals
named David Meggyesy bowed his head and held the face mask of his
helmet with one hand, letting it rest between his knee and hip, as a protest
against the war in Vietnam. Thinking back on that moment, Meggysey
later said: "I was more pissed about their response of militarism, patriotism and all that more than anything. . . . And the overt burden of the
players, saying, 'You're the chattel out here, and you've got no say how
we're going to do it and salute the flag."[20] Meggysey went on to be an
anti-war activist and write an explosive book on professional football, *Out
of Their League*, which took on such taboo subjects as racism, drug abuse,
and extreme violence in the NFL.

It was in that period, the mid and late 1960s, that the heavy-handed
transformation of the professional football field into place of military
spectacle began; the US government, for one, understood perfectly well
that it had a huge, captive, television audience. As early as 1965, the NFL
had started sending players on goodwill tours to visit military personnel,
which also had the effect of giving the Vietnam War the imprimatur of
the NFL; no one trying to voice the opposite opinion was allowed to go.
The Super Bowl also hosted its first military flyover that year, which established the NFL's relationship with the Department of Defense. The
1969 Super Bowl included a halftime show with the theme "America
Thanks." And in 1970, halftime ceremonies included a reenactment of
the 1815 Battle of New Orleans. Decades later, as the wars in the Middle
East wore on, the NFL's brand of patriotism would place the military at
the fore of its charitable efforts. When the United States launched the war
in Afghanistan, President Bush's speech announcing the campaign played

on the immense video boards in NFL stadiums. Military tributes became pervasive at games, so much so that the Marines used footage of them in recruitment commercials, and in turn played recruitment commercials during halftime. In 2009, Army general David H. Petraeus flipped the Super Bowl's opening coin at midfield.

Author and former Army Ranger Rory Fanning, who became a vocal critic of America's Middle East wars, put it this way:

> It almost feels like it's a mandatory patriotism that is pushed down the throats of anybody who wants to attend a game. . . . By trotting out veterans, patting them on the back, I don't think it does justice to the actual experience of veterans, particularly over the last 18 years. There certainly isn't an opportunity for veterans to talk about their experiences in combat. So many veterans don't feel like the heroes the NFL wants to present them as.

In 2015, a Congressional oversight report revealed that the NFL was one of several leagues that accepted Department of Defense funds to stage military tributes, a practice known as "paid patriotism."[21] This is not to say that many fans do not welcome the presence of military ceremonies or even advertising on the field. But it also means that many who do not are forced to witness the displays and be unwitting stage props and cheerleaders by their very presence.

We have to understand that the battle over sports activism is a battle between well-financed owners, backed by US taxpayer contributions to the military budget, and protesters armed with nothing besides their celebrity and individual courage. What activist athletes are doing now is similar to what Jackie Robinson did long ago: they are taking the standard values of the sports world—individual talent and initiative, competitiveness, courage, and commitment—and using them for social justice. There is absolutely no contradiction. And the more athletes that have started to act on their conscience, the more others have stepped forward, inspired by their examples.

Soon after Kaepernick took a knee in September 2016, US women's soccer star Megan Rapinoe knelt in solidarity during the national anthem. She said being a "gay American" helped her empathize with the struggle for minority rights.[22] The protest spread beyond professional sports, to US high schools and abroad—soon a German soccer team also knelt in solidarity: "We're no longer living in the 18th century but in the

21st century," Hertha Berlin defender Sebastian Langkamp told Sky TV at halftime. "There are some people, however, who are not that far ideologically yet. If we can give some lessons there with that, then that's good."[23] The gesture was also soon adopted to protest other kinds of bigotry and state suppression. At a South African middle school in 2018, two students knelt in protest during the playing of "Hatikvah," the Israeli national anthem. While it is common for such events to include the singing of both the South African and Israeli national anthems, and not unusual in the past for students opposed to the school's Zionist stance to either sit or stay silent during the singing of the Israeli anthem, it is worth noting that through these gestures the protesters were explicitly aligning themselves to the #BLM movement. Kaepernick's act of defiance had become part of a global symbolic system of protest.[24]

Athletes have also increasingly refused to play the political roles that team owners, politicians, and conservative media pundits wish them to play. Not only have professional athletes declined to participate in Israel's exercises in propaganda, thinly disguised as "goodwill" missions, but even amateur players have resisted being used as pawns or backdrops.[25] Consider the case of the women's softball team, the Texas-based women's softball team Scrap Yard Fast Pitch. Each and every member quit the team after its general manager tried to use it to promote racist Trump tweets. And, as remarkably, their opponents, USSSA Pride, also walked off the field in solidarity.[26]

Not only that, but just as Carlos and Smith did in 1968, athletes had, over the preceding decade, begun to connect the dots between racism and economic and social injustice.[27] In 2010, the NBA's Phoenix Suns protested Arizona Senate Bill 1070, which aimed to criminalize anyone suspected of being an undocumented immigrant, and twenty Major League Baseball All-Stars threatened to pull out of the All-Star Game if it were held in Arizona. In 2011, several members of the Green Bay Packers, the only non-profit, fan-owned team in all of major US professional sports, protested Wisconsin governor Scott Walker's "Act 10." Walker portrayed the bill as a "budget repair bill," but his "repair" involved stripping public sector workers of their collective bargaining rights. The players issued a statement declaring: "Governor Walker is trying to take away their right to have a voice and bargain at work. The right to negotiate wages and benefits is a fundamental underpinning of our middle class. When workers join together it serves as a check on corporate power and helps ALL workers by raising community standards."[28] Relatedly, in 2011, DeMaurice Smith, head of the NFL Players' Association, spoke of solidarity not only with Wisconsin workers, but also striking workers in Egypt.[29]

This willingness of athletes to use their voices to make political statements on and off the playing field also had an effect on spectators: many followed suit. At one of Major League Baseball's 2019 World Series games, when Trump's presence was announced, it was not professional athletes who rose up to start booing, calling for him to be "locked up"—it was the fans in the stands. The moment was captured on dozens of cell phones and blasted across Trump's favorite platform, Twitter. And at that moment, the sports stadium was returned to the people.[30] As Trump's term wore on, more and more athletes took highly public stands, issuing scathing critiques.[31] In 2020, Jalen Rose, a retired NBA player and ESPN analyst, posted a statement on Facebook that evoked the idea of "voice" in exactly the way we have been talking about it in this book: "We need people who aren't Black, we need people who aren't brown. When you know these things are happening in your society . . . have a voice, a legitimate one, lock and step with us, protest with us, post with us, not just when it's convenient, [but] when it can be uncomfortable."[32]

Of course, these cases do not erase the dominant symbolism behind sports, or sports arenas, nor should they necessarily. What they do accomplish is to break taboos about who can protest, and where they can protest. No place is presumed off-limits, and thus, no one is presumed to be without political voice. And, just as important, we discover that "political voice" can take all sorts of shapes. Fundamentally, these brief moments on the football field exist on the same political spectrum as longer-term instances when space has been remapped by means of mass occupations and protest camps.

Occupations

In the introduction, I talked about the Aventine Hill episode in the days of the Roman Empire, when a band of plebians dared to stage a unique protest over the denial of their political voice and rights. In modern times, such takeovers of specific places as a way to voice grievances—people's occupations—can be traced at least as far back as the days of the Great Depression, when in 1932 a group called the Bonus Army set up what would become known as Hoovervilles in Washington, DC. This group consisted of veterans of the First World War who insisted that the government make good on the benefits promised to them. These camps were combination military bases and shantytowns, and that admixture highlighted the precarious lives of military personnel trying to make ends meet during the recession. The Hoovervilles were encampments where the veterans created ad hoc communities of mutual support and protest, and their choice of the nation's capital was of course strategic—they knew the press would take an interest, and their shameful treatment was made all the more graphic by the proximity of their tent cities to iconic federal buildings. In so doing, they rescripted public space—making it a place for their voices to call out the failures of the government. They broke apart the solemn status quo of those places, and imposed their own agenda and their own histories. Over thirty years after the Hoovervilles were torn down, Dr. Martin Luther King Jr. revealed that "Resurrection City," the encampment set up on the National Mall during the 1968 Poor People's Campaign, took direct inspiration from them. Baptist minister Jesse Jackson declared, "Resurrection City cannot be seen as a mud hole in Washington, it is rather an idea unleashed in history." In making this bold statement, Jackson was doing more than gesturing back in time, or even just pointing to the current moment; he was saying that his own campaign was part of a much larger movement that would continue well into the future. The spirit of "Resurrection City" has also been evoked to instill a radical stance in the midst of tepid liberalism.[33] To mark the fortieth anniversary of that occupation, organizers at the 2008 Democratic National Convention set up "Resurrection City Free University," paying homage to the city's efforts to bring together the nation's ethnically diverse poor to protest economic injustice.[34] Such forms of protest mark both the present and the past; they carry an ethos and inspire others to act, to learn tactics and invent new ones as necessary.

This form of protest—of "taking place" and creating political voice—intensified after 1968, from the international anti-nuclear movement of the 1980s to the anti-roads movement in the UK of the 1990s, the counter-summit mobilizations of the global justice movement in the early 2000s, and a wave of climate camps during the late 2000s—first in Brazil and then across the world.[35] In each of these cases, the gatherings embodied the values they promoted. For example, climate camps not only staged discussions, workshops, and seminars; they were also built with recycled materials, used composting toilets and bicycle-powered laundries, and derived energy from solar panels and wind-driven turbines. This ethos spread into the organization of social and political life: the camps amounted to neighborhoods with deliberative, democratic structures.

The 2011 Occupy Wall Street movement was exemplary of this bold, participatory approach, and its participants drew parallels to the historic movements on which its foundations were built. As John Carlos himself remarked during a speech at New York's Zuccotti Park: "There was no more important place for me to stand up in 1968 than the Olympic medal stand. And given the economic injustice in the world, there is no more important place today for people to stand up than Wall Street."[36]

The French Marxist theorist Henri Lefebvre conceptualized the relation of people, place, and politics in ways that speak directly to this way of creating social and political space. Rather than assume we all simply move through and inhabit a prefabricated landscape, Lefebvre saw space as a product of a three-part act, comprising "perceived," "conceived," and "lived" space. Perceived space is that which we see before us—the actual physical environment. Conceived space is that which we come to understand—ideas, concepts, representations. This is where people are given the freedom to make something symbolic out of the given; in so doing, they grant it meaning, which might be radically different from the meaning conventionally given it. Finally, lived space is that which people actually experience—a combination of prefabricated space and the concepts they use to understand it in their everyday lives.[37] Now, what does this mean for political voice?

Consider the case of the 2011–12 "Indignant" protests at Syntagma Square in Athens, Greece. The protests were part of a movement against harsh austerity measures imposed by the government that had eviscerated the social safety net of thousands. For almost two months, demonstrators occupied the square, a site they had chosen specifically for its symbolic value. As researchers Anastasia Kavada and Orsalia Dimitriou explain:

> Syntagma Square is the main statutory public space of Athens, a spatial
> relationship between state and public. The square was named after the
> constitution that King Otto, the first King of Greece, was forced to grant
> after the popular and military uprising of 1843. The most prominent
> building, and the one that dictates the character of the square, is the
> former Royal Palace and current parliament building. . . . By 1860 it was
> the center of political and social life. The symbolic significance of the
> square and its central location in front of the Greek parliament offered
> a prime site of protest for the Indignant Movement. . . . As one inter-
> viewee put it, "the Parliament is there, the ex-palace is there, even if you
> are unaware of the history of the place it has great importance for the
> collective imaginary and what you perceive that is happening there."[38]

In choosing this site, like the Bonus Army and like the Poor People's
Campaign, the Indignants were drawing on the already existing symbolism of a specific place and stamping it with their protest. The Indignants
showed both their celebration of a critical democratic victory of the people, and their outrage over how those historical democratic principles had
been disgraced in the present. Such occupations hold the present up to
scrutiny, in order to assess how the foundational values of the nation are
in any way still alive.

The Syntagma occupation has striking resonances with the Wisconsin
protests that took place that same year, when between seventy and one
hundred thousand protesters took over the state capitol building to voice
their opposition to the governor's anti-union, pro-austerity agenda. In
both cases, while those pressing for "austerity" claimed that "we are all in
this together," protesters gathered to declare emphatically that this was
not the case. They drew attention to the manners in which public services
were being cut to cover the costs of private speculation. In critical ways,
the protests at Syntagma Square and the Wisconsin state capitol were
themselves microcosms of the worldwide protests over the suffering unleashed by the 2008 global economic collapse and the efforts of politicians
to foist the cost of economic recovery onto the backs of the working poor
and the unemployed. Here is historian Harvey Kaye's riveting first-person
account:

> We hope [to] block the passage of the anti-labor, indeed, anti-democratic
> budget repair bill proposed by governor Scott Walker—a bill that not
> only slashes public workers' incomes, but also strips them/us of their/
> our democratic rights to bargain collectively. . . . Moving with others

into the Rotunda area, beneath the great Dome, I could not help but look up and around and what I saw and heard maybe tearful, joyfully so . . . at the center of it all was the "people's microphone." There, one by one, people young and old spoke: students, Wisconsin unionists, and labor delegations from across the USA. Teenagers spoke in support of their teachers and parents. Workers of every trade decried the Republicans' so-called Budget Repair Bill and the corruption of democracy by billionaires such as the Koch brothers; recounted how their own parents and grandparents struggled to organize unions and secure their democratic rights; and declared their determination to fight on. . . . And folks from New York, Florida, Michigan, and points West registered their own unions' solidarity with Wisconsin.[39]

Despite the protests, Walker prevailed, and the state legislature passed the bill. While it is important to note this failure, we must also remember that the struggle is long, and that even failures can have positive results. Most important for this book, the people's microphone, by which a crowd amplifies the words of a speaker, has entered our political imaginary precisely as an instrument that gives democratic voice to the collective, over and against the false democracy of entrenched, suborned politicians. Even situations that seem like defeats can serve to lend a phenomenon new representation in language, thus transforming it into a weapon for political voice—we come to "know" something precisely because it is communicable and shared. Consider, for example, the term "the 1 percent" and its popularization through Occupy Wall Street. As Mark and Paul Engler have observed:

Occupy's shortcomings were real. But reflection on them should not obscure the impact that the movement did have. It is important to remember that Occupy was a drive that started with extremely minimal financial resources, no staff, no officers, and no established membership lists. . . . A *ThinkProgress* report showed that the month before activists arrived in Zuccotti Park, news outlets such as CNN, MSNBC, and Fox News were mentioning government debt some 15 times more often than problems of unemployment. Two months later, with the movement in full bloom, the trend had reversed.

When SEIU president Mary Kay Henry went door to door to canvas voters, she told a reporter, "every conversation was in the context of the 99% and the 1% come this discussion sparked by Occupy Wall Street. . . . The Occupy movement has framed the fight. They've totally changed the debate within a 30-day period.

As the *New York Times* reported, state legislators "lauded the Occupy
Wall Street movement for changing the political climate in Albany."
California governor Jerry Brown had pushed forth a similar measure [to
New York's "millionaires' tax"] in his state the same month, prompting
the AP headline reading, "you can thank the Occupy movement for
these new taxes on millionaires in California and New York."[40]

Even beyond those acts of legislation, we must note that the phrase "the
1 percent" has become part of everyday speech. Not only does it name
the ultra-rich; it also recognizes a moral, ethical, and political stance toward the extreme concentration of wealth we see in this country, and
this stance now has a kind of shorthand expression that has become a
permanent fixture in our conversational speech.

The fact that the state is so ready to violently put down these instances of
speaking out of place shows that civil disobedience truly frightens them—it
upsets their sense of reality and entitlement, and what's more, it threatens
to loosen the state's monopoly both on the right to speak and on the truth.
I will never forget as a young man hearing Ronald Reagan, then governor
of California, say in response to the unrestrained crackdown on the 1969
Berkeley People's Park protest, "If it takes a bloodbath, let's get it over with."
I was in Berkeley when Reagan sent in the National Guard to suppress the
demonstration, which had started when young people took over a vacant lot
and set up an alternative community, organic garden, and help center. The
National Guard shot dozens, arrested hundreds, and tear-gassed thousands
of protesters and innocent bystanders. In the ensuing military occupation, a
helicopter launched a chemical attack on the university campus, and adults,
young people, and children who were with their parents were surrounded
by soldiers with rifles and bayonets.[41] One young man, James Rector, who
was simply sitting on a roof on Haste Street, was shot to death.[42]

Those events, which would come to be known as "Bloody Thursday,"
illustrate the ways those in power have historically refused to tolerate the
reclamation of public space. And the reason for their intolerance is clear:
such "autonomous zones" are vivid testaments to the possibility of living differently, of speaking differently, and of "taking place" differently.
Occupations broaden the idea of the "political event" to include the addition
of one's own symbolic content to the commons. As we have seen, this often
entails the contestation and displacement of existing forms of language,

authority, and occupation. Political events take place when the course of history, or historical stasis, become intolerable—when the destruction of democracy, or an infinite delay in granting it, arrives at a day of reckoning. At these junctures, there is an eruptive moment of political recognition, and even as these moments of eruption are met with demands for "civility" and "patience," people persist in the creation of alternate articulations of their grievances and demands, reinventing the places from which they speak.

Eruptive Voices

A remarkable essay by writer and activist June Jordan titled "Civil Wars" tells of her impatience with self-appointed leaders who consolidate power and energy, and her appreciation for the eruptive energy of the Miami uprising of 1980, which followed the acquittals of four police officers who had beaten to death 33-year-old Arthur McDuffie, a Black insurance sales-man and Marine:

> It was such good news. A whole lot of silence had ended, at last! Misbegotten courtesies of behavior were put aside. There were no lead-ers. There was no organization and no spokesman. There was no agenda. There were no meetings, no negotiations. A violated people reacted with violence. An extremity of want, an extremity of neglect, and extremity of racist oppression had been met, at last, with an appropriate, extreme reaction: an outcry and a reaching for vengeance, a wreaking of havoc in return for wrecked lives, a mutilation of passers-by in return for genera-tions mutilated by contempt and by the immutable mutilations of pover-ty. Miami was completely impolite.[43]

In Jordan's narrative, this eruptive moment coincides with a dispute she was having with her good friend and fellow activist, Frances Fox Piven. For some period of time, they were not on speaking terms. Nevertheless, the essay closes with this moment:

> I decided to let it stand: to let the failures of the friendship stand and to reach out, instead, to Frances in areas of mutual, urgent concern, to engage once again in talk about tactics of struggle. . . . If the essence of a peoples' movement is its spontaneity, then how can you sustain it? But I hesitated. I thought again about all the other things that we would not talk about and all the arguments that would persist between us, and my feeling was, "What the hell; friendship is not a tragedy; we can be polite." And so I called her up, to talk.[44]

Jordan's essay moves beautifully on this parallel track, between friendship and allyship, between the language and sociality we use in all cases. She gives weight to the need for explosive, impolite speech and action, and grants such "incivility" an essential personal and political value. "Speaking out of place" is the only correct moral response to repeated acts of silencing and harm. But crucial, too, is the moment when that eruptive energy needs to be channeled into organization and sustained. And because Jordan recognizes this, she calls on Piven.

In her book *Challenging Authority*, Piven addresses precisely the phenomenon of eruptive protests, such as we saw after the May 2020 murder of George Floyd. At these moments, she observes, people "rise up in anger and hope to defy the rules that ordinarily govern their lives, and, by doing so come disrupt the workings of the institutions in which they are enmeshed. . . . [T]he drama of such events, combined with the disorder that results, propels new issues to the center of political debate."[45] Possessing scarce resources and little if any organizational infrastructure to rely on, protesters use "weapons of the weak" such as boycotts, highway blockages, and rent strikes. They garner media attention and use social media as well; they call out and shame bad people and bad practices in both conventional and unconventional speech. In many cases, such eruptions come about as the expression of long-term historical grievances, and thus they also mark—and spark—a new public political consciousness that can result in material change. As journalist Sarah Jaffe asserts:

> The key to understanding how to make change is to understand how power operates. Being able to donate millions to a single candidate is power, but so is shutting down the busiest shopping district in Chicago on the busiest shopping day of the year, as activists did in 2015 to protest the police shooting of Laquan McDonald. The action is estimated to have cost retailers 25 to 50% of their sales that day. Refusing, collectively, to pay millions of dollars in debt, is also power, as is closing the schools in Detroit for days in "sick out" protests in a kind of informal strike against abysmal conditions, as teachers did in early 2016 to force out the emergency manager appointed by the governor. Disruption is power when it is used strategically.[46]

Political scientist Aristide Zolberg describes these atypical, eruptive states as "moments of madness," by which he means periods of political exuberance when "human beings living in modern societies believe that 'all is possible."[47] Veteran activists often cite such moments as decisive in forming their own political commitments, and they can lead to long-term, sustained involvements, organizations, and movements. Again, with the #BlackLivesMatter protests of 2020, we witnessed a sea change in public attitudes regarding police violence. Long-held skepticism with regard to #BLM was transformed into solid belief in its justness, a change in feeling brought about not only by the brutal evidence placed before people's eyes, but also by the fact that when people saw just how many others were outraged by the murder, they gained confidence in their own reevaluation of the movement. The fact that the protests erupted in cities, suburbs, rural areas, and in every state of the Union inspiring protesters old and young, and of many races, should not be overlooked; nor should the fact that the demonstrations spread beyond our borders, even in the midst of a global pandemic that made public gatherings dangerous.[48]

As people around the world witnessed this crisis in America, not only did tens of thousands take to the streets in solidarity; they also linked racist state practices in the United States to those in their own countries—Australia, Britain, France, Germany, and elsewhere. What started in Minneapolis became a referendum on police violence everywhere, all through the power and moral energy of the protests.[49] When politicians and governments are held accountable for defaulting on their promises to support democracy and to practice it, the streets become a place where unofficial, yet highly visible plebiscites can take place. Notably, June 2019 saw demonstrations on an unprecedented global scale, in far-flung places such as Czechoslovakia, Hong Kong, Kazakhstan, and Palestine.[50] As researchers at the Tricontinental Institute noted:

> It is impossible to anticipate the spur for rebellion. In Lebanon, it was a tax on the use of WhatsApp; in Chile, it was the rise in subway fares; in Ecuador and in Haiti, it was the cut in fuel subsidies. Each of these conjunctures brought people to the streets and then, as these people flooded the streets, more and more joined them. They did not come for WhatsApp or for subway tokens. They came because they are frustrated, angry that history seems to disregard them as it consistently favours the ruling class.[51]

They go on to point out:

> It is important to ask why people have taken to the streets, to ask about their political orientation. In each of these cases—Chile, Ecuador,

Haiti, and Lebanon—the core issue is that the people of these countries have been defrauded by their own bourgeoisie and by external forces (pointedly, multinational corporations). The protests have targeted their governments, but that is only because these are protests that want to uphold democracy against capitalism.

Make no mistake—it is impossible to predict either the short-term or long-term effects of such protests. My focus here is not on the conventional (and often short-sighted) political markers of success or failure, but on the larger question of changing a people's attitude about their ability to speak and be heard, in both conventional and unconventional ways. While it is foolhardy to overvalue perceptual changes or small instances of hope, history has shown us that large things can gradually emerge out of smaller things. As critic John Berger puts it in his 1968 essay "The Nature of Mass Demonstrations": "A demonstration, however much spontaneity it may contain, is a created event which arbitrarily separates itself from ordinary life. Its value is the result of its artificiality, for therein lies its prophetic, rehearsing possibilities. . . . A mass demonstration distinguishes itself from other mass crowds because it congregates in public to create its function, instead of forming in response to one."[52] I want to pay particular attention to Berger's assertion that a demonstration as something that "separates itself from ordinary life." For the argument of this book, "ordinary life" is the life we have become habituated to—and the habits we have adopted include "knowing our place." Demonstrations eruptively set those habits aside; in fact, the best ones obliterate them. These demonstrations put on display, as the plebs did on the Aventine Hill, a rejection of policing the boundaries of whose voices count, and whose do not.

Policing Political Voice

The French political philosopher Étienne Balibar similarly envisions politics as something that creates a rupture in the calm of everyday life. Rather than subscribing to "eschatological visions of the time and place of politics" that conceive of politics as located in "an ideal situated beyond the realm of necessity," Balibar asserts that, like demonstrations, politics itself "inscribes risk and discontinuity in everyday life."[53] "Everyday life," or as Berger puts it, "ordinary life," exists in a world where people are slotted into specific spaces, each one containing different privileges of voice, of speaking.

Segmentation of people into those who have voice and those who do not is part of the logic of deferral, and obstruction, of democracy. Indeed, Balibar believes that "the state has never been democratized without demands, resistance or an upsurge of forces from 'from below,' designated by the political tradition precisely in a manner at once extensive and specific, with the name *demos*, the egalitarian component of the 'constituent' people."[54] While the state needs to maintain a monopoly on power, it cannot do so and at the same time claim to be a democracy. Therefore, it distributes bits and pieces of democracy, strikes seeming compromises, and allows non-threatened elements of democracy to appear from time to time, as needed. All of this is done to deter and contain the "eruptive" moments described above. In order to manage that perfect balance between the maintenance of their monopoly on power and allowance of brief or reduced moments of "democracy," state actors insist on and enforce a practice of "civility." This boils down to people's internalization of which sorts of language, expression, and action are sanctioned, and which are not. And, even more insidious, it can include the instillation of constant doubt as to whether one is entitled to speak or not.

When one censors oneself too quickly, that is, if one gives into habits of mind or social instincts too readily, one is stopped from engaging in serious political thinking. Indeed, many political thinkers have conceived of a healthy body politic as reliant on conflict and abrasiveness. For instance, James and Grace Lee Boggs insist: "You have to have a conflict before you can have politics. Only when you struggle over an idea do you reach the level of politics in the sense in which we are discussing it."[55] The essential point is to make the distinction between conflict for its own sake and conflict in order to reach a better progressive politics. The big question is: What are we fighting for? At the start of this chapter, we looked at a succession of worldwide protests against neoliberal agendas, though the manifestations of those agendas took different forms. We thus considered the need to see both the forest and the trees.

In April 2020, historian Rebecca L. Sprang asserted that the level of struggle—of taking sides, of stepping outside the roles assigned to us, and likewise radically reappraising "ordinary life"—had reached a historical high. Although she refrained from saying we were in the midst of a revolution, she declared that we were at a critical point of transition. While many people still feel atomized and powerless before crises in world health, the environment, and social and political upheaval, she argued that we had started to break out of stark neoliberal individualism and economic singularity and single-mindedness, and had begun to take sides, together. She uses a historical example to make her point:

> People sometimes imagine yesterday's revolutions as planned and carried out by self-conscious revolutionaries, but this has rarely, if ever, been the case. Instead, revolutions are periods in which social actors with different agendas (peasants stealing rabbits, city dwellers sacking tollbooths, lawmakers writing a constitution, anxious Parisians looking for weapons at the Bastille Fortress) become fused into a more or less stable constellation. The most timeless and emancipatory lesson of the French Revolution is that people make history. Likewise, the actions we take and the choices we make today will shape both what future we get and what we remember of the past.[56]

If we apply this lens to our own historical moment, we can see a number of different causes that form an impressive (if still unsolidified) constellation of resistance and progressivism. Before, I spoke about what I perceived to be a "war on difference"—that is, a broad repression of those who dare to declare, and act on, political agendas, identities, and beliefs that challenge the norms. Challenging norms is not in and of itself revolutionary or even desirable. The value of presenting such challenges comes when these norms are meant to block people from fully enjoying their rights, their protection under the law, and their full participation in fashioning a democracy. When people protest against state violence, economic and environmental injustice, systemic racism, and misogyny, we can see a common set of liberatory values that are aimed toward social justice. These values, and voices, have heretofore been silenced, segregated, and fragmented. Now they are coming together, and joining in a purposeful and self-conscious manner. We need to nurture and develop them, and concretize this constellation through persistent action. I thus end this chapter by looking at some other examples of people stepping out of their assigned roles to reinvent public space. My recommendation is that we begin to stitch these different moments together, so we can see just how much power we have, collectively.

Taking Control of the Streets

Sometimes protests erupt not in response to something the state has done, but rather in response to something it has failed to do. When governments fail to uphold their duties and responsibilities, the people can and do act to protect themselves, to demonstrate both the government's failures and to show their own capacity to protect themselves and their fellows. This is another important dimension of "speaking out of place," and one that is inflected in the last set of examples I offer in this chapter. As we delve into these instances in which people have taken over the streets, and made them safer, I want to remind us of the plebs on the Aventine Hill who demonstrated their ability to rule themselves. That example contained a dramatic element: the plebs "performed" an audacious act, taking on roles that were prohibited to them. In a similar manner, the following cases show protesters as vital political actors and people capable of doing something the state claims it alone is licensed to do.

In 2018, I reported in *Truthout* about the demonstrations in Dhaka.[57] During the summer, the capital of Bangladesh, which has a population of over eighteen million people, was rocked by protests that effectively shut down the city. The demonstrations were sparked after two young people were struck by a bus and killed. These tragic deaths were just the latest to be added to the thousands of similar fatalities each year that stem from government corruption and weak enforcement of the law. As *US News* reported: "Corruption is rife in Bangladesh, making it easy for unlicensed drivers and unregistered vehicles to ply the roads. At least 12,000 people die each year in road accidents often blamed on faulty vehicles, reckless driving and lax traffic enforcement."[58] While the immediate cause of the protests were those deaths, the reaction of the government unleashed widespread anger at government corruption and reignited long-standing fears about state violence: "Repression has been a trademark of this government over the past five years," Omar Waraich, the deputy director for South Asia at Amnesty International, told the *New York Times*. "Whether it is journalists, the opposition or peaceful protesters, dissent has never been tolerated."[59]

The protests grew for several days, and so did government repression. All social media platforms were strangled; the government suspended 3G and 4G telecommunications. People rushed to download photos, videos, and all other information available before Facebook and Twitter were completely shut down. An internationally famous photojournalist named Shahidul Alam was abducted from his house by Bangladeshi detectives and held because of Facebook posts and remarks he gave to *Al Jazeera* about the situation. Journalism platform *Muktiforum* claimed: "With reports of Internet slowdown, that hampers livestreaming and evidencing of the brutal attacks, and the government's warning to the media, that has made many local outlets back away from covering the events, Dhaka city has now turned to a war zone."[60]

What, exactly, were the student's demands? Nothing radical: improved road safety and justice for those who died in traffic and during violent clashes over the weekend. In fact, these young people left their roles as high school students and took up the roles of traffic enforcers: they set up checkpoints and established safety measures across the city. As the *Sydney Morning Herald* reported: "The demonstrations have been leaderless so far, with students gathering at their schools or universities in the morning before funneling out onto the street to block roads and erect makeshift checkpoints around their respective institutions. . . . On some days the protests have attracted up to 15,000 students, with parents leaving work to join their children and restaurants offering free food to demonstrators."[61] The high school students tapped into something powerful that clearly drew others to their cause. They felt an urgent sense of duty, as they saw government corruption leading to more and more deaths of ordinary people simply trying to carry on their lives in safety. Several students reached out to me when they learned I was working on a news article. One told me: "In Bangladesh, students have historically been the people who bring about change."

I want to draw attention not only to the fact that these protests erupted when two young people became the latest fatalities of a lax and corrupt system of traffic control, but also to point out how these actions showed a much broader anger over government corruption and lack of care. These lives were dispensable. Both the site and the manner of protest were eminently public, and made people literally stop. The protests indicted the status quo.

One finds in many of these protest camps and occupations that what political scientist Margaret Levi called a "community of care" emerges—and sometimes social roles and statuses are transformed or put to new uses. And, most consequential for my argument in this book, people create a community where their opinions and actions count. They create a new sense of space, in Lefebvre's terms, to meet their needs and pleasures, and in accordance with the values they bring and they learn.

In scholars Özge Yaka and Serhat Karakayali's description of what happened in Istanbul's Gezi Park protests of 2013, we see another group of demonstrators who took over responsibility for public welfare and safety. The protests began in May, in opposition to the government's plan to redevelop the park; by June, they were also focused on preventing the eviction of a protest camp that had been established. Like the Dhaka protests just discussed, the Gezi Park occupation expressed long-standing grievances against the Turkish government's crackdown on unions, teachers, dissidents, and others. At their height, the protests consisted of five thousand separate protests involving over three and a half million people. At the encampment,

> [t]he emergent forms of division of labor were based entirely on voluntary participation and were flexible to include "non-experts." Of course, medics built infirmaries within the park or the football Ultras and the radical left activists went to build barricades on the roads surrounding the park. However, established roles were increasingly negotiated by non-experts assuming new roles. Non-doctors providing basic medical care was a common example. Another interesting example was Demet Evgar, a famous actress without any credentials in pedagogy, who decided to establish a children's atelier, noticing the number of children in the park. The result was amazing in terms of giving children a venue to express how they understood, felt and experienced what was happening. . . . [N]ot having a professional, organizational body to orchestrate infrastructures and practices did not result in chaos but encouraged people to participate and take initiative. This particular organization of things engendered a new understanding of the park as a public space, which challenged the established codes of behavior.[62]

The Gezi Park demonstrators not only reclaimed the park precisely as a public place, reinstating the symbolic language that was historically its public identity; they also challenged who belonged where, who was authorized to do what, and whose voices could be heard. In both word and deed, this protest, and many others through history, showed people's rejection of the scripts and roles set out for them, and remapped social and political life as participants created new roles and responsibilities together.

In this chapter, we've looked at moments where people break with scripts that have been placed before them, using the occasion instead to say the unexpected and the unwanted. In so doing, they break the illusion that places can only accommodate certain kinds of speech, and certain kinds of people. In such acts of reclaiming, not only do people come together to form a chorus of voices; they also form communities of care and mutual support, thus remapping those places and leaving indelible marks upon them—be they sporting arenas, city streets, plazas, national monuments, restaurants, or schools. And this sharing has extended across national borders into the international sphere.

In the following chapters we will continue this discussion, turning to the places where we spend our lives with others: first to city spaces, then to the global, and finally, to the planet itself.

CHAPTER 2

RIGHTS TO A PLACE TO LIVE

In chapter 1, we saw powerful examples where both experienced activists and organizers, as well as ordinary people acting politically for the first time, put their voices and bodies on the line to stake out alternative political and social possibilities. These instances showed the ways that "speaking out of place" involves thinking, speaking, and how, if we are to learn to act in such alternative ways, we must relearn intellectual and political habits and break down the barriers to which we have become habituated—"partitions" that are anything but natural.

One of the most important of these barriers to break down is the one that lies between intellectuals and oppressed peoples. We must learn to speak with each other and to imagine common values and interests. On this dimension, the following quote from Marxist geographer David Harvey is worth contemplating, particularly in its call for us to focus on the very local and palpable scale of the city:

> The relationship between city and citizenship—the city as an object of utopian desire, as a distinctive place of belonging within a perpetually shifting spatio-temporal order—all give it a political meaning that mobilizes a crucial political imaginary . . . there are already multiple practices within the urban that themselves are full to overflowing with alternative possibilities. . . .
>
> The idea of the right to the city does not arise primarily out of various intellectual fascination and fads. . . . It primarily rises up from the streets, out from the neighborhoods, as a cry for help and sustenance by oppressed peoples in desperate times. How then do academics and intellectuals (both organic and traditional as Gramsci would put it) respond to that cry and demand?[1]

These lines take up the idea of place as something that is both malleable and the object of utopian thinking for people who are intent on building a space for a just and decent life.

In a moment I will describe in greater detail what the "right to the city" meant originally and how it became adapted by a range of activist groups here in the United States and globally. For the moment, let us use this shorthand description: the right to the city puts forward the notion that those whose labor makes the city possible should shape the environment in which they work and live. This right is both an aspiration and a call to action. Though the city itself has morphed under the regime of neoliberalism (and continues to do so), the logic and moral urgency of this right remain constant, if not even greater.

In this chapter I explore the notions of place and voice in the context of housing, segregation, race, and labor. I argue that de facto segregation has never ended, and has even intensified. The idea that those of a certain race and class belong in certain places, and that it is duty of the state to enforce those boundaries, regardless of what the law says, is alive and well. The policing of bodies extends to the attempt to control the voices of those people—some of whom are heard, and others not. The right to the city is effectively segmented, parceled out, and suppressed, often violently, in response to racist notions of who belongs where and how they must speak and act. This policing, both by state actors and by ordinary people acting as vigilantes, has often treated those marked by race and class as threats; and when these state and nonstate agents enact violence against marginalized groups, they have proven largely immune from prosecution, let alone serious consequences for their actions. This phenomenon has been a feature of American life for well over a century.

For example, years before Derek Chauvin, surrounded by three other officers, killed George Floyd by putting his knee on the prostrate man's neck, the news media showed a similar image—this time of a young Black girl, lying on the ground, with a policeman kneeling on her back. This happened in June 2015, in a Texas suburb. The girl's crime? Swimming in a public pool. The violence, which ended with a heavy-set, fully armed white male police officer throwing a 15-year-old Black girl clad only in a bikini to the ground and holding her down with his knee on her back.

Tatiana Rose, nineteen years old, who hosted the community pool party with her siblings, said that the weekend confrontation was sparked by
angry white neighbors. She said the cookout at the Craig Ranch housing
community in McKinney, Texas, was a public event she and her sisters
had held for their young friends from the neighborhood. A group of white
neighbors began cursing at the party attendees, telling them to "return
to their Section 8 housing" and hurling racial slurs at the children; at one
point, a white woman slapped a Black teenager in the face.[2] This remarkable event serves as a reminder that we are still living in a world of de facto
segregation, and that the "fact" of segregation is enforced not just by the
police, but also by members of the public. In these people's minds, the
only place for Black youth is in neatly segregated public housing, not in
a public space. The fact that the police officer was clearly acting not only
unprofessionally but also illegally, that he had stepped outside his role as a
police officer and into that of a vigilante, should make us think too of the
2012 killing of Trayvon Martin, another Black teenager who was deemed
to be "out of place."

But more than a century before his killing, or those events in McKinney,
we find another deadly combination of self-deputized enforcers of the
assumed "public good," along with the enforcement of racial barriers
by renegade police and security personnel. This resulted in one of the
most significant uprisings in American history. It all started on a Chicago
beach in 1919 and resulted in thirty-eight dead, five hundred injured and
six thousand National Guard troops called out in what became known as
Chicago's Red Summer. Importantly, the term "Red Summer" pointed
both to the blood spilled, and also to another term in currency, the "Red
Scare"; it was an image in which race and class were melded into one.

In stark contrast to the democratic sentiments expressed in the Treaty
of Versailles, which was signed the same year as the Chicago uprising,
segregation was alive and thriving in the United States. Black World War
I veterans who had recently risked their lives for their country returned
to find not only an abundance of racism still in place, but also unemployment and poverty. In Chicago, the Twenty-Ninth Street Beach was for
whites, while the Twenty-Fifth Street Beach for Blacks. On July 27, Eugene
Williams, a Black teenager, was on a raft that drifted across the unmarked

barrier. Whites began throwing rocks, and Williams drowned, sparking the Chicago rebellion.

In his study *Red Summer*, journalist Cameron McWhirter explains that in 1919, the country had been rocked by a series of bombings by a group of Italian anarchists. On one June night, ten bombs exploded in eight cities across the nation, targeting judges, legislators, and a Catholic church.[3] One of the homes bombed was that of A. Mitchell Palmer, Woodrow Wilson's attorney general. While he escaped harm, the event caused Palmer to start a wholesale attack on radicalism, which became known as the Red Scare. Along with anarchists, Black activists became associated with the unfolding social violence. McWhirter notes:

> Palmer and his agents came to believe Blacks were susceptible to communists and anarchists because of their subservient status, so they set out to prove that revolutionaries were recruiting Blacks. Palmer defined radicalism broadly, and would include the legitimate political efforts of black activists. President Wilson was predisposed to make such a connection. That March, he remarked . . . that "the American returning from abroad would be our greatest medium and convening in conveying bolshevism to America." American soldiers were being treated as equals by the French, he worried and "it had gone to their heads."[4]

The attacks that Palmer led became known as the Palmer Raids.

The "Bolshevism" Wilson had in mind had recently been manifested in some of the largest labor strikes in US history. They included a strike of four hundred thousand steelworkers organized by the American Federation of Labor. In response to this strike, because Boston police were on strike, Massachusetts governor Calvin Coolidge sent in the state militia.[5] Palmer proceeded to whip up public rage against both Black protest and labor protest, claiming that the two groups were acting in unison (which was hardly true, as most US labor unions excluded Black workers, along with other minorities). At the height of the frenzied Red Summer, "pundits and politicians offered up analysis of and solutions for the escalating 'problem period.' At one point, William Monroe Trotter's National Equal Rights League pushed for the United States to take over some or all of Imperial Germany's African colonies and encouraged black Americans to colonize them."[6]

What the Red Summer brings to the fore is the tight interlinkage between race and class—between those who can participate in shaping their environments of work and play, education and health, political engagement and cultural life, and those who cannot. It comes down to an issue of democratic participation in the creation of the conditions of one's life. That right would seem to be noncontroversial. But not only has that right been erased for so many; this silencing has also become naturalized and embedded in our expectations of life.

The white neighbors in McKinney who screamed curses at the young Black pool goers in their neighborhood did so because they felt an injurious breech had been made in their notion of "public" space.[7] The revision of public space into private space, in what American studies scholar George Lipsitz has called the "white spatial imaginary," stretches back in time, and as Black people have always been seen as exploitable sources of labor in the United States and elsewhere, it is no surprise that racial and class segregation are closely entwined.[8]

In this chapter I trace how people have conceived of the right to public space, the right to be public citizens, the right to shape the environment that has been built by their labor—that is, the right to the city. I also discuss how people have historically adapted it and organized around it. The forces that act against this struggle are enormous, and I make no claim that victory is around the corner. What I do argue is that we should not downplay our capacity to claim our rights, especially if we act in solidarity. Indeed, the small but significant victories should be taken as evidence of our collective powers.

The Right to the City

In 1967, even before the tumultuous events of May '68 in Paris, Henri Lefebvre wrote his seminal essay "The Right to the City," a text that not only had an immediate effect in France but has come to have global import. Its continued importance is easily explained. Dismayed by the increasing deterioration of urban life under capitalism, a deterioration marked by the increasing alienation of urban life, Lefebvre's essay urged a radical rethinking of what a city was considered to be and what it could be, as well as the relationship between human beings and what he conceived of as "space." One of his basic concerns was the increasing atomization of life, via consumerism and the phenomenon of de-collectivization. No wonder, then, that as the very trends Lefebvre noted in 1967 have developed, unabated, and become amplified under the regime of neoliberalism, more and more people today embrace "The Right to the City," even while reinventing it. The following passage neatly encapsulates Lefebvre's main argument:

> Until now, only those individual needs, motivated by the so-called society of consumption (bureaucratic society of managed consumption) have been prospected, and moreover manipulated rather than effectively known and recognized. . . . The human being has the need to accumulate energies and to spend them, even waste them in play. He has indeed to see, to hear, to touch, to taste and the need to gather these perceptions in a world. . . . The need for creative activity, for the *oeuvre* (not only of products and consumable material goods), of the need for information, symbolism, the imaginary and play. Through these specified needs lives and survives a fundamental desire of which play, sexuality, physical activities such as sport, creative activity, art and knowledge are particular expressions and *moments*, which can more or less overcome the fragmentary division of tasks. Finally, the need of the city in urban life can only be freely expressed within a perspective which here attempts to become clearer and to open up the horizon. Would not specific urban needs be those of qualified places, places of simultaneity and encounters, places where exchange would not go through exchange value, commerce and profit? Would there not also be the need for time for these encounters, these exchanges?[9]

As opposed to capitalism's construction of the individual as solely an economic actor—a person whose only function is to provide labor and then spend their wages on commodities—Lefebvre sees people as those whose energy can and should be expended outside the circuits of capitalism. Humans can and should create and enjoy pleasure on their own, and most significantly, in encounters with each other unmediated by the exchange of money or wage labor.

The idea of the "creative," so perversely appropriated by today's neoliberal city planners, is here regarded as a collective investment in a shared better life—something as yet unscripted. In Lefebvre's usage, the oeuvre, or "work," is an existential project, aimed at changing the circumstances of one's life and those of others. Lefebvre argues: "The *right to the city* cannot be conceived of as a simple visiting right or as a return to traditional cities. It can only be formulated as a transformed and renewed right to *urban life*. It gathers the interests (overcoming the immediate and the superficial) of the whole society and firstly of all those who inhabit."[10]

Again, this requires people to reorient themselves away from and out-side the compartments and roles assigned them by capitalism. Crucially, these compartments and roles are prescribed in the blueprints and build-ings, pathways and diversions, that constitute the city, guiding, channe-ling, and blocking the movements and actions of our bodies. The passage from Harvey quoted at the top of the chapter underscores this point, as he describes the city "as a distinctive place of belonging within a perpetually shifting spatio-temporal order—all give it a political meaning that mobi-lizes a crucial political imaginary."[11] Through a new political imaginary, we can envision a different space and time, and a different expressive and political voice. Here I am referring to what Lefebvre calls "social space." As he defines it, "social space incorporate[s] social actions, the actions of subjects both individual and collective who are born and who die, who suffer and who act *from the point of view of these subjects*, the behavior of their spaces at once vital and mortal: within it they develop, give expres-sion to themselves, and encounter prohibitions; then they perish, and that same space contains their graves. . . . Social space thus remains the space of society, of social life. Man does not live by words alone; all subjects are situated in a space in which they must either recognize themselves or lose themselves, a space which they may both enjoy and modify."[12]

I emphasize "from the point of view of these subjects" because one of the key arguments of this book is that we need to reauthorize ourselves as empowered actors in the world; we must question any expert or pundit or political ideology that has shouted over us until we have simply remained silent. We must let ourselves speak. Please note that I am not advocating for some radical, libertarian vision à la Ayn Rand. What I am proposing is a democratic socialist endeavor that sees the value of our social and intellectual independency, and of our collective existence and collective action. One manifestation of this is what Harvey calls "participatory budgeting,"

> in which ordinary city residents directly take part in allocating portions of municipal budgets through a democratic decision-making process, has been so inspirational has everything to do with many people seek-ing some kind of response to a brutal neoliberalizing international capitalism that has been intensifying its assault on the qualities of daily life since the early 1990s. No surprise either that this model developed in Porto Alegre, Brazil—the central place for the world social forum.[13]

Such examples are vital to this book's central argument: we cannot and must not leave "alternative thinking" to experts and pundits. Only everyday people, whose lives are most impacted by the decisions of those in powerful places, can see the uneven applications of those economic, social, and political decisions. Only everyday people have the knowledge needed for democratic decision making. We need to instill and nurture a sense of collective, democratic ownership of the decisions that create the conditions under which we live together.

The first formal collective to be created around Lefebvre's concept was the Right to the City Alliance, founded in 2007.[14] It consisted of forty urban and community-based organizations who came together to fight the gentrification of working-class communities of color.[15] Joining these groups were individuals from many walks of life, including students, teachers, health care workers, and clergy. As the organization grew, its mission came to include a spectrum of areas that have been under constant attack, squarely at the intersection of "place" (urban land use, community development, environmental justice) and "voice" (human rights, civic engagement, criminal justice) clearly intertwined. With the 2008 financial crisis, neoliberalism spread its toxicity in forms such as so-called austerity programs that converted private corporate debt into public debt and public misery. In response, the idea of the right to the city became the focal point of a resurgence of global activism. As urbanist Margit Mayer explains:

> The claim for the right to the city has turned into a viral slogan across Europe, North America as well as Latin America, because it fuses and expresses a variety of issues that had become highly charged over years of neoliberal urban development and even more so through the effects of the financial and economic crisis. They have made the loss of social, economic and political rights painfully tangible not just for traditionally disadvantaged and marginalized groups, but increasingly also for comparatively privileged urban residents, whose notion of the good of urban life is not realized by increasing privatization of public space, in the "upgrading" of their neighborhoods, or the subjection of their everyday lives to the intensifying interurban competition.[16]

Another concept that helps us see how the dispossessed can, even with scarce means, fight back in multiple and inventive ways is what Sarah Keenan, co-director of the Centre for Race and Law, calls "subversive property." Keenan evokes the work of feminist geographer Doreen Massey to portray an idea of "space" that taps into both Lefebvre's "social space," and what I am calling "place" and "voice":

> Massey understands space as "the simultaneity of stories so far"— this simultaneity of multiple and different stories of subjects, streets, mountains, communities and empires; stories which are, importantly, unfinished. These stories are practiced, embodied and relational—to understand space as the "simultaneities of stories so far" is not to reduce space to narrative, but to capture its multiplicity, is vitality and its interconnectedness. . . . Spaces where subjects belong, or "spaces of belonging," are spaces of propriety—spaces where *some will smoothly fit because they are "in place" and proper, while others will be "out of place," improper and thus repelled, unsettled or realigned.*[17]

Keenan's and Massey's ideas are invaluable to the present study because instead of thinking of space and place solely as something dictated and managed from above, according to the logic and the demands of the state, they see space as produced by multiple voices emanating from different spaces, centering on a shared project to which they belong. This is a space where their voices are heard, rather than demoted or silenced—an inversion of the "placement" of peoples and voices. In this contestation of who belongs where and how they should speak, we see a struggle over the right to shape the conditions of one's own life.

The idea of "subversive property" is not, in fact, a radical departure from classic liberal notions of property. It is, rather, a radical revision of these notions. Keenan makes this point by revisiting the seventeenth-century English philosopher John Locke's famous assertion that the land belongs to the people whose labor makes the land productive. In the fifth chapter ("On Property") of his *Second Treatise of Government*, Locke writes: "That the earth and all inferior creatures be common to all men, yet every man has a property in his own person; this nobody has any right to but himself. The labor of his body and the work of his hands we may say are properly his. Whatsoever, then, he removes out of the state that nature has provided and left it in, he hath mixed his labor with, and joined to it something that is his own, and thereby makes it his property."[18] Keenan takes this foundational notion of property and human beings' relationship to it to claim the collective right of all those who actually produce the city and live in it, feed it, care for it in multiple ways. What we see in capitalist societies is exactly the opposite—instead of the city belonging to those whose labor makes the place productive and nurturing, it belongs to the owners of the workers' labor. It is those people's labor that is exploited and appropriated by capital and capitalists who claim to be the ones "really working," which is evident in the tremendous differentials in compensation—a 2018 study found that CEOs now make on average 278 times the average worker's salary.[19]

Crucially, as Harvey writes, "[t]he right to the city is not an exclusive individual right, but a focused collective right. . . . It seeks a unity from within an incredible diversity of fragmented social spaces and locations within innumerable divisions of labor.[20] I argue that the very unity of which Harvey speaks is only possible if all voices are enfranchised to speak from their different places and different roles as workers—or better yet, as the collective *makers* of the city. Indeed, the very etymology of the word "nation" is founded on the idea of labor, and in the erasure of that labor by those who seek to claim the land as actually theirs.

The word "nation" derives from the Latin verb *nascor* (to be born, formed, destined, arise in). Hannah Arendt appeared to focus on the idea of "formation" when she introduced the notion that the nation comes into being along with the territory that bears a particular mark: "[The nation] is attached to the soil which is the product of past labor and where history has left its traces."[21] In this sense, "natives" are those original peoples whose labor on the land has created its space. Yet in both settler-colonial states and in capitalist societies, rightful ownership of and proprietorship over the land is claimed by those who are, in fact, parasitic on the work of others. The battle for the right to the city is nothing less than a reclamation of the value of one's own labor, and that of one's coworkers, in the broadest collective sense possible. In declaring its right to the city, this collective names itself, rather than accepting the definitions of the state—definitions that are intent on separating, segregating, and rendering weak the voices that threaten its power. "Segregation" thus is not simply the separation of people from other people; it is the systematic "placement" of people into zones of exploited labor, alienation, and the purposeful creation and exacerbation of antagonisms based on race and class.

Housing and Race

The physical landscape of the United States is segmented by more than mountains, rivers, and state and city boundaries. Aerial photographs vividly display large swaths of degraded land, impoverished communities, crumbling infrastructure, abandoned farms, and deserted, rusted deindustrialized spaces.[22] But there are also patches of green, luxury homes on large landscaped lots, high-rise apartments, gated communities, chrome-and-glass office buildings, clean and modern structures and facilities, golf courses, swimming pools, and massive areas dominated by agribusiness. The categories that drive the production of these differential spaces are class and race, each of which are exploited by capitalist growth, extraction, and abandonment. Especially after the Second World War, the US government engaged in a massive project to "rebuild" cities, ostensibly to improve life for everyone. In fact, its benefits flowed along racial and class lines.

Postwar urban development programs manifested the necessity for a proactive government, engaged in assuring that cities developed in profitable and efficient manners. As scholars Roger Friedland, Frances Fox Piven, and Robert R. Alford write:

> The capitalist state must provide the infrastructure and subsidies which will ensure the profits of monopoly capital; it must subsidize and protect the accumulation process, while continuing to permit the private appropriation of profits. . . . Government agencies provide the authority to make and enforce decisions affecting the spatial efficiency of the urban economy, in the form of zoning plans, the development of industrial parks, urban renewal projects and, increasingly, metropolitan planning activities.[23]

We see here the systematic reinvention of "public works," characterized by an inherently private enterprise benefiting from public dollars. Redevelopment had a particular impact upon ethnic neighborhoods, as these spaces became embroiled within a sweeping program to reformulate American urban space for the late twentieth-century economy according to the demands of transnational capital. This postwar urban redevelopment was characterized by a strategy that removed "undesirable" populations from potentially valuable land and used public funds for private goals instead of direct funding of social programs. The impetus for renewal was twofold: the need to make the new city economically vital and competitive, and the desire to eradicate "urban blight." This term has a special history and application. Its close cousin, "urban renewal," has many of the same properties, but the long history of the word "blight" lays bare both the intense racism that informs the displacement and destruction of poor neighborhoods and neighborhoods of color, and the manners in which these communities were necessarily connected to "urban blight"; in this view, their intrinsic character was itself a "blighted" form of humanity.

As architectural historian Andrew Herscher observes, "removal" projects differed from the usual urban renewal projects in one important way: blight removal was a "totally subtractive demolition project," that is, "renewal" was not on the planning board's agenda.[24] In an article titled "Black and Blight," Herscher gives a detailed account of how the destruction of Black communities and ethnic communities was facilitated by declaring them spaces of "blight." The stigma, of course, equally indicted the inhabitants of those spaces; they were found unworthy of simply living there because of their supposed disregard for peace, hygiene, and the proper upkeep of property. He notes that a fundamental contradiction is evident in these acts of stigmatization:

> [The] conceptualisation of blight and practice of blight removal have productively obscured the fundamental needs of industrial capitalism for a population of reserve labor and for urban space to accommodate that population. When defined as blight, the urban spaces that forces of reserve labor occupy are discursively and practically expelled from the system that produced them. These spaces were framed as obstacles to property development, as opposed to products of a disavowed form of de-development premised on maintaining reserve labor in a precarious condition.[25]

We can see this phenomenon in the light of our discussions of the right to the city and "subversive property." If, drawing on Locke's notion of personhood and property, the land belongs to those whose labor transforms it, and the right to the city includes the basic right to shape and determine the environment that relies on one's own work, then we can see in "blight removal" the expulsion of the very people whose labor was brought in to build the environment from which they are now to be ejected. Their homes and their places of community, and their bodies themselves, are relegated to a past and expired time. However, this degradation of their lives is not blamed on the workings of capital, but on some inherent trait of their own. These debasements of life and labor exert a kind of "shame" tax: one's worthiness is called into question, and when that happens, one's ability to protest and argue for rights is removed as well. One is thought to have defaulted on precisely that right.

In tracing the deep history of the uses of "blight" to degrade and displace Black bodies and livelihoods, Herscher tells of Frank B. Williams, a New York lawyer, zoning advocate, and future cofounder of the journal *City Planning*, who declared in 1912: "[A] blighted district tends to become an unsanitary district, and where the blight goes far enough in time it may even tend to become a slum district."[26] A little more than a decade later, Stanley McMichael and Robert F. Bingham lay bare the racist foundation of "blight": "Southern cities have a method of taking care of the problem which is well known, and seems to be entirely effective. . . . Colored people must recognize the economic disturbance which their presence in a white neighborhood causes, and must forgo their desire to split off from the established district where the rest of their race lives."[27] Then, nearly a hundred years later, in 2014, we had Dan Gilbert, billionaire founder of the online mortgage lender Quicken Loans speaking in his new role as cofounder of the Detroit Blight Removal Task Force. He drew on exactly the same rhetoric: "Blight is a cancer. Blight sucks the soul out of everyone who gets near it. . . . Blight is radioactive. Blight is contagious. . . . Blight serves as a venue that attracts criminals and crime. It is a magnet for arsonists. Blight is also a symbol of all that is wrong and all that has gone wrong for too many decades in the once-thriving world-class city of Detroit."[28]

"All that is wrong and all that has gone wrong" is a pretty sweeping accusation to essentially lay at feet of the city's Black and poor residents. It is not hard to see that in Gilbert's view it is *they* who are the "cancer" that has to be excised. And his racist proselytizing ignores a fundamental point, to which I return: it is the people whose labor transforms the land that are its proper owners, and it should be up to them to decide its future. From the brutal logic of settler colonialism, to racist "development," to the appropriation and destruction of Indigenous peoples' lands, each instance is preceded by and incorporates a regime of degradation—one that enables the displacement of bodies and the silencing of voice.

Scholars Norman and Susan Fainstein say that one of the rationales behind urban development was that it would "maintain and reestablish racial and class territorial segregation through locational decisions involving clearance, zoning, public facilities (especially schools), transportation routes, and publicly subsidized housing [and] encapsulate the lower classes in peripheral locations."[29] To facilitate the acquisition of land, cities such as New York declared "special districts" that altered zoning laws in unpublicized hearings. The wholesale delegitimation of poor and minority communities was facilitated under the pretense of attacking the universally abhorred condition of poverty. This was a thinly disguised strategy of class and race warfare. Sociologist Herbert J. Gans's 1961 essay "The Balanced Community" shows the social, economic, racial, and "cultural" segregation that lay behind "urban renewal," supporting an agenda for redevelopment that would spatially maintain strict class divisions:

> Architectural and site plans can encourage or discourage social contact between neighbors, but . . . homogeneity of background or of interests or values [is] necessary for this contact to develop into anything more than a polite exchange of greetings. . . . Positive, although not necessarily close, relations among neighbors and maximal opportunity for the free choice of friends both near and far from home [are] desirable values, and . . . a moderate degree of homogeneity among neighbors [is] therefore required.[30]

Further into his essay, Gans tries to argue that class, not race, is of central importance. Without common "values" and tastes, neighborhoods will be sites of "cool" politesse, not communities. He suggests that the state pay greater attention to improving the economic status of the poor, rather than forcing open housing and depriving the American citizen from their inalienable right of choice. But whether or not the cause is primarily race or class, we should not lose track of the fact that Gans merges them together. Gans's proposal is that urban redevelopment would actually benefit everyone—better housing for the poor and Black communities who would, like middle-class whites, appreciate being with "their own." But after the bulldozers had done their work, the historical reality of urban redevelopment set in. While urban decay had been uprooted and slums torn down, municipalities were not required to replace housing units demolished under renewal programs. Space clearing was performed by invoking the power of eminent domain, which allowed city governments to seize land and then sell it to private developers, who in turn were sub-sidized by federal monies. Thus, segregation and displacement without compensation is the true legacy of urban redevelopment.

We find exactly this pattern, amid racist accusations of "blight," in the construction and the subsequent destruction of the massive Pruitt-Igoe housing project in St. Louis. Built in 1954, this federally funded project was heralded as the harbinger of enlightened city planning and federal–city cooperation. But by the 1960s, the project had become crime-ridden and poorly maintained, and vacancy rates skyrocketed. By 1972, St. Louis began tearing the project down, and by 1976 all thirty-three towers were gone. The blame for its failure was placed solely on the Black communi-ty; it was argued that they carried urban blight into even these pristine, modern housing projects. Chad Freidrichs's award-winning documenta-ry *The Pruitt-Igoe Myth* shows that the failure was in fact the result of a confluence of conditions, including a changing labor market, the overall decline of the city, the desertion of the area by services and amenities that make life livable, and a shift in state welfare policies.[31] In 1973, President Richard Nixon had declared that the urban crisis was over, and withdrew federal funding for education, transportation, and public health; in turn, cash-strapped cities and states did so as well. Nixon's 1968 presidential win had been based on a "law and order" platform that would pour money into law enforcement, surveillance, and harassment of Black and brown communities. As his war on Black and brown communities materialized, it took many forms. One, of course, was mass incarceration. Another was the depletion of wealth from Black communities—precisely those communities that had started to make some headway economically. This historical shift had profound effects on urban life, on race relations, and on the financing and economies of cities.

After the early 1970s, urban redevelopment took on an entirely new dimension, although its basic premises remained the same. Development policy shifted from direct federal aid to block grants in 1975, simultane-ously giving over administrative power to "virtually autonomous redevel-opment authorities."[32] Federal oversight decreased, and the private nature of this public enterprise became more clearly evident. As more and more public funds were devoted to subsidies and incentives for private business, they were diverted specifically from social programs aimed to help the poor. The compensatory logic behind this, again, was that a healthier business climate would produce better jobs for all. Yet, as public policy scholar Gregory Squires argues, "the principal beneficiaries are often large corporations, developers, and institutions because the tax burden and other costs are shifted to consumers. And perhaps the most important public benefits—jobs—are either temporary and low-paying or, in the case of good jobs, go to suburbanites or other out-of-towners recruited by local businesses."[33] The selling point for urban development, while including an appeal to civic duty, was largely the redistribution of public monies to select private enterprises that did not pass on their profits to the public. Instead of improving the public lot, urban redevelopment usually created greater inequities. For example, more jobs were created in New York City in 1983 than in any year since 1950; however, the city's poverty rate increased 20 percent between 1979 and 1985 because the jobs created paid worse than the (usually unionized) manufacturing jobs they replaced.[34]

In *Race for Profit*, Princeton University professor Keeanga-Yamahtta Taylor notes another critical element of the policy changes enacted in the 1970s that had profound effects on Black communities: the Federal Housing Administration ended the segregationist policies known as redlining, and started low-income lending programs to encourage Black homeownership:

> Predatory inclusion describes how African American home buyers were granted access to conventional real estate practices and mortgage financing, but on more expensive and comparatively unequal terms.... The benignly named "public private partnership" obscured the ways that the federal government became complicit with private sector practices that promoted residential segregation and racial discrimination.[35]

This shift in policy was of a piece with what I described above, in terms of the shift in federal policies and the fusion of government agencies and the real estate industry. This extremely cozy relationship (individuals sometimes held appointments to both real estate boards and municipal or federal offices) bred lax oversight and maximized exploitation, extortion, and profiteering, all in the name of removing "blight," making America beautiful, and offering people the chance to own their own houses.

These strategies of exploitation continued well into the twenty-first century, reaching their apex in the run-up to the 2008 economic crisis. UCLA professor Gaye Theresa Johnson points out:

According to the 2007 annual Minority Lending Report, about 47% of Latinos and 48% of Blacks who purchased mortgages in 2006 got higher cost loans, as compared with about 17% of whites and Asians. The predatory lending the targeted minority communities resulted in what the Kerwin Institute for the Study of Race and Ethnicity has called "extreme geographic concentrations of foreclosures." In 2008, United for a Fair Economy estimated that the results of predatory lending would be disastrous for Black and Brown people and by the time the recession was over the loss of wealth for people of color would total between $164 billion and $213 billion: it is the greatest loss of wealth for people of color in modern US history.[36]

This trend, which as we have seen started in the 1970s with urban redevelopment driven by state, municipal, and real estate interests working together and exploiting public monies for private gains, continued through the 2008 economic crisis and its continued aftermath. David Harvey and David Wachsmuth note:

At the top, $32 billion accumulated, and at the bottom 2 million people lost their houses in what has been described as one of the biggest asset losses of all time for the African-American marginalized population. The losses of those at the bottom of the social pyramid roughly matched the extraordinary gains of financiers at the top. . . . Value was stolen from one segment of the population and accumulated by another.[37]

As I have argued throughout this chapter, the disenfranchisement of Black people, other racial minorities, and the working class and poor was frequently enacted by the same tactics of eviction, debt, and segregation that robbed people of both their voices and their homes. These cases show us, once again, how the structural violence that capitalism enacts in its path to "development" not only does not distinguish between race and class, but leverages bigotry against both to achieve its aims.

Displacement, Not Just "Gentrification"

In this book about place and voice, we have observed, time and again, that language truly matters. The word "gentrification" is no exception. When one uses the word, one erases the human forces behind it. "Gentrification" simply names a mechanical process; it obscures who makes it happen, how they make it happen, and whom it effects. So, who drives the process? It is there in the name: the gentry, or, even better, the ruling class. Following the logic of "blight" that we explored earlier, and the ways it was used to stigmatize Black livelihoods, the poor, and other subaltern groups, with "gentrification" we have the reverse. Here we have a process of "space production" by genteel, wealthy people who by their very presence "improve" the land with their capital investments. And these investments return to themselves and their class. What we lose sight of is that they are there only because the levers of public-private interests have been pulled in their favor, and to the detriment of the people and lives they have displaced and exploited. Chester Hartman's classic of urban planning, *Displacement: How to Fight It*, defines "displacement" as "what happens when forces outside the household make living there impossible, hazardous, or unaffordable."[38] While here Hartman prefers the word "displacement" over "gentrification" because the former names the forces that enact displacement, activist and essayist Jeff Chang criticizes "gentrification" because it erases those who are thrown out of their homes: "[G]entrification offers a peculiarly small frame for trying to understand these paradigmatic shifts. . . . But what of those who are displaced? Gentrification has no room for the question, 'where did the displaced go?' instead the displaced joined the disappeared."[39]

Besides the demolition of old buildings and the construction of sterile, shiny new city center centers, publicly funded arenas and entertainment facilities, and luxury apartments, we also find the burgeoning of electronic surveillance, private security forces, and policing. These apparatuses serve to secure the "production" of capitalist space so that it does not slip into disrepair, and so that no one who does not "belong there" stays more than their allotted time. The entire facade and structure of the new cityscape is meant to be unwelcoming to those whose time is not used primarily spending money or working for their bosses.

In his important study *How Racism Takes Place*, George Lipsitz tells the story of the construction of a new football stadium for the St. Louis Rams in the early 2000s, where the city's priorities became clear: "Downtown redevelopment for the Rams stadium followed clear precedents established previously by a variety of slum-clearance, highway-building, and urban-renewal policies in the mid-twentieth century, as well as by neoliberal public-private partnerships in subsequent decades."[40] Thus,

[w]hile the Rams and their fans in the expensive luxury suites are housed lavishly inside the Dome, Black children in St. Louis face the consequences of a segregated housing market. . . . Poverty and a disastrous shortage of adequate dwellings forced some children to have to move and change schools so often they were never exposed to any one single teacher, pedagogy, or curriculum for very long.[41]

Ironically, the gentry come to invade city spaces on the basis of their history, edginess, creativity, and vitality, and then purposefully scale all those things back into constrained and defanged versions of their former selves. Most immediately, this happens by making the city too expensive for ordinary people, the very people who built those communities, to live in. Chang tells of one instance: "When in 2013 the famed artists René Yanez and Yolanda Lopez—Yanez had helped found Galeria de La Raza as well as the famed Diá de Los Muertos parade and Lopez had created some of the most compelling art of the Chicano movement—were evicted from their apartment, artists gathered to raise funds to help them and to mourn what the city had become."[42] Flooded by mostly white, young tech workers, San Francisco—formerly home to the beats, jazz, the blues, the countercultural scene, street art, the Magic Theatre, the Mission, and so much else—had become an inhospitable, even threatening place. Chang goes on to note, "Where you live plays a significant role in the quality of food and the quality of education available to you, your ability to get a job, buy a home, and build wealth, the kind of health care you receive and how long you live, and whether you will have anything to pass on to the next generation."[43]

Both Chang's and Lipsitz' understandings of "place" are closely connected to the ways in which I have been using the term in my study. Here is how Lipsitz describes "place": "When I say that racism 'takes place' I mean it figuratively, in the way that historians do, to describe things that happened in history. But I also use the term as cultural geographers do, to describe how social relations take on their full force and meaning when they are enacted physically in actual places."[44] To this, I add the idea of the "production of space" that Lefebvre coined to designate that alongside the physicality of a place, people produce a sense of how this place is inhabited and animated by people—purposefully, or in play, or simply in residing there, filling out physical space with meaning. So when people are displaced, it is not a matter of simply picking up and starting over again. Displacement involves the destruction of meaning, of significance, and an environment that bears the signs of one's life, one's energy, one's dreams, and one's social and cultural life together with others. And that is why being displaced, evicted, expelled, exiled is immensely destructive not only to individuals and families, but also to communities. And this is especially true for those who cannot easily reproduce their lives materially and spiritually, and for ones who are forced to live that much further from their workplace, or possibilities of work, separated from their neighbors and loved ones, wrenched out of places and habits that, in their sheer being, secured a pattern of living. Sarah Keenan describes something like this when she speaks of space "holding people up": "[H]olding up invokes a wide range of social processes, structures and networks that give forced relations of belonging."[45]

In *Evicted*, sociologist Matthew Desmond notes what happens when this support of "place" is removed:

> Suicides attributed to evictions and foreclosures doubled between 2005 and 2010, years when housing costs soared. Eviction even affects communities that displaced families leave behind. Neighbors who cooperate with and trust one another can make their streets safer and more prosperous. But that takes time. Efforts to establish local cohesion and community investment are thwarted in neighborhoods with high turnover rates. In this way, eviction can unravel the fabric of the community, helping to ensure that neighbors remain strangers.[46]

It is not just the unemployed who suffer. The National Low Income Housing Coalition's annual *Out of Reach* report found that "[f]ull-time minimum wage workers cannot afford a two-bedroom rental anywhere in the U.S. and cannot afford a one-bedroom rental in 95% of U.S. counties. In fact, the average minimum wage worker in the U.S. would need to work almost 97 hours per week to afford a fair market rate two-bedroom and 79 hours per week to afford a one-bedroom, NLIHC calculates. That's well over two full-time jobs just to be able to afford a two-bedroom rental."[47]

But even people who might be able to afford to stay in place are not immune from the effects of the housing crisis. People may be homeowners, but their grown children can't stay nearby them because they can't afford to rent. Housing rights activist Tony Roshan Samara told me that activism for fair housing policies is not restricted to just the renter population:

more and more people who are not directly affected by high rents fight for fair housing because it is needed to preserve their entire communities, and their sense of place. This shows a sign of concern with community stability, insofar as it widens the sphere of those affected and hence calls for greater democratic processes. And yet, Samara said: "Another challenge is the breakdown of democratic representation—city councils are refusing to act in the interest of the overwhelming number of their constituents. In San Mateo, three out of the five council members oppose any rent control and just cause, but 72 percent of the constituents are supportive; these politicians are acting as realtor proxies."[48]

Writer and activist Lacino Hamilton explains how eviction often leads to incarceration, in what he calls the "gentrification to prison pipeline." In a 2017 essay, he shows precisely the importance of community as a place of social, cultural, and economic support, and what can happen when those anchors of stability are removed. Hamilton also notes how these acts of destruction are coupled with what we heard about from Samara—the erosion of democratic voice:

> In the mid 1980s, Detroit Mayor Coleman Young announced that city dollars would be used to finance the development of downtown hotels, so that Detroit could attract convention business. Homes were foreclosed. Businesses were dismantled. And every day decision-making power was shifted from families and local business owners to state legislators, venture capitalists and a combination of financial institutions and interests.
>
> Forcing people to evacuate a neighborhood or entire section of a city cannot be achieved by democratic means. It is inconceivable that anyone would vote to displace themselves, right? This explains why police, courts and prison are often used to remove and disappear some people. I was either stopped, arrested and/or conveyed to the police station once or twice a month for the entire 10 years I lived in and frequented the Cass Corridor, supposedly for "identification purposes," by regular beat police. Mind you, these same beat police worked the area for decades and were familiar with me, my friends and extended members of my family. I was told that if I did not like the treatment, I could always move.[49]

Displacement is not only a process of destruction and human violence; it also brings about the alienation of human relationships, and the re-placing of people into constrained and confined political and spatial worlds.

Nevertheless, we should bear in mind that these processes are not lin-
ear and do not unfold smoothly. Rather, as we will continue to see in the
remaining chapters of this book, people have pushed back in a variety of
powerful ways. They have reclaimed space, directly and indirectly, and
have used their new senses of political struggle to develop new voices
to meet the historical challenge. And in reinventing "place," they have
authorized themselves and their communities to speak out. One of the
most important things to do in this respect is to contest the very terms
that are used to distort social realities. For instance, earlier in this chapter
we looked at how the term "blight" was used to stigmatize and deval-
ue Black and poor communities, and their space in the city, and how it
has continued to be used to legitimize projects that displace and destroy
communities. But as the term became established and used in this manner, two Black scholars radically revised its sense and made its use highly
problematic—no longer could people use the word innocently, without
acknowledging it as a racist euphemism. They accomplished a revolution
in language and invented a new voice.

In 1945, a doctoral student in anthropology at the University of
Chicago, St. Clair Drake, and a graduate of Chicago's sociology department, Horace Cayton, published *Black Metropolis: A Study of Negro Life in
a Northern City*.[50] Rather than accepting the concept of "blight" as it was
conventionally understood and applied, whenever they used the word in
their study they put it in scare quotes. They accomplished two key things
by doing this. First, the authors boldly challenged the worldview of the
white scholars who had coined the term—in effect, Drake and Cayton
were telling them that *they* were speaking "out of place," that the language they were using to describe this phenomenon was inappropriate
and misleading. Second, in so doing they also affirmed their own right to
dispute their predecessors and teachers. They claimed the right and their
obligation to describe the Black city in their terms:

> Over half of Black Metropolis lies in that area which the city planners
> and real-estate interests have designated as "blighted." . . . The super-
> ficial observer believes that these areas are "blighted" because large
> numbers of Negroes and Jews, Italians and Mexicans, homeless men
> and "vice" gravitate there. But the real-estate boards, city planners, and
> ecologists know that the foreign-born, the transients, pimps, and pros-
> titutes are located there because the area has already been written off

as blighted. . . . Black Metropolis has become a seemingly permanent enclave within the city's blighted area.

That is to say, rather than follow the pattern of saying these populations carried "blight" with them, Drake and Cayton indicted "real estate boards, city planners, and ecologists" for creating, in the first place, these areas that were cast aside as the detritus of industrialization and modernization. Again, these populations were originally brought into the city to serve as an expellable reserve labor force, and once the need for their labor was suspended or ended entirely, they were relegated to the degraded spaces of the city.

Drake and Cayton gave a radically different explanation of history, and in so doing, they both added knowledge and gave activists indispensable tools for fighting back. And so, when skeptics say that nothing "revolutionary" can take place in the academy, they are only half right. The academy is certainly antagonistic toward challenges to its mode of knowledge production. But that certainly does not mean that one has to be intimidated by that antagonism. Progressive academics must not waste their students' time with dull repetitions of what has been sanctioned, but rather teach them to find their own voices. And the best way to do so is to model it—as Drake and Cayton, and others, have done. Sometimes, this is done by setting the scholarly record straight. Other times, it can take place simply by acting in ways that demonstrate the very possibility of breaking barriers.

Breaking Barriers and Forming Connections

While it may not at first appear to be a momentous event, the historian Anne C. Bailey tells of a moment that crystallizes much of what we have looked at in this chapter, and does so in an intimately personal manner— the partitioning off of space, the locating of people in specific places that contain the roles and actions deemed appropriate for them, but then, as well, the human capacity to identify those forms of containment and constraint, and to break through them to forge moments of solidarity, understanding, and common humanity. She explains that in 1985, during her junior year at Harvard University, "I got a call from the masters of my house, an older white couple, who asked me to join them for dinner with none other than James Baldwin, the famous writer, civil rights activist and one of my heroes." But upon arrival, she was directed to the kitchen: "Now here I was, here to meet James Baldwin, the only other Black person in the room, and I was being ushered to the kitchen. . . . Suddenly, the hostess caught herself and somehow turned it around and invited me instead to stay and have dinner with them. But it was too late. I was crestfallen." Here is what happened next:

> James Baldwin, ever the astute writer and observer of life, especially life in America, looked across the room and knew it. He was far enough away that he could not have heard our exchange, but he felt it and he saw it for what it was and gave me the most knowing look with his large piercing eyes that I remember to this day.
>
> The next thing I knew he was ushering me to his side, to his table. I was to sit next to him at dinner. I was to be his guest. . . .
>
> I can still see James Baldwin's eyes—fixed on me and my predicament— which was also his predicament and the one he dedicated his life to writing about—those eyes that pulled me in and out of history.[51]

That Bailey chose to write about this instance, and to write about it in this manner, is evocative of the intersection of personal and collective histories. In this piercing anecdote we see a tiny enactment of so much— something that "pulls" the author "in and out of history." It is a history that includes at its heart the history of exclusion, of containment, and of prejudice. It is a history that has become hardwired into a society, where "natural assumptions" about which people belong where, and the actions that are "appropriate" to them, mask the violence that they rehearse each time they are manifested. Only through Baldwin's extraordinary sense of humanity is the situation re-placed into a humane narrative—he does not embarrass the hostess, but neither does he embarrass Bailey by calling attention to his act. He acts graciously, preserving a social space of openness and connection, in spite of the racist presumption of his hosts. Nevertheless, I need to add this: Baldwin's act fits the moment; but at any moment, a different response might be called for, depending on the specifics of the case. In other words, in learning to use "voice" in "place," we need to become fluent in understanding the ways we have come to believe that space has to be partitioned just so, and people placed differently. So too do we need to find the best ways to open up the space for free movement, and freedom writ large. While Baldwin's life-changing act took place with hardly a word being spoken, others fighting for racial and economic equality have adopted raucous and space-destroying voices.

Gaye Theresa Johnson's *Spaces of Conflict, Sounds of Solidarity* is a powerful study in precisely this kind of solidarity across assigned place and space, using a very different set of tools. As I noted above, the destruction of neighborhoods, evictions, and gentrification not only move people "out of place;" they also destroy the social fabric and a sense of connection among individuals. Along these lines, Johnson writes: "[S]truggles for spatial entitlement flow from the recognition that a community requires more than physical space to survive. Spaces have soulful meetings. They function to maintain memories and to preserve practices that reinforce community knowledge and cohesiveness."[52]

Johnson tells the story of how people reclaimed and reinvented the spirit of their community. Noting how as postwar urban renewal projects and traffic arterials ate into neighborhoods, segmented neighborhoods, and razed homes, businesses, and schools, Johnson tells how "youth from the aggrieved communities expressed their claims to meaningful space in ways that were available to them, particularly through the production and consumption of popular music. Because they were limited in their ability to interact in physical places, they turned to sonic spaces as sites of mutual recognition."[53] In this phrasing, we hear an echo of the story we just heard from Bailey and see at the moment her eyes meet those of Baldwin—a similar instance of "mutual recognition."

In arguing that "[s]onic aspatial articulations in this era refer to the transformation of the ways in which people moved themselves through space, shaped the spaces where they congregated, and inserted their entitlements with the cultural currency they created," Johnson is in essence describing the "production of social space" that Henri Lefebvre advocated in "The Right to the City."[54] As Lefebvre argued, such productions can take many different forms. We saw one kind in the story Bailey told of her encounter with James Baldwin—a "production" dependent on nothing more than an act of generosity. Here we have something very different, at least on the surface: the use of available technologies and musical forms to transect barriers and exclusionary practices. In her study, Johnson explains that while

> whites became increasingly spatially separated from nonwhites, barricaded behind walls of wealth and municipal spaces far away from

the center of the metropolis. . . . Radio broadcasts from Dolphins of
Hollywood transmitted an invitation to enter a multiracial discursive
space of listenership emanating from a new physical space of interracial
contact, despite the calculated efforts of the LAPD and Los Angeles
City Council members to curtail interracial music events on Central
Ave, afraid that whites, Blacks, Mexicans, and Filipinos might be allowed to dance together.[55]

The politics of voice and place I emphasize in this book are spaces where
voices echo and resonate with shared experiences and dreams, across the
barriers and constraints that seek to disunify and co-opt them into silence
and immobility. If a road is torn up, or a legal border is established to separate us, we need to find the sound, sights, and words to reconnect and
grow, and to incorporate others. And this is exactly what occurred in my
next example, which regards one of the longest eviction cases in US history.

As noted above, the case of San Francisco's redevelopment in the 1970s
exhibited many familiar features of structural violence. The city's early
transformation toward a service economy and its position vis-à-vis the
emerging "Pacific Rim" worked to its advantage during the postwar years.
During that period, there was a tremendous boom in high-rise construction
in the central business district. The city's business elites looked forward to
reaping huge profits from San Francisco's strategic location in the state,
nation, and Pacific by transforming the city into a hub of transnational
capital. With a mixture of fear, fascination, and hungry anticipation, journalists Frank Viviano and Alton Chinn wrote in 1982: "The simple truth
is that San Francisco's economy is no longer unfolding in the boardrooms
of New York, the committee rooms of Washington, or the back rooms of
Sacramento. . . . The Bay Area is slowly being drawn into a second great
frontier of new possibilities: a transpacific urban community that will be
the globes' most formidable economic powerhouse by the end of the decade."[56] This restructuring had a profound effect upon ethnic and racial
minorities and the poor, who were to have no place in this reinvention of
the city. To clear land, San Francisco redevelopers targeted the Western
Addition (occupied by an older Japanese American population), Hunters
Point (largely African American), the heavily Latino Mission District, and
Chinatown. Indeed, the actual term used by developers to describe this
land grab was "Negro removal." And one of those structures that had to
be destroyed, and its inhabitants dispersed, was the International Hotel.

In the late 1960s, the hotel was home to about two hundred elderly Filipino men. They had been recruited to labor in the United States, and later fell victim to Asian exclusion: unable to bring over Filipina women and subject to anti-miscegenation laws, these men formed a unique community within the larger enclave of "Manilatown." It was not long before the hotel, located in precisely that area that was to become the expanded and renovated Financial District of this new Pacific Rim city, was targeted by developers. In 1968, Walter Shorenstein of the Milton Meyer company initiated demolition proceedings in order to turn the site into a multi-level parking garage. Filipino tenants marched in protest, represented by the United Filipino Organization. Because of this strong community resistance, Shorenstein backed off from that plan and was compelled to sign a new lease agreement.

Between 1969 and 1970, thousands of individuals and various groups from around the Bay Area came together to completely renovate the hotel. Nonetheless, in 1974 the hotel was sold to the Four Seas Investment Corporation of Hong Kong, and in September of that year the the hotel was again ordered demolished. This announcement was protested by a large coalition of tenants' rights groups from Japantown, Hunters Point, the Western Addition, and the South of Market area; indeed, racially diverse tenants' rights advocates were perfectly aware of the larger structural consequences of local redevelopment. In July 1976, the state supreme court ordered a stay of eviction, and Mayor George Moscone proposed that the city exercise its right of eminent domain to buy the hotel from the Four Seas group and sell it back to the tenants as a nonprofit venture. Under tremendous pressure from the mayor's office and the community, the board of supervisors ultimately agreed to this plan, but the Four Seas group refused to accept an offer that would have provided them with a 50 percent profit. Instead, they insisted on going forward with the demolition of the hotel.

On January 16, 1977, six thousand people formed a barricade around the entire block; while the number varied over the next several months, there were always several hundred protesters present. Superior court judge Charles Peery rejected the city's attempt to exercise eminent domain, and in July the state supreme court lifted its ban on the eviction. On August 4, 1977, the San Francisco Police and Sheriff's Departments deployed over three hundred armed officers in full riot gear to remove three thousand people who had maintained a vigil against the eviction for several days. The police cordoned off a two-square-mile perimeter to prevent tens of thousands of other protesters from joining the vigil, and, using fire trucks and axes, battered down the doors at both ground level and higher floors, smashing down apartment doors, and removing protesters and tenants. The "fall of the I Hotel" marked the destruction of the last piece of Manilatown, which had slowly been eroded and consumed by urban expansion. Yet the story does not end there.

For the next twenty years, if one visited the site of the I Hotel, one would not have found a high-rise, or even a parking garage. Instead, a huge gaping crater marked the site for two decades. The Four Seas corporation discovered that, ironically enough, the protest had forestalled development until the site became less profitable than they had envisioned. The corporation was therefore content to simply let the land stay vacant. In 1994, the US Department of Housing and Urban Development awarded the city $7.6 million for low-income housing. The San Francisco mayor's office promised to add $5.5 million to that for the construction of a new International Hotel, which would ultimately provide housing for seniors as well as serve as a community school and a museum for Manilatown. Activist and scholar Estella Habal points out that a central component of community organizing was the connection between younger Asian American activists and the elderly Filipino tenants. While the media attempted to portray the tenants as innocent dupes of rabble-rousers who were seeking an issue, Habal stresses the fact that the tenants themselves initiated the protest and were in many cases themselves well-versed in labor activism. The history of the I Hotel manifests at once the interrelationship between economic restructuring, public-private enterprise, and community resistance, cast within the redefinition of local space as nodal point on the Pacific Rim. The "Asian" identity of San Francisco was thus battled over by two groups with entirely different visions of Asian America.

By the time of the mass eviction defense of the I Hotel, resistance and coalition building around this issue were already well underway. San Francisco's identity was shifting, and with it the homes, neighborhoods, and communities that constituted it. Here I look at three people who, through different media, attempted to capture the facts and human truth of the events between 1968 and 1978: Curtis Choy, a documentary film-maker; Estella Habal, a historian; and Karen Tei Yamashita, a novelist. Each of them was involved in giving a voice to this dramatic and violent evacuation of space, and what followed. Each was focused on a specific historical event—the eviction of elderly tenants from the I Hotel. The battle over the hotel escaped the gaze of the mainstream press, which was focused on such national-scale issues as the Vietnam War and demonstrations in Chicago and elsewhere. The struggle of a handful of elderly Filipino men apparently did not have the dramatic appeal required for mass media attention. Our archive, as it exists today, is solely the result of the efforts of those who wanted to preserve the images, sights, and sounds of the struggle, such as Choy, and those (mostly nameless) who kept mementos: ragtag pamphlets, buttons, posters, mimeographed notes, postcards, personal photographs, and diaries.

Choy's 1983 film, *The Fall of the I-Hotel*, contains the immediate, graphic recording of the demonstrations and eventual demolition, but alongside that newsreel material it offers a probing analysis, using archival film and photographs, of the forces and histories that drew these men to the United States, and of the textures of their lives here. Choy, along with the poet and activist Al Robles, went into the rooms of the tenants and interviewed them. In one of the most remarkable interviews, a man tells of his work as a sailor, boasting proudly of his numerous romantic encounters, and when the interviewer seems to disbelieve him, the man pulls out a thick album with, indeed, pictures of him and his various lovers in Brussels, Paris, Rio, Finland, and elsewhere.

This archive is multilayered: after Choy records the man's stories, the man displays his own archive. In the poetic composition of these layers, we see the significance of this one tiny room in this residential hotel for the interviewee; we also see how his oceanic and now land-bound histories are imbricated in Asian American migration and labor, and in the spreading phenomenon of global capital, as the hotel passes through the hands not only of local developers with strong Washington connections, but also of multinational, transpacific Thai-based finance. Choy weaves all these strands into his narrative.

Habal was there, too. She was a young single mother then, working as a member of the leading Filipino radical organization, the Katipunan ng

Demokratikong Pilipino (KDP) or Union of Democratic Filipinos. As she puts it, the struggle was "a fight for housing rights versus private-property rights; for a neighborhood's existence versus extinction and dispersal; and for the extension of democratic rights to the poor and working class."[57] When the decade-long struggle ended, Habal decided to get a college degree, which culminated in a doctorate in history from the University of California, Davis. The path from activist and organizer to PhD was not an easy one for her; nor was it easy to transform her dissertation into a published book. That the story was a history seemed to rule out her narrative voice as a participant; yet from the start the struggle itself was motivated, among other things, by her firsthand witnessing of and participation in the events, and by her personal commitment to get the story out. The resulting book, *San Francisco's International Hotel* (2007), received high praise and serves as an indispensable document, full of historical data that would otherwise have been lost.

While Habal was finishing her book, Yamashita was writing hers: the novel *I Hotel*, a 2010 National Book Award finalist. She had researched her book for more than a decade, delving into all manner of archives and interviewing more than 150 people. She told me that she wanted to write the history of the Asian American movement. What emerged is exactly that, but it is also much more. *I Hotel* rightly recognizes the struggle as a local event driven by global forces. The movement is seen politically and geographically, as the book moves from Oakland to Moscow, the Tiao Yu Tai island protests, Beijing, Paris, the Native American occupation of Alcatraz, and the Japanese American internment at Tule Lake, as well as the critical work that Filipinos (known as the Delano Manongs) did with the United Farm Workers.

Habal's and Yamashita's books complement each other. If Habal had to be reticent in places to preserve objectivity, Yamashita imaginatively sketched out thoughts that lay behind the actions taken. Likewise, if Yamashita needed a more complex sense of how the facts were experienced at ground level, she had Habal and a hundred more witnesses to draw from. At the launch of the novel, at the new International Hotel (which was built in 2005, and is now the Manilatown Heritage Foundation), the comment after Yamashita finished her reading was from Habal: "As a historian, I have never seen until right now how literature can keep history alive." By this she meant that the events and stories from that decade, over forty years ago, were reframed and extended into the present through their imaginative representation in Yamashita's novel.

In the spring of 2010, I was working on a community-based learning course that would combine in-class learning with work at the Manilatown Heritage Foundation. My students and I watched Choy's film and were visited by my Stanford colleague, historian Gordon Chang; the poet, critic, and essayist Hilton Obenzinger (who owned the print shop that produced many of the publications of the movement); Estella Habal; the novelist Fae Myenne Ng; and Karen Tei Yamashita. Obenzinger suggested that I meet someone from the San Francisco Art Institute who was then artist in residence at Stanford, Jerome Reyes. We made an appointment, and one afternoon he came to my office. After we shook hands, he reached into his backpack and pulled out a brick. The minute I saw it, I looked at him and asked, "Is that really . . . ?" He nodded: the brick was from the original International Hotel.

Reyes had acquired (literally) a ton of those bricks for the installation he was working on. He then unrolled the 1906 blueprints of the hotel on my desk and explained how he had scanned and uploaded them, and how he planned to reconstruct the hotel digitally in order to pose the question: What would have happened if it had not been demolished? He not only imagined the repopulation of the hotel, but also thought of what social services might be put into place. He spoke passionately about how he would visually represent the flows of energy and community that passed through the hallways, and he showed me some samples of how he imported imagery from thermodynamics, wave technology, and oceanography into the reimaging of the structure and the community it could house. He also told me what he intended to do with the bricks. Many of them would be used in the installation. But when he asked the original activists if he could break up some of the bricks and use that material for modeling and other plastic artifacts, they said, "No, that is all that remains." Undeterred, he noted that there were mounds of brick dust—could he use that material? That was fine, they said. Reyes felt the dust was a historical artifact of migrant labor, exile, diaspora, and displacement. He thus reworked that brick dust into something that both recognized history and looked to the future.[58]

Among other things, Reyes made a fedora similar to those that many of the residents sported in the 1960s and 1970s, adding a feather to the hat-band—a common feature. But he did not stop with one; he made precisely 2,005 feathers, in reference to the Manilatown Heritage Foundation's 2005 opening of its center at 848 Kearney. He told me that he would watch as people came into the exhibit and approached the table to look at the hat. They would step onto the carpet of feathers and brick dust, not realizing that the feathers and dust were part of the exhibit, and quickly step off in horror. He would tell them not to worry—in fact, he wanted them to leave traces of the dust across and through the building as they continued through the exhibition space. It was a way of bringing the event and its telling to a wider set of participants. The paths marked by the dust traced the narrative of observation and travel. A review of the exhibit in *Art in America* magazine shows this metaphoric intent:

> The elderly tenants would collect in the hallways of the boarding house to mingle—their private rooms were too small for guests. Their fraternization was more than habitual and casual social gatherings, it was also a manifestation of the powerful yet muted tactics of resistance inherent in everyday life—walking the city streets, or in this case, organizing in the hallways of the hotel. The tenants unconsciously took over and refigured these common and unexceptional walkways that were meant for movement, passing, and transition and instead turned them into fleeting zones of autonomy, collectivity, and resistance. *Until Today* is an elegiac reminder of the forgotten social and political wars fought at home.[59]

In their art and scholarship, Reyes, Choy, Habal, and Yamashita both reconstruct the history of what was destroyed and create a new place of community. Not only that; their particular efforts lean on those of others and incorporate their audiences into the production of this space.

When the Public Reclaims Its Space

One of the lessons we have learned is that it has become common for people to be told they have no right to the city, and no right to space that is in fact public. Neoliberalist ideology has driven the belief that property only belongs to private interests, both by law and by habit. The slow but steady conveyance of public land into private hands, and the transformation of private debt into public obligations have been a hallmark of our perverse age. But at least two recent events have shown the power of the people to put the "public" back into the idea of the public good.

In 2020, homeless families in the Los Angeles area saw huge numbers of publicly owned properties lie vacant, even as the pandemic threatened the health and welfare of those without shelter. These families organized themselves into a group called Reclaiming Our Homes, declaring themselves rightful members of the public, and entitled to occupy public property in that time of crisis. These families then moved into 11 of the approximately 163 vacant properties and "demanded that public officials use these homes and other publicly owned vacant properties to shelter people immediately, especially as the threat of a global pandemic looms."[60] In this way, these people "took place" and raised new voices. That same year, homeless activists in Philadelphia reached an agreement with the Philadelphia Housing Authority to have it turn fifty properties over to a community land trust administered by housing advocacy groups.[61] As part of the deal, "[t]he two homeless protest encampments" would "remain in place while residents transition into the vacant homes and others explore alternative housing options."[62] Here is an excellent example of activists beginning a series of transformations that each bring space back to its public ownership—an empty public space was converted to a protest encampment that in turn became a transitional space to adequate housing. Again we see the power of people to occupy space, rename it and reinvent it, and make it serve a purpose that enhances their right to the city.

Finally, let me mention one of the small but deeply meaningful events that took place during the protests over the killing of George Floyd—a telling moment of spontaneous solidarity. In early June 2020, as reported in the press, "When the march reached the corner of 15th and S streets . . . a line of D.C. police officers was blocking the road. Someone who seemed like an organizer suggested the protesters head west on Swann Street. But within a few seconds, the marchers realized that they were now boxed in by officers in riot gear on all sides." At that point a resident, Rahul Dubey, opened his door and shouted out to the protesters to come in. Here is what happened next: In his words, the "crowd came racing through like a tornado" and he "flung the door open and let them inside." He added: "I opened a door. You would have done the same thing."[63] That last sentence cannot be proven, but it is a call to conscience. This sharing of sanctuary, another production of space where one voice calls out to others in solidarity and gathers and protects, is, as I said, small in scale and short in duration. It should remind us as well of the story Anne C. Bailey told of the gesture of hospitality James Baldwin extended to her—he shared his place of honor with a person who he had just seen relegated to second place. Again, a large part of this message of this book is that we each need to reimagine our relation to politics, and to never dismiss out of hand the importance of what we can do. Such examples, momentary as they are, help point the way. As the historian Howard Zinn famously said, "[S]mall acts, when multiplied by millions, can transform the world."

In the next chapter, we turn from urban space and the right to the city to the world stage and a discussion of international borders. We will engage in a critical reflection on the production of borders, the reasons behind them, and the ways people have sutured those violently demarcated places back together—and, in so doing, reimagined how we can live together.

CHAPTER 3

GLOBAL HOME

In the previous chapter, we saw how Black and poor households, along with other racial minorities, were "relocated" both by what seemed beneficent and enlightened liberal policies, and by outright segregation and violence, and had their homes and resources plundered. But we also saw how people have risen up and taken back what was rightfully theirs— how they have created ways to resist discriminatory boundaries and speak back, using voices both permissible and impermissible. We saw how people formed communities of solidarity, large and small, and advanced and expanded the notion of the right to the city.

In this chapter, I move to the global scale, considering the planet itself as a home to all. I first show how it has been carved up into spaces of rich and poor, healthy and ill, entitled and disenfranchised, and make the argument that each of these partitions presents major challenges to our capacity to see the interconnectedness of our struggles for democratic justice. In much the same way as I handled similar issues at the urban scale, I will talk about borders, labor, homes, camps, and place. Here, I argue that the phenomena we looked on the domestic front are reflected in global capitalism, and particularly the effects of displacement and gentrification—the destruction of communities and the remapping of urban space away from human needs and desires and toward the interests of capital. In these operations, the very rhythm, intimacy, and sociality of life are disrupted and replaced by a zone of immense alienation and exploitation.

The increased distance between the place of work and the place of home, and the off-work time it eats into, exacerbates the degradation of life under capitalism. In his classic essay "New Globalism, New

Urbanism," radical geographer Neil Smith examines this phenomenon in terms of today's "global cities." Smith writes, "More than anything else, the scale of the modern city is . . . calibrated by something quite mundane: the contradictory determinations of the geographical limits of the daily commute of workers between home and work."[1] According to Smith, the distance between home and work has never been greater: "[I]n 1998, the New York City Department of Education announced that it faced a shortage of mathematics teachers and as a result was importing forty young teachers from Austria. Even more extraordinary, in a city with more than two million native Spanish speakers, a shortage of Spanish teachers was to be filled by importing teachers from Spain."[2] He goes on to remark that the underlying logic of twenty-first century neoliberalism is "galvanized by an unprecedented mobilization not just of national state power but of state power organized and exercised at different geographical scales." In other words, the "global" does not simply exist in large financial hubs and metropolitan spaces—it also permeates the corridors in between big urban spaces; it reaches into the remote areas where workers live; it floods the shelves of local markets forced to trade in neoliberal capital's commodities. Smith describes this in terms of social processes and relations that create "new amalgams of scale replacing the old amalgams broadly associated with 'community,' 'urban,' 'regional,' 'national,' and 'global.'"[3]

Each different manifestation of the global adjusts to the function it plays in the neoliberal economy. Again, it would be wrong to imagine that the remedy to this is somehow to return to past times; rather, as Lefebvre argues, the task is to recognize one's historical location and to see the most important kinds of rights and freedoms to work for and give voice to. For example, Smith describes in these terms the very basic and necessary phenomenon of travel to work:

> The daily commute into São Paulo, for example, can begin for many at 3:30 a.m. and take in excess of four hours in each direction. In Harare, Zimbabwe, the average commuting time from black townships on the urban periphery is also four hours each way, leading to a workday in which workers are *absent from home* for sixteen hours and sleeping most of the rest. The economic cost of commuting for these same workers has also expanded dramatically, in part as a result of the privatization of transportation at the behest of the World Bank: commutes that

consumed roughly 8% of weekly incomes in the early 1980s required
between 22% and 45% by the mid 1990s.[4]

I underscore the phrase "absent from home" because it is so germane to
the problems of political participation and voice I address in this book.
How can one have any political life at all when one is not at home, with
others, in a community? How can one have the physical strength to do
political work, having wasted unpaid hours in transit? In such precarious
work situations, when labor can be drawn from many different places,
who has the freedom to ask for a change in one's condition?

Cities are hardwired into networks that resonate with the previous
chapter's discussions of displacement and gentrification. Smith notes the
tremendous penetration of the "global" into the local. Using a condo-
minium building on New York's Lower East Side as an example, Smith
notes that "it was built by nonunion immigrant labor . . . the developer
is Israeli, and the major source of financing comes from the European
American Bank. The reach of global capital down to the local neighborhood scale is equally a hallmark of the latest phase of gentrification."[5]
That is to say, global capital's ripple effects are not only facilitated by neoliberalism—they are manufactured by it. Its needs for labor, resources,
and infrastructure all override the efforts to retain a sense of belonging.
After all, belonging is achieved through investing one's spirit and energy
into a place, and finding that it, and the others it houses, reflect something
of oneself—one's energy, values, commitments, visions of the future.

One of the more startling creative works to depict the alienation of
labor from place is Alex Rivera's 2008 film *Sleep Dealer*. The central premise is that workers in Mexico, unwelcome in the United States, labor in
huge hangers literally hooked into a vast computer network. Wearing VR
glasses and attached to wires snapped into nodules fixed on their bodies,
as they lift their hands, turn their heads, stoop to pick up items, those
same movements are replicated by robots in the North. Rivera also draws
a parallel between the extraction of labor from Mexico and the extraction of natural resources as, especially with regard to minerals and water.
Made on a shoestring budget, the film earned major international awards
due to its cinematic brilliance and globally resonant message.

What I want to focus on here is not just the generation of work in
the First World performed by the labor of people anchored in the Third

World or other spaces; I also want us to pay equal attention to the devastated landscapes those bodies still reside in. Rivera pointedly shows us
how people's futures are mortgaged based on some hope that their work
will improve their own homes, communities, and families. He shows that
natural resources like water have been taken over by multinational corporations, and that people must trudge miles to a water station, to pay for
whatever amount of water they can afford, then carry it home with them
on their backs. Along with the extraction of labor and natural resources,
their spirits and intellect are marketed. Students are forced to pay off student loans at exorbitant rates—one does so by selling her memories.

Again, in *Sleep Dealer* there is no sense that we could or should return
to some nostalgic world of tradition. Rather, the aim of the film is to
focus on empowerment: in Rivera's vision, it is the residents of the city
who should have the guiding hand in imagining and constructing their
environment. Rivera is not suggesting that one could simply dismantle
the "network" of global labor and replace it with something organic and
local, or something neatly contained within the form of a traditional
nation-state. Rather, he is challenging us to imagine both a local and organic "place" and a way to connect to other such places in a just and humane manner, outside the circuits of transnational capital. Our efforts as
activists should go beyond identifying egregious inequities; we need also
to disabuse ourselves of the so-called solutions that neoliberalism offers
us. They are, as we say, precisely part of the problem, not the solution.

In his article, "The West Is, in Fact, the World's Biggest Gated Community,"
satirist Frank Jacobs points to a map drawn more than a decade ago:

> This map [showing that 14 percent of the world's population holds 73
> percent of the world's income and live in one common area of the globe,
> while 86 percent of the world's population holds only 27 percent of the
> world's income] is a decade old, but it feels increasingly topical with
> every passing year. More than ever, we live in a Walled World. . . . The
> US-Mexico border is far away from "Fortress Europe," and both are dif-
> ferent from Israel's security wall. . . . [O]ther, similar barriers have their
> own peculiarities. But in the end, they all do the same thing: keep the
> poor, huddled masses from the shantytowns off the manicured lawns
> of the First World.[6]

This reality connects up with the premise of Rivera's dystopian, futuristic
film—the First World does not want to be bothered by the presence of Third

World or other international workers; on the contrary, it wants to keep them trapped behind border walls while it extracts their long-distance labor.

And like the many technological apparatuses that spy into the bodies and even minds of workers in *Sleep Dealer*, today's very real economic apartheid is maintained by a global security apparatus; as one journalist observes, "The walls of the future go beyond one administration's policies . . . they are growing up all around us, being built by global technology companies that allow for constant surveillance, data harvesting and the alarming collection of biometric information."[7] Under these conditions, no place is really "home," and there is no sanctuary, no safe space. And even worse, as human and civil rights are increasingly stripped from ordinary people, they are bestowed upon global markets. And so, the rights of a "free market" have taken precedence over the rights of a free people.

In this regard, sociologist Saskia Sassen argues that today, individual "citizenship" is in an outmoded concept. A true democracy counts on the enfranchisement of everyone, and this applies both to our notion of national democracies and to our imaginary of a global civil society. Sassen argues that today there is indeed a global citizenry, but it is compromised not of peoples, nor even of an ecumene of states, but of transnational capital. This is what she calls "economic citizenship," which

> does not belong to citizens. It belongs to firms and markets, particularly the global financial markets, and it is located not in individuals, not in citizens, but in global economic actors. The fact of being global gives these actors power over individual governments. . . . The global financial markets, in particular, represent one of the most astounding aggregations of new rights and legitimacy that we have seen over the last two decades . . . they have taken on more of the powers historically associated with the nation-state than any other institution over the past decades. . . . These markets now exercise the accountability functions associated with citizenship: they can vote governments' economic policies up or down.[8]

Here is the legal infrastructure that protects the prerogatives of capital to displace, remove, rearrange, and destroy people, their homes, and their communities, and to make sure the bulk of their waking hours are devoted to its enrichment. The welfare of the people does not even register in the interests of these "economic citizens." People are, in Sassen's view, reduced to being simply sources of labor and consumption. Despite all the outcry from ethno-nationalists about "invasions" of foreign workers, Sassen notes, "[i]mmigration is really more of a management problem than a crisis."[9]

Central to "managing" migration is the exploitation of ethnic and racial divisions to obstruct any sort of international solidarity among workers: for the consolidation of racist and anti-worker sentiment has been fed by right, center, and liberal ideologies alike. Nearly everywhere we see the readiness to fall back on retrograde nation-state (and indeed, ethno-nationalist) ideology to remedy this situation of inequity. There is no better example of this politically cynical thinking about labor and immigration than Angela Nagle's oddly named essay, "The Left Case against Open Borders." Claiming to speak from the place of "the Left," Nagle argues:

> Today's well-intentioned activists have become the useful idiots of big business. With their adoption of "open borders" advocacy—and a fierce moral absolutism that regards any limit to migration as an unspeakable evil—any criticism of the exploitative system of mass migration is effectively dismissed as blasphemy. Even solidly leftist politicians, like Bernie Sanders in the United States and Jeremy Corbyn in the United Kingdom, are accused of "nativism" by critics if they recognize the legitimacy of borders or migration restriction at any point.[10]

I do not wish to spend time critiquing Nagle's reactionary and hopelessly anachronistic essay, and its narrowing of the Left's horizon to the local politics of the nation-state; indeed, there are many other very capable dissections.[11] Instead, I here deploy it as a negative example of the kinds of thinking in which we *should* engage, as exemplified in the following from *Viewpoint Magazine*:

> If we step outside media narratives, think beyond the immediate electoral horizon, and train our sights on migrant organizing and solidarity, the basis for such a politics becomes demonstrably clearer. Just as the right's strategy of white fear-mongering has highlighted new, more visible tactics among migrants in the form of the caravan, we propose to respond by centering migrant struggles, particularly from the perspective of "migrant autonomy" that was so well illustrated by the democratic decision-making of caravan members over their collective fate. With this perspective, it becomes evident that to consider class politics in the United States today means considering a working class whose composition crosses geographical borders and weaves together the exploited and the dispossessed from across a much broader region.[12]

Let us consider this more realistic way of looking at labor and justice. To do this we need to seriously address both the cases of those who are contained and exploited by borders and those caught in the stateless places of refugee camps. A large part of my argument is that we need to focus on how the figure of the "illegal" migrant worker connects to the figure of the "international refugee" in terms of neoliberal economics and labor, as well as state practices that feed neoliberalism. And as we have done throughout this study, I want to insist on the connection between race and class as we turn to the manners in which borders and camps are constructed and resisted, and new places of voice opened up—voices that speak a different sort of language.

Borders, Immigration, Concentration Camps

To start with, there is no way to address the issue of borders without addressing the issue of violence, and violence on multiple scales and in various forms. The very attempt to draw a border is an act of violence and domination. The militarization of borders, which has formally existed at the US–Mexico border since the establishment of the Border Patrol in 1924, has traditionally involved military operations in the production of flows of peoples across borders; in fact, with the founding of the Border Patrol we see the beginnings too of experimental surveillance technologies at the border.[13]

The militarization of borders is legitimized and advanced by use of the language of war, which casts those to be prevented from crossing as enemies, militants, radicals, or criminals. This has been a constant feature of immigration management. Consider this contemporary report, published in *The Nation* during the Trump presidency:

> Last week, President Donald Trump admitted that his administration's deportation agenda is "a military operation." The United States is "getting really bad dudes out of this country. And at a rate nobody's ever seen before," he announced at a meeting with manufacturing-industry CEOs. "And it's a military operation because what has been allowed to come into our country, when you see gang violence that you've read about like never before and all of the things—much of that is people who are here illegally." Trump's words, however rambling, summed up the aggressive, wide-ranging policy being put into effect by his

administration's executive orders and the Department of Homeland Security's recent memorandums.[14]

Contrary to Trump's assertion that this war is meant to protect the United States from gangs and "bad guys," the vast majority of those detained and deported are in fact low-wage laborers. In her study *Deported: Immigrant Policing, Disposable Labor and Global Capitalism*, sociologist Tanya Maria Golash-Boza argues:

> [T]he reality . . . is that immigration policy enforcement targets Afro Caribbean smalltime drug peddlers and Latino undocumented workers— not hardcore criminals or terrorists. Nearly all deportees—97 percent— are from Latin America and the Caribbean. DHS rarely deports any the approximately 25 percent of undocumented migrants in the United States there are from Asia and Europe. . . . On April 6, 2014, the *New York Times* reported that nearly two-thirds of the 2 million deportations since Obama took office have involved either people with no criminal records or those convicted of minor crimes.[15]

Thus, the real targets are not the "gangs" of "bad guys" to which Trump constantly refers, but the people who grow and harvest our produce, clean our buildings, work in our restaurants, care for our children—all major contributors to our communities and households. They are also essential contributors to our society and pay billions of dollars in taxes a year. A 2016 study found that "[o]ut of that $11.64 billion total, undocumented immigrants pay $6.9 billion in sales and excise taxes, $3.6 billion in property taxes and about $1.1 billion in personal income taxes. ITEP estimated that if America's 11 million undocumented immigrants were granted citizenship allowing them to work legally, current state and tax contributions would be boosted by over $2.1 billion a year."[16] Despite all these contributions, neoliberalism requires docile workers willing to work for less than a living wage. Noncitizens in the United States provide the necessary labor force in a neoliberal economy, and their "removability" as the demand for their labor shifts is a gift to capitalist production. Their precarity makes them less likely to strike, protest, or in any way challenge their bosses—they are deprived of voice. It is clear that these "military operations" are much less about national security and much more about neoliberal labor management. Nevertheless, the suspension of human rights has been euphemized under the pretext of national "states of emergency," the favorite tool of autocrats to control both external and internal "threats."

While the Right likes to portray those seeking to cross the borders as motivated solely by criminal interests (of various sorts), in reality both the flows of refugees seeking asylum and migrants seeking work are products of the United States' "adventures" in Latin America. According to Christy Thornton, a sociologist focused on Latin America at Johns Hopkins University, "The destabilisation in the 1980s—which was very much part of the US Cold War effort—was incredibly important in creating the kind of political and economic conditions that exist in those countries today."[17] One can point to the 1954 US-backed coup against democratically elected president Jacobo Árbenz in Guatemala, and the subsequent genocide against the Indigenous population that killed roughly two hundred thousand people between 1990 and 1996; and to the 2009 coup against Manuel Zelaya, Honduras's reformist president, which was facilitated by then–secretary of state Hillary Clinton. These acts of anti-democratic violence created the dangerous and often deadly conditions from which migrants and refugees seek to escape. And to some degree, the US welcomed them, if provisionally.

Golash-Boza argues that these "involvements" were part of the US mission to facilitate the entry of countries in the global South into the global economy, thereby integrating national labor into transnational labor:

> During the 1950s and 1960s, the United States helped to install governments in the Dominican Republic and in Guatemala that were more favorable to global capitalist production. In the 1980s, the United States supported Jamaica's and Brazil's integrations into the global economy. As these and other countries became part of the global chain of production and consumption, their economies experienced disruptions. Economic and social turmoil often lead to increased emigration. Emigration, in turn help to thin the ranks of the unemployed in the sending country and cushion this transition through remittances.[18]

Two of the main ways that migrants and refugees are managed and channeled through this cycle are deportation and internment. Although separate tactics, both serve the same basic purpose: to manage the flow of labor into and out of the United States. Golash-Boza locates this push-pull within the logic of what she calls the "neoliberal cycle," whose elements include "outsourcing; economic restructuring; cutbacks in social services; the enhancements of the police, the military, immigration enforcement; and the privatization of public services." Taken together, these strategies "lead to and reproduce one another" in ways that produce exactly the global economic apartheid we noted earlier. Golash-Boza writes,

> This cycle of restricted labor mobility and deportation is crucial to the maintenance of global apartheid—a system where mostly white and affluent citizens of the world are free to travel to where they like whereas the poor are forced to make do in places where there are less resources. Global apartheid would not be feasible without deportation, as deportation is the physical manifestation of policies that determine who is permitted to live where.[19]

One of the many strengths of Golash-Boza's book is that, rather than report on this historical phenomenon solely through data and analysis of information or secondhand reporting, she centers on the human experience of moving through this neoliberal cycle, as told by workers themselves. Having interviewed over 140 workers, she writes, "I contend that deportees' stories are the best way in which to capture the nuances and complexity of mass deportation and the impacts of neoliberal reforms on their overall migration trajectories."[20]

Another book that does the deep work of listening to the voices of those compelled to follow these dangerous paths is journalist Rubén Martínez's *Crossing Over*. He begins his tale with a funeral of three brothers who die crossing the US–Mexico border. From this end point, he retraces their journey, living in and through those places and others, and interviewing people along the way. One of the most startling and evocative passages comes when Martínez visits the graves of three brothers whose path he has retraced:

> The cemetery is at the western edge of town, a few hundred feet below the level of the plaza, bordered on three sides by the highway. The deathscape is as divided along the lines of class as is the town. The rich get elaborate tombs of polished stone; the poor, simple wood crosses rarely more than a foot tall, which disappear after only a few years or into the wet climate of the highlands. The tragedy will give the Chavez brothers a middle-class existence, albeit in death. The three are buried in a spot usually reserved for the illustrious, under a cherry tree at the very center of the crowded cemetery, affording them shade every day of the year, especially welcome at midday, when the tropical sun is punishing summer and winter alike. A stonecutter in the state capital of Morelia heard of the tragedy and offered to build, free of charge,

three large monuments in the shape of church steeples, the preferred
style—for those who can afford it.[21]

There is so much one could say about this remarkable passage, but what
I want to focus on is the juxtaposition of both the dream and the nightmare. The dream that informs the "migrant spirit," a spirit that has both a
deep emotional element as well as a material one—the aspiration for personal and familial safety, security, home. Martínez speaks here of class,
and that is of course central, but I want to go beyond class to address
the different kinds of life that class indicates—wants and needs of much
different magnitudes, depending on one's wealth. The nightmare, which
includes the "deathscape" of which Martínez speaks, is both the danger
and precariousness of the journey, and of the labor to be found. But most
of all, I want us to note that the brothers' "dream" is achieved only in
death and, crucially, only due to the empathy and care of the stonecutter
who bestows upon them the markers they have earned but will never
enjoy. Embedded in the language of this book we see yet another instance
of the revision of the meaning of "place" through a different sort of imaginary of who belongs where, and the establishment of a different claim to
meaning and worth. It is a struggle against being told one is not worthy
of honor, despite one's labor, and a "production of space" that accommo-
dates the voices and dreams of the dead.

One can think, too of Woody Guthrie's elegiac song "Deportee," which
tells of the deaths of twenty-eight Mexican workers being sent back over
the border by plane in 1948. The song centers on many aspects of the workers' lives, and deaths—aspects that are erased from the historical record:

Some of us are illegal, and some are not wanted,
Our work contract's out and we have to move on;
Six hundred miles to that Mexican border,
They chase us like outlaws, like rustlers, like thieves.
We died in your hills, we died in your deserts,
We died in your valleys and died on your plains.
We died 'neath your trees and we died in your bushes,
Both sides of the river, we died just the same.
The sky plane caught fire over Los Gatos Canyon,
A fireball of lightning, and shook all our hills,
Who are all these friends, all scattered like dry leaves?
The radio says, "They are just deportees."[22]

The bodies of the four crew members were shipped to family members, but the remains of the twenty-eight Mexicans were buried in an unmarked mass grave at the edge of a cemetery.

There is much to comment on in this song: the way the press reduced those who died to their degraded status as migrants ("just deportees"), forgetting their names; the singer's act of restoration in naming them, as he imagines them, in parallel to the stonecutter's gesture; and the final verse, a not-so-subtle indictment of capitalist production. We are reminded of the government's payment to farmers to let their crops rot so as to maintain market prices, just as the bodies of the workers are disposed of. The wholesale perversion of work, nurture, and nature runs through this song.

The erasure of identity and life that Guthrie memorialized was miraculously rectified, at least in part, some sixty-five years later. Writer Tim Z. Hernandez, whose parents and grandparents were Mexican farmworkers, came across the story. "When I saw the newspaper stories, Woody Guthrie's lyrics became real to me," he said. "I thought, someone somewhere must have those names." As a story in the *New York Times* documents, along with Carlos Rascon, the cemeteries director for the Roman Catholic Diocese of Fresno, Hernandez "dug through records at the Fresno County recorder's office and coverage of the crash from a local Spanish-language newspaper. Where he could, Mr. Hernandez filled in information and double-checked name spellings by talking with surviving family members." A memorial service was then held at the cemetery, where their names were finally read aloud. Nora Guthrie, one of Guthrie's daughters said, "Sometimes, songs leave behind questions which ultimately can, and will, be answered by someone whose heart is pulled into the mystery."[23] Here we witness a chain of events that began with a singer noting a human tragedy—not only of death, but of anonymity. Then, half a century later, those who were killed in that tragedy were finally given a proper memorial by a writer, a priest, and a community. The anonymity of the mass grave is replaced by the naming of the dead, but the history of loss and recovery remains a narrative of the dehumanization of the workers, in life and in death. Importantly, this is a dehumanization that "takes place." We find a similar process of dehumanization in the places that hold migrants and refugees.

In his study of the concentration camps people are placed into as they await processing by Immigration and Customs Enforcement (ICE), journalist Jack Holmes picks up on two of the keywords of this chapter: "All this has been achieved through two mechanisms: militarization and dehumanization." He quotes from Andrea Pitzer's book *One Long Night: A Global History of Concentration Camps*, where she describes such camps as "a deliberate choice to inject the framework of war into society itself."[24] In these camps, all who are forced to live there are stripped of their civil and human rights. While legal and narrative distinctions are often drawn between migrants, refugees, and stateless people, and international human rights regimes afford them different sorts of protections (or lack thereof), one thing that makes each of their cases complex and difficult is their relation to what is called "national security" and the neoliberal demand for labor.

One of the major human rights violations that occurs at the US–Mexico border involves the construction of concentration camps to "hold" those being "processed." This processing can take an indeterminant amount of time, and the conditions under which those imprisoned live are barely human. The excruciating circumstances of separation from family members (especially of children from their parents or guardians), combined with a lack of sanitation, healthy food, adequate medical care, communication with the outside, or education, stand beyond any sort of oversight. Ensnared in the histories of imperialism and neoliberal exploitation, refugees are caught within various "management" situations—hovering in place between states, humanitarian organizations, and international law. Crucially, we should remember, as anthropologist Liisa Malkki notes, that "refugees suffer from a peculiar kind of speechlessness in the face of the national and international organizations whose object of care and control they are. Their accounts are disqualified almost a priori, while the languages of refugee relief, policy and 'development' claim the production of authoritative narratives about the refugees."[25] Thus, to be placed in the category of "refugee" is to be named a passive victim of history, not a living subject making history. To believe them to be passive is of course a mistake; by defying borders or living as unauthorized inhabitants of certain places, refugees and migrants are both taking part in the neoliberal cycle and violating the terms of their participation. And for their defiance, they are stripped of rights. Let us look more closely at the places that are constructed both to deprive these individuals of rights and to exploit their labor.

The Place of Refugees

Since its invention in the late nineteenth century, the concentration camp has been a place of rightlessness, and the suspension of life. It is a holding cell for those who, according to the rulers, belong nowhere. Of them, Arendt declared, "[T]he human masses sealed off in them are treated as if they no longer existed, as if what happened to them were no longer of any interest to anybody, as if they were already dead and some evil spirit gone mad were amusing himself by stopping them for a while between life and death before admitting them to eternal peace."[26]

In November 2007, Italy enacted an emergency decree that brought Arendt's words into the twenty-first century. The measure allowed local prefects to expel from Italy citizens from other European Union states. This decree effectively overrode previous reciprocal agreements within the EU, and ushered in a new, and continuing, set of policies designed to strip people of basic human rights. The Italian decree denied these immigrants any possibility of appealing an expulsion order. In sum, it made their very presence in a court of law a matter of their being "out of place." As legal scholar Ayten Gündoğdu says: "What was denied . . . was not merely access to law. The Italian case exemplifies how the unmaking of legal personhood often goes hand in hand with the destruction of political and human standing. The deportation order and the levelling of homes endeavored to remove the Roma immigrants from the political and social fabric of Italy."[27] In these camps, refugees are unable to discern any of the features of normal life—they cannot find work to organize their days around; they have no access to independent housing, and, of particular importance to the present study, they cannot create "public *spaces* where one can act and *speak* in the presence of others."[28]

The deprival of access to a public space where ideas, grievances, or arguments can be voiced runs contrary both to any idea of human rights, and also to the professed values of the humanitarian organizations that are often put in charge of the campus. Gündoğdu notes: "If humanitarian organizations are willing to encourage certain forms of self-sufficiency (for example basket-weaving), they strongly discourage initiatives that challenge the administration of life in camps. When refugees barter or trade food, for example, they risk confiscation of that food or even arrest by local police. Their attempts to lead ordinary lives can be stunted in various ways due to the structural conditions of camps."[29] If refugees are released from these camps, argues migration scholar Loren Landau, they should be given the means through which to recuperate these rights:

> This means providing them with not only legal status to work, which is the first stage, but also the opportunity to organize politically to challenge discriminatory obstacles and, more importantly, to enhance the social networks there is so important in improving welfare and security. . . .
>
> In this model, we no longer measure success solely in nutritive or legal status but by evaluating whether the refugees are progressively able to expand the opportunities to achieve levels of welfare and security in line with local standards and their own heterogeneous objectives.[30]

To deny refugees the right to participate in the determination of their life conditions is, again, a deprivation of what Arendt calls the most fundamental human right: the right to be part of a community where one's opinions count, or in the language of this study, *a place where one's voice matters.* Yet it is precisely this ability to voice grievances, especially when it comes to the conditions of one's work, that is most endangered by the neoliberal cycle.

The concretization of the relationship between refugee camps, humanitarianism, and the exploitation of refugee workers has been a primary feature of refugee camps, almost from their inception. Consider, for instance, that between 1925 and 1929, the International Labor Office functioned as a "refugee labor exchange."[31] In that context, as Katy Long notes, "refugee exile was just one part of a broader concern to tackle the much greater project of global unemployment through targeted migration." States therefore understood the granting of asylum from persecution through the lens of their employment needs: "rather than insisting on a program of admission as a humanitarian good, refugees were essentially presented as productive economic migrants."[32]

In his book *Displacements*, architectural historian Andrew Herscher gives a comprehensive overview of the history of these camps, and the connection between architecture and ideology, especially with regard to the transit between refugee camps and workplaces:

> Contemporary refugee spaces are increasingly housing refugees, locating housing in camps, and connecting camps to urban labor markets all at the same time. Established in 2016, the "Refugee Cities" project, which proposes to construct refugee camps as special economic zones were refugees could become "productive generators of income, jobs, and foreign investment," perhaps most vividly demonstrates the emergence of new refugee spaces that can be described as housing, camp, and city simultaneously.[33]

Herscher notes how the path from "dependence" on humanitarian shelters to independence as a member of the workforce ignores that housing itself is not a neutral place, but one entirely integrated into the capitalist market. However, this integration is uneven in terms of access to housing and work: refugees are forced to compete for substandard housing with working-class renters, with the effect of

> benefitting property owners in the form of increased housing demand, along with increased social suffering to communities denied affordable housing. This became apparent in Jordan, where for a time an estimated 80 percent of registered Syrian refugees were residing outside of refugee camps, for the most part the country's most impoverished municipalities. There, refugees competed with poor and working-class residents for affordable housing. Subsequently, at the beginning of spring 2015, reports began to emerge of Syrian refugees moving from Jordanian cities back into refugee camps: *these were camps that began to provide refuge not from war zones but from cities without affordable housing.*[34]

As we saw in the previous chapter, and at the start of this one, vulnerable populations are subjected to displacement, eviction, detention, imprisonment, and more. They are meant not to have a "place" of stability, autonomous growth, and self-determination. They are not meant to have voices, but only working parts. Because of their class status, their race, their ethnicity, and in some cases their nationalities and their religions, they are identified as "blight," "criminals," "bad guys," "terrorists," and more. They are "enemies within," undeserving of being treated as human beings.

Enemies Within

I began this chapter speaking about an invariable element of all borders—violence. I now want us to think about the drawing of borders within the United States itself, especially as they pertain to the US government's war on its own people, and the resistance to concomitant forms of state violence posed by "sanctuary cities" and "autonomous zones." It came as no surprise that the person who ran for the presidency on the slogan "Build the Wall" began his term by working to fortify the country's borders, and to do so in ways that targeted certain populations. Donald Trump's policies took the form of the so-called Muslim ban, the attack on Deferred Action for Childhood Arrivals (DACA), and the unleashing of ICE and other federal law enforcement agencies for the sole purpose of harassment, incarceration, and deportation of immigrants, refugees, and other suspect populations. These affronts were immediately met by resistance in several forms. Beginning just a week after Trump's January 2017 inauguration, ordinary people clogged major airports in protest for days at a time, immigration lawyers and their staffs worked overtime, and local churches and other community organizations set up shelters.

In his first one hundred days in office, Trump coordinated an unprecedented throttling of immigration quotas, poured hundreds of millions of dollars into the state's attacks on undocumented immigrants, and funded a brutal expansion of the US deportation infrastructure. The force and viciousness of this new immigration regime led even a federal judge to remark on its inhumanity.[35] In his opinion on one case, Judge Stephen Reinhardt of the Ninth Circuit Court wrote, "The government forces us to participate in ripping apart a family . . . three United States citizen children will now have to choose between their father and their country."[36] These new policies and practices had immediate and often profound effects on the way immigration law was practiced at the grassroots level. In 2017, I interviewed a number of pro–immigrant rights lawyers and activists.[37]

Ilyce Shugall, directing attorney of the immigration program at Community Legal Services in East Palo Alto, California, confirmed the new intensity and aggressiveness of the Trump regime. She told me in an interview for *Truthout* that in immigration court, the ICE Office of the General Counsel was opposing "essentially every motion—basic motions for continuance are being opposed, motions for administrative closure or motions to terminate in cases of children who are eligible for Special Immigrant Juvenile Status are being opposed when those were routinely agreed upon previously." Lucas Guttentag, a professor at Stanford Law School and founder of the ACLU's Immigrants' Rights Project, said that the Trump administration was also trying to gradually change the culture within the Department of Homeland Security. "Everything's gone out the window—it's a free for all," he said. He explained that even though the Trump administration retreated somewhat in the face of legal challenges to its sweeping orders, damage had already been done in the message sent to ICE and Customs and Border Protection officers.

The Trump administration also threatened to expand the use of the "expedited removal" initiative—under which it can deport people unchecked by any immigration court. The initiative had previously been used only at the border, but now the government was applying it in the interior—it allowed ICE agents to make extrajudicial decisions to deport individuals on the spot. Another aspect of this new mode of enforcement and judgment has been that more people seeking asylum are being denied parole and kept in detention. As a result, the non-detained, non-priority cases get dragged out. During the Trump administration, that included children's cases, which were deprioritized. Consequently, people were, and remain, reluctant even to apply for asylum protections they may well qualify for.

As all these actions were threatened, and many of implemented, there was a widening disconnect between the goals of the federal government and the aims of local law enforcement. Shugall gave the example of San Mateo County, where the sheriff's department did not want to deputize its law enforcement officers as immigration agents, for fear that doing so would decrease the safety of the community. The sheriff's department had expressed fear that doing so could "prevent immigrants from reporting crimes and it could very well prevent people in mixed-status families from reporting crimes," Shugall said. In that 2017 interview, he also told me: "We've already seen statistics coming out of Los Angeles that there's been a decrease in reporting of domestic violence and sexual assault. And the belief is that it's because people are afraid to work with law enforcement." Ultimately, as Guttentag noted, there was an even larger issue at hand—something that went to the heart of what we are as a nation: "I don't think it's just about undocumented immigrants. I think it's about changing the perception and the reality of America and its composition. I think the Trump administration wants to change the immigration laws far more deeply than just what we're talking about now," he said. "It feels like we are in a period like at the beginning of the 1900s that lead to the 1920s National Origins Quota Act. That was—as you know—an openly racist and exclusionary law designed with the explicit goal using immigration to return to an era of America as a white, northern European, Christian nation. Barring all Asian immigration, and virtually no Jewish, Southern or Eastern European immigration."

In the face of the retrenchment of racist exclusionary practices, however, the Trump era also sparked new forms of popular resistance. In Guttentag's words, the movement against these practices "broadened and deepened the voices in support of immigrant communities, and made those communities feel there is a larger movement supporting them and that immigrants are not alone." Some municipalities established themselves as sanctuary cities, meaning that they refused to take on the role of federal immigration enforcers. Doing so would both make them complicit with blatantly unconstitutional practices and also erode whatever positive relations they might enjoy with their communities. Similarly, in September 2017, the California State Legislature passed, and Governor Jerry Brown signed into law, Senate Bill 54, which prohibits state and local law enforcement agencies from "using money or personnel to investigate, interrogate, detain, detect, or arrest persons for immigration enforcement purposes, as specified, and would, subject to exceptions, proscribe other activities or conduct in connection with immigration enforcement by law enforcement agencies."[38]

In response to these political moves by the Trump administration, undertaken in the name of "national security," activists created autonomous zones—places within towns and cities where people took charge of space and social organization. Such places are driven by a spirit of independence and creativity, where, as writer Ezra Marcus says, "[o]ne simply wants to live differently within the parameters of what's possible. . . . It's about a strategy where you develop the institutions on your own," she said, the goal being to "develop the collective capacity to take care of yourself."[39] The creation of such spaces is not new; they go back to the Paris Commune of 1871 and the Free Derry nationalist area of 1969, set up by Irish Republican Liam Hillen. The spirit of these prior enactments, as we saw with the way Martin Luther King Jr.'s 1968 Resurrection City was inspired in part by the Bonus Army of World War I veterans, lives on: in 2020 a protester in Seattle put up a tribute to Free Derry at the city's Capital Hill Autonomous Zone. The "Black House Autonomous Zone" in Washington, DC, was also set up in June 2020, and evoked the typically violent response by the Trump, who tweeted that the zone would be met with "serious force." The tag "BHAZ" was placed on the white pillars outside the historical St. John's Episcopal Church—the very place where, weeks before, peaceful protesters demanding justice for George Floyd had been tear-gassed by federal law enforcement.[40]

These examples epitomize the struggle over space, in terms of the people's right to produce space that is commensurate with their values, and to create a place where silenced voices can be heard. Such spaces have proven to be intolerable to the state, and have been dubbed "war zones," a rhetorical move that shifts the focus from external enemies to enemies within; those who dissent, protest, and resist are deemed worthy of arbitrary arrest, confinement, and even extrajudicial execution.[41] In sum, the border moved within, and divided people in terms of not only nationality, but also race, ethnicity, and political belief. And again, this is nothing new; local police and federal agents have long acted on invisible borders that are often left entirely up to them to perceive. We saw this in the previous chapter with the racialization of space. Without doubt one of the most blatant examples of the militarization of the border within took place on May 13, 1985, when police dropped a bomb made of C-4 plastic explosives—the sort widely deployed in Vietnam—on a Black neighborhood in Philadelphia, killing eleven people, including five children. The supposed reason: to clear out a house suspected of housing members of MOVE, a group devoted to Black liberation and environmental justice. But even after killing those people inside the house, the police commissioner, Gregore Sambor, ordered that the fire be allowed to spread across the entire neighborhood, where it destroyed sixty more houses and left 250 people homeless.[42]

In a sick twist of fate, the legal leverage for so many violations of the US Constitution and of human and civil rights turns out to be the exhumation of "American Indian laws"—laws used to control, contain, and destroy Indigenous peoples. With these legal instruments, the federal government turned to wreak the same damage not only on Indigenous peoples, but also on racialized peoples and political dissidents on public streets. Indigenous legal scholar Maggie Blackhawk notes: "The last three administrations have pointed to the Indian Wars as precedent to justify executive action in the war on terrorism, with the Trump administration invoking the plenary power doctrine as justification for family separation, migrant detention camps and religious persecution."[43] In sum, the government showed its willingness, and even desire, to turn against its own people and against international human rights, in a dizzying remapping of borders and boundaries.

Setting a dangerous new precedent of the militarization of these internal borders, in July 2020, the Trump administration took advantage of the one-hundred-mile "border zone" that extends inward from the country's coasts to send the Border Patrol Tactical Unit (BORTAC) into Portland, Oregon, where its elite troopers broke up peaceful demonstrations, including autonomous zones. Reporter Trevor Timm began his account with these words: "A remarkable and nightmarish scene playing out in Portland should terrify anyone who cares about the US constitution: unmarked vans full of camouflaged and unidentified federal agents are pulling up next to protesters on street corners, then snatching and arresting them with no explanation."[44] In Portland, and then in other cities, Trump launched an all-out, unconstitutional military assault on democracy. Even some military leaders objected to their troops being transformed into symbols of fascism, or their own offices' exploitation as props for Trump's militaristic strongman image. It soon became clear that much of the violence that was blamed on the protesters was actually perpetrated by so-called alt-right militias, most notoriously the extremist "boogaloo" groups, and by police infiltrators.[45] These provocations allowed Trump to claim that entire cities were aflame due to Antifa fires.

The fact that it was DHS troops that were deployed was not lost on commentators and activists, who noted that those who patrol the national border have been taught to dehumanize immigrants and refugees, to use deadly force without provocation, and to suspend constitutional and international human rights law. Hungry for targets and trained to target broadly, and given a federal mandate to do whatever they deemed necessary, DHS troops turned on domestic subjects with alarming alacrity and joy, even beating and macing older people. Trump himself publicly condoned the police violence against unarmed protestors that summer, including those in Buffalo, New York, who shoved a 74-year-old pacifist to the pavement, causing internal bleeding; of course, Trump claimed the man was a member of "Antifa."[46]

Despite these violent crackdowns, the summer of demonstrations, protests, and occupations demanding justice for George Floyd and an end to police impunity continued. When state violence reaches a certain point, two things can happen: first, people who ordinarily call themselves "apolitical" can become politicized, even radicalized; and second, people can decide that there is simply too much to lose by staying quiet. Earlier I talked about the idea of "eruption"—a spontaneous uprising and expression of dissent. Such eruptions are highly significant symptoms of social malaise, although it can be very difficult to sustain the intensity of such momentum. One of the keys to keeping that momentum, I have argued, is to reclaim space: to open up possibilities and make things happen in places where they are not supposed to. This takes imagination, courage, and solidarity. And it is precisely to those things that I now turn, as they have emerged in people's struggles against borders and remapped space.

Erasing Borders

It would be wrong to downplay or underestimate the violent and destructive power of borders, real and imagined, especially when those borders are enforced by the full weight, and will, of the state. And it is important to recognize that any breach in such a wall can be closed quickly. Nevertheless, despite the claims of those who build walls, it has become clear that human ingenuity, imagination, and cooperation far exceed the capacity of any wall to completely seal off people and goods. As former secretary of homeland security Janet Napolitano famously said of the border wall, "[S]how me a 50-foot wall, and I'll show you a 51-foot ladder at the border."[47] Throughout this book, I have given examples of work people have accomplished individually, but more often in groups, that challenges and overcomes the ways power has placed them, trying to either fix them in place or manage their movements according to the needs and demands of neoliberal, ethno-nationalist, or other anti-democratic forces. I have shown how this "placement" has been accompanied by a silencing of voices, and how people relegated to these spaces are deemed to have less importance, less authority, less learning, less to offer. But there is something incredibly resilient about human beings, and this book has tried to remind us of that conceptually, philosophically, and historically. And the failures of the past to breach these kinds of barriers and restrictions of the imagination and political will should not be seen as defeats, but as lessons for the future.

This reality is illustrated by a small but telling example. Citing the Border Patrol's use of high-tech devices to track and trap those crossing over, Rubén Martínez tells of an interview he did with a cab driver in Cherán, in central western Mexico:

> [F]or every high-tech weapon the *migra* employ, Marco says, there's a guerrilla-like response from the wetbacks and coyotes. Take the laser traps, for example, grids of beams that, when breached, immediately alert the *migra* to movement. One wetback crew Marcos crossed with was equipped with spray cans. You sprayed ahead of you in an area already known to be a problem from previous busts. The beams glittered in the mist, and you made your way around the grid. The coyotes claimed that the Border Patrol constantly relocates its tracking equipment. But each group of migrants that gets caught actually helps new migrants cross. Each bust is valuable intelligence gathered.[48]

Despite the fact that in the decades since the 1986 Immigration Reform and Control Act was passed, over $187 billion spent on immigration control and border security, geographer Michael Dear says something that both seems to agree with the above quote from Napolitano, and also goes further in understanding what drives human ingenuity:

> These are irrational proposals because, simply stated, walls won't work. . . . Walls won't work because the border has long been a place of connectivity and collaboration. The border zone is a permeable membrane *connecting* two countries, where communities on both sides have strong senses of mutual dependence and attachment to territory. The inhabitants of this in-between place—what I call a "third nation"— thrive on cross-border support and cooperation, which had flourished in diverse forms over many centuries.[49]

In other words, even while acknowledging the virulent forms of racism that exist at the border, one should recognize that ultimately, people need to live together. That should be recognized as a kind of force of nature—we are social beings.

In a moving essay titled *"Recuerdos*/Souvenirs: A Nuevo Grand Tour,"* Ronald Rael provides photos and illustrations of dozens of ways people on both sides of the border have penetrated it. Each one of these involves collaboration and cooperation, and each one has had success. He shows photos of "portable bridges," consisting of a steel ramp that creates a pathway for automobiles to drive over the fence: "There are several types of movable bridges. Some are attached to the backs of pickup and flatbed trucks, making them highly portable. Others must be hand carried and put in place by several people. Ironically, vehicular walls, specifically designed to stop automobiles, are the easiest walls to cross because they are typically quite low, and ramps can easily be placed on both sides, allowing vehicles to drive across them."[50] Such practical techniques have inspired more fanciful tributes, as well, such as the shoes Argentine artist Judi Werthein's designed specifically for migrants planning to journey through the desert and traverse the wall. These shoes served several purposes at once; they were creative and imaginative art objects that spread the artist's message about migration to the art world, they were put up for sale at boutiques, and they were also distributed at a migrant shelter for free:

> These cross trainers are called "Brinco," the word used by immigrants for their "jump" over the wall to the other side. A compass and a flashlight are attached to shoelaces, as most immigrants attempt to cross at night. The shoes have a small pocket for hiding money from coyotes and also include Tylenol to alleviate pain from injuries sustained in the journey. Printed on the removable insole is a map of the border showing the most popular routes from Tijuana to San Diego.[51]

Rael's book *Borderwall as Architecture* offers a photo of these shoes next to another, very different kind of footwear. Those crossing the border sometimes attach remnants of carpet to the soles of their shoes, which disguise and partially erase their footprints as they walk. These modified shoes give us an important example of how people can apply their imagination to create low- or no-cost tools made out of materials they find at hand, and start traditions of resistance. In this case, migrants transform places of surveillance into ones of disappearance and invisibility.

In response to the manners in which walls seek to destroy human connections, people have also imagined ways to transform walls into objects that can allow forms of human closeness. Rael's book tells of the creation of "yoga walls," "communion walls," "volleyball walls," and "confessional walls" at the border, as well as "friendship parks" in which friends old and new, and extended families, create new places for themselves outside of the logic of borders and walls. In this sense, they claim a "right to the border" in every way possible. One of the most radical artistic and political acts in this regard occurred in 2016, when Palestinian artist Khaled Jarrar constructed a ladder out of the wall itself. Rael explains:

> He ripped away a portion of the border wall in Tijuana—an 18-foot-long post—and transported it to New Mexico State University where he cut the steel into pieces. He used the pieces to construct a ladder, which he transported to Juarez, Mexico and had installed near the border wall as a monument "to connect communities and explore comparisons and common concerns between this wall and the wall I live with every day in my home city of Ramallah, Palestine."[52]

The forms of resistance and solidarity we find with regard to borders and walls sometimes take place in migrant detention centers and in refugee camps. In these camps, people do not simply accept their conditions as passive victims, but struggle actively to overcome them. Despite the stripping of their right to work, they engage in various commercial activities, such as barter for or sale of their rations, in response to the inadequate quantity or bad quality of the rations doled out by camp administrators.

Like autonomous zones, protest camps are repudiations of anti-democratic forms of place, and provide a pathway for people to live together in mutual support and dignity. In both cases, people reject the forms of identity and the assignments of value and voice that the state places upon them. Researcher Elisa Pascucci points out:

> Over the past decade, migrant and refugee protests have emerged as one of the most significant phenomena through which citizenship and belonging are contested and redefined from the margins, both in Europe and along its externalized borderland. The sit-ins held by undocumented migrant workers in Murcia, Southern Spain in 2001 and the African refugees protests in Tel Aviv's Levinsky Park, as well as the camps set up by rejected asylum seekers in central Vienna and in Berlin's Oranienplatz in 2012–2013 and the collective known as "Lampedusa in Hamburg" are all examples that highlight how political mobilization against migration governance is increasingly taking the form of protest camps.[53]

These camps are not simply sit-ins; they become places where people can claim a right to the city in a microcosmic fashion—determining their own forms of collective governance and their own political economies. The Marconi Occupation in São Paulo, Brazil, which came into being in 2012, was a particularly remarkable repudiation of extractive capitalism. Marcella Arruda writes:

> [E]veryday relations between people were transformed to come with the aims of achieving a glimpse of a more just, sustainable and equal society. By creating other ways of being in the world, Marconi became an example of a social movement protest strategy providing housing but also challenging the capitalistic status quo and encouraging a search for individual and group identities. . . . Issues were intertwined and collided in the everyday existence of the inhabitants of this social laboratory. Despite the short life of the initiative, it still reverberates and the experience is still embodied in the people who are involved.[54]

Arruda points out something urgent and important: when people "take place," creating new spaces where new ways of living together can be imagined and carried out, they put something new into the world and take that spirit and ethos with them, modeling a new way of life that can inspire others. Crucially, this new modality of living together is manifested in new language and new voices.

Often the placement of protest camps is planned in order to "produce space" that symbolizes the stark contrasts between justice and injustice, between democratic and autocratic forms of governance, and between established institutions and those created on the spot by the people themselves, according to their immediate wants and needs. For example, in September 2005, a small group of Sudanese refugees started a three-month sit-in at Mustapha Mahmoud Square, located directly across from the offices of the United Nations High Commissioner for Refugees (UNHCR) in Cairo, Egypt. While at first the demonstration gathered only a few hundred protesters, sociologists Carolina Moulin and Peter Nyers observe,

> the sit-in quickly grew to numbers in excess of three thousand protesting Sudanese refugees of varying degrees of status. Among the protestors' key demands was to be included in discussions about the politics of their status, the terms of their care and protection, and the future possibilities for international resettlement. Perhaps symptomatic of the enormous challenges of refugees today is that the protestors' demands

were all but ignored by the UNHCR. The mere presence of political voice by the refugees evoked strong hostility.[55]

Once again, we find an instance of people insisting that their voices should be heard, that they have a right to shape the conditions of their existence. Yet this act of speaking out of place was met with antagonism from officials who jealously protected their authority to distribute human rights as they saw fit.

In North America, Indigenous forms of protest have centered on the reclamation of unceded territory. In the United States, the history of the American Indian Movement and the resurgence of tribal sovereignty struggles in the 1960s and '70s is inextricably wrapped up with occupations: Alcatraz from 1967 to 1971, the Bureau of Indian Affairs Building in Washington, DC, in 1972, and the town of Wounded Knee, South Dakota, in 1973. In Canada, in 1995 Ontario provincial police violently raided Ipperwash Provincial Park, which had been occupied by members of the Stony Point Ojibway band as part of a decades-long land claim. This standoff overlapped with an occupation near Gustafsen Lake in British Columbia, between August and September of that year. And both these protest camps followed on the heels of the most well-known standoff featuring blockades and occupations in Canadian history, the 1990 Oka Crisis.[56] Researchers Adam Barker and Russell Myers Ross note: "When Indigenous communities take up visible presence on the land, especially presence that disrupts the mobility of the capitalist economy of the settler state, this disruption forces issues of Indigenous discontent and struggles for freedom into the settler Canadian public discourse. In short, Indigenous re-occupations assert Indigenous identity across the boundaries of settler colonial space, which frustrates the drive for invisibility or transcendence of the settler colonial form."[57]

This assertion of Indigenous identity can also be seen in the final example of protest camps I will discuss in this chapter: the Aboriginal Tent Embassy in Canberra, Australia, the world's longest-running Indigenous protest camp to date. On January 27, 1972, the day after the national holiday that commemorates the landing of British colonizers, a group of Indigenous activists set up the Embassy. The Embassy, like the plebians' forum on the Aventine Hill, displays wit, imagination, and a parody of state power. Part of the reason it stood for so long is that the

Embassy presented the Australian government with a public relations nightmare—how to remove it without reenacting the founding act of colonialism? The protest simply grew. As the editors of the anthology *Protest Camps in International Context* write: "The inability for the government to remove this embarrassing protest from in front of their parliament house captured the imagination of not just indigenous Australia. Within days the site had established an office tent and installed a letter box in front. Tourist bus operators became aware of the new attraction in town and began bringing their busloads of tourists to see the aboriginal embassy before escorting them across the road to Parliament House."[58]

I want to turn now to an event that displays the solidarity, intelligence, creativity, and humaneness that each of the above instances have incorporated. The 2019 film *The Infiltrators*, directed by Alex Rivera and Cristina Ibarra, tells the true story of a group of young undocumented activists who purposefully break the law (or claim to have) in order to be detained at the Broward Transitional Center in South Florida, a notorious detention facility. The film begins by documenting the lives of the young activists and their planning sessions. They create a communications network that allows them to work together and also to feed important information to their comrades who have been detained at the facility. At points, the filmmakers are not able to gain access to the center, and so they employ volunteers actors, also activists, to play the roles of their comrades. A key element of the film is the smuggling of petitions and official documents into and out of the center. The activists get a sense of each of the detainees' situations, working through the communication network to send and receive information to National Immigrant Youth Alliance activists on the outside. In turn, the NIYA activists create savvy PR events and media assets to bring specific stories out to the public, and in many cases these stories result in a halted deportation.

There are moments when things go wrong—plans have to be rescheduled, people are unexpectedly transferred, or the routine at the detention center changes. But each time, we see the community reform and reinvent itself around all these contingencies. One of the most interesting aspects of this work is the sheer imagination and intelligence that arise solely because of a shared sense of empathy. With regard to the work of these activists, Diana Flores Ruíz notes: "Spanning a period from the late

2000s through the early 2010s, their organizing tactics must respond to changing immigration regulations, largely during the Obama administration. The group's intervention successfully liberates Claudio and a few other detainees, yet the film reminds audiences that detention is merely one cog in a broken, highly profitable machine."[59]

In their interview with Ruíz, the directors offer important insights into the production of the film. First, there is this account by Rivera of how they created the space of the film from disparate sources:

> Our journey of trying to go from a space we didn't know at all to a space that we re-created and made physical, that materialized in front of the camera, had a lot of way stations. One step was archival: looking at images of the interior of the facility. There's not many, but there are some, and we found them on . . . a clearinghouse for the U.S. Department of Defense. There, they have B-roll footage of Department of Defense and Department of Homeland Security activities. They even have some images from the inside of Broward. And we had our interview material from all of the formerly detained people who had been inside Broward. But it was really living and working with Claudio Rojas for a month that brought everything to life.

This act of creation is part of what we have been describing, following Lefebvre, as the production of space. That is, a people's ability to fabricate, even out of oppressive source material, a place where they tell a story that is not supposed to happen. The center assigned each detainee a role, a function, and set of authorized words and actions, and through this multilayered act of solidarity, those assignments were all breached, violated. The words and voices that were created displayed the same kinds of collaboration and solidarity that informed the reinvention of "place." Ibarra explains:

> We depended on Marco's, Viri's, and Claudio's descriptions of life in detention. We had to get them on board with this creative approach because they were the ones who were going to open up that part of the film for us. . . . A large part of the story is set inside the detention center; all of that had to be imagined and re-created. Alex drew storyboards of the scenes to illustrate those things that we couldn't see. . . . Once we had focused on specific moments of the story, we'd ask them to re-create them with us. We had a measuring tape, and we drew out the geography and were able to get a lot of details in a very visceral way because they were able to take themselves back inside together.[60]

Summing it up, Ibarra called this a "backwards process" in which the norms of film production had to be violated on account of the topic, the real-life events, and the specific constraints of working both within and without a detention center. Yet the "backwards process" worked perfectly to accomplish both its goals, and to capture the real events. Most powerfully, the "memory workshops" form an indispensable archive of knowledge—knowledge that stems from and feeds back into not only the collective memory of the immediate participants, but also the memories and future actions of all of those faced with similar constraints and injustices. In this regard, the film echoes the historical patterns of solidarity we have traced throughout this book. In making the film, the directors had to try to make sense of a divergence between what President Obama was saying, and what he was doing with regard to detention and immigration:

> What we ended up seeing under Obama was an administration that built a massive infrastructure on the ground. The detention center where the film is set is a part of it. But there was daylight between what was happening on the ground and what Obama was saying about immigrants—sympathetic things. That was the chasm that the activists threw themselves into. They were exploiting the dissonance between what Obama was saying and what he was doing. That was fascinating to watch.[61]

One of the tasks of this book is to trace the variance of "voice" wielded by those in power, and to show instance after instance in which people have "exploit[ed] the dissonance" created by liberalism and neoliberalism. What we find in Rivera and Ibarra's film is young undocumented activists risking everything to infiltrate a detention center and create a new place from within, linked to activists and the broader public on the outside. In *The Infiltrators* we also identify an especially powerful example of how people can recreate space in accordance with their needs, demands, and desires, and from within that space broadcast a liberatory voice.

I conclude this chapter with an account of two acts that are, once again, small but significant. Above, we considered the terrible challenges of "crossing over"—challenges presented by the state, and by the state's exploitation of the harshness of the terrain and the heat. We saw sophisticated inventions, from border-crossing bridges to modified footwear that erases footprints. But here we find one individual simply offering water and shelter to two people.

In 2018, a 37-year-old geographer named Scott Warren was charged with giving two young men from Central America a place to sleep for a few days and some food and water. They had arrived at a humanitarian aid station in Ajo, Arizona, with nothing. Warren told them he could offer what he could offer, but he could not shield them from the law. As Ryan Deveraux reported for the *Intercept*: "Border Patrol agents descended days later. Warren was arrested along with the two young men. He was charged with two counts of harboring and one count of conspiracy and faced up to 20 years in prison."[62] Only after two years of trials was he found not guilty. The case hung on whether or not the prosecution, aided by a high-powered prosecutor dispatched by Trump, could prove criminal intent, rather than the fact that Warren was acting on his religious and humanitarian beliefs. But the very fact that offering food to someone could be regarded as a criminal act beggars belief. Here, the modest action of a single person gathered worldwide attention because it awakened our conscience, and dramatically showed the inhumanity of US federal law. Scott Warren shone a bright light on this cruelty and created a backlash against more than just his prosecution.

For my second example I turn to Pia Klemp, a biologist and the former captain of the refugee rescue ship *Juventa*, who together with her crew saved thousands of migrants in the Mediterranean Sea. In August 2019, the Socialist Party mayor of Paris, Anne Hidalgo, decided to honor Klemp for her actions. But instead of using the occasion to accept the honor, Klemp posted this statement on her personal Facebook page:

> Madame Hidalgo, you want to award me a medal for my acts of solidarity in the Mediterranean Sea, because our crews "work daily to save migrants in difficult conditions." At the same time, your police steal blankets from people forced to sleep on the street, while you repress demonstrations and criminalize those who defend the rights of immigrants and asylum seekers. You want to give me a medal for acts that you oppose within your own borders. I'm sure you will not be surprised to see me refuse your Grand Vermeil medal.[63]

Like several of the other acts we have discussed, this one also takes advantage of media attention to bring broader awareness to an injustice; instead of offering Paris the opportunity to demonstrate its beneficence, Klemp used the media spotlight to point out *systemic* injustice. As in Jackie Robinson's appearance before the House Un-American Activities

Committee, Klemp accepted the state's invitation, only to go off script and speak with a different voice. In so doing, she reshaped that space of voice in order to send a powerful message.

In the final chapter, I move from discussing human-made borders and the ways we need to, and can, re-imagine living outside both the legal lines and the invisible lines of prejudice and bigotry that the powerful use to segment us off from each other, and turn to the relation we have to the planet. In moving to the planetary scale I ask us to observe, and act against, systemic injustices that are depriving us and future genera-tions of our common place. While every chapter of this book has dealt with the idea of political voice in terms of new imaginings of place and living together, the issue of planetary well-being is an existential one that links humans, non-human animals, flora, and the material and spiritual forms of the earth in an dilemma of immense proportions. And we have precious little time to rethink, in the profoundest ways possible, how we can survive the effects of our mishandling of what we have inherited as a planetary home.

CHAPTER 4

PLANETARY HOME

Before moving into the main body of this final chapter, let's review what we have covered in our study and the line of reasoning we have followed. In chapter 1 I suggested we could learn from the historical examples of the 1968 Olympics, the #BlackLivesMatter protests in sports arenas, and several other occupations of space and eruptions of voices around the world, to see how various people "spoke out of place," transforming what was possible to transpire in places that had been declared out of bounds for any sort of dissent, and indeed, out of bounds for any political action. The things activists made happen were not supposed to be able to take place, and the fact that they did shows the power of the political and social imagination. In chapter 2, we began developing this idea of place and looked at the right to the city as a powerful concept with which to imagine people taking charge of their surroundings, their work, their habitat, and their community. We saw how displacement, gentrification, and invisible lines of racism supported by a combination of real estate, corporate interests, and government bodies work against this sort of empowerment, and how people have fought back. In the previous chapter we moved onto the global stage, building on Neil Smith's conception of globalization, labor, distance, and place. We looked into the violent divisiveness of borders both within and without, and the specific places of detention and concentration camps. And once again, we saw ways in which people have resisted, remapped, subverted, and reinvented places and voices to mark the possibilities of different ways of living together.

Now, in this final chapter, I wish to move from the scale of the global to that of the planetary. We turn away from urban spaces and national borders to address the ways that not only human beings but also parts of the planet itself have been parceled out, segmented, and assigned different values and rights. We will look at both causes and effects, but also at other ways of imaging our relationship to the planet—ones that stand in stark contrast to the mandates of neoliberalism and capitalism. It is urgent that we take on these new ways of thinking if we are going to truly understand the peril in which our planetary home has been placed. The following passage from journalist and activist Naomi Klein frames these concerns well.

> A decade ago, Australian philosopher and professor of sustainability Glenn Albrecht set out to coin a term to capture the particular form of psychological distress that sets in when homelands we love and from which we take comfort are radically altered by extraction and industrialization, rendering them alienating an unfamiliar. He settled on "solastalgia," with its evocations of solace, destruction, and pain, and defined a new word to mean, "the homesickness you have when you are still at home." He explained that although this particular form of unease was once principally familiar to people who lived in sacrifice zones—lands decimated by open-pit mining for, for instance, or clear-cut logging—it was fast becoming a universal human experience, with climate change creating a "new abnormal" wherever we happen to live. "As bad as local and regional negative transformation is, it is the big picture, the Whole Earth, which is now a home under assault. A feeling of global dread itself himself as the planet heats and our climate gets more hostile and unpredictable," he writes.[1]

Klein touches upon the key topics of this chapter—the sense of a loss of home, the psychological and physiological stress of that feeling, and the need to act on these feelings of alienation—with others—before it is too late. Instead of accepting inevitable catastrophe, as corporations and oligarchs and governments ask us to do in any number of ways, we need to recognize the strength we have together, to repudiate "gradualism," and to use every means necessary to put forward an entirely different view of the planet and our relationship to it, and to ourselves. We must expand our sense of the places where we belong, and where we live with other beings. This means we have to identify the ways we have become detached from each other, and even set against one another, as well as the ways we have become alienated from planet.

Consider Henri Lefebvre's extension of his study of the production of space to the idea of nature:

The fact is that natural space will soon be lost from view. Anyone so inclined may look over their shoulder and see it sinking below the horizon behind us. Nature is also becoming lost in *thought*. For what is nature? How can we form a picture of it as it was before the intervention of humans with their ravaging tools? Even the powerful myth of nature is being transformed into a mere fiction, a negative utopia: nature is now seen merely as the raw material out of which the productive forces of a variety of social systems have forged their particular spaces.[2]

Recall that Lefebvre's seminal essay "The Right to the City" drew the connection between one's environment and the conflicting forces of capitalism and democracy. In the above passage, Lefebvre expands this notion to the planetary scale to incorporate the nonhuman animal, flora, and all elements of the planet in an urgent attempt to lessen the great damage of "the fragmentation of space for sale and purchase" and the parallel devastation of not only human social life, but all natural life as well. This urgency is pressed upon us by the increasingly rapid and visible damage that capitalism and other forms of human domination have wrought and continue to wreak.

Lefebvre's prediction that "natural space will soon be lost from view," has striking resonance with Klein's more recent observation that our whole sense of home and being at home in nature is fading before our eyes. In this chapter I will address the destructive ways of seeing each other and the world that capitalism has promoted, as well as explore how people have and can continue to keep the "myth" of nature alive. For such myths and stories have shown us very different ways of being together in the world, ways that increasingly appear more healthy, sane, and just. Even in a globally connected world (or perhaps because of it), people still need a sense of common life, a humane life that is shared with others and with the planet. It is possible to return to life's rhythms—marked by the movement of the sun, the seasons of the year, the cycles of nature—that all beings share. But to do so will require capacious acts of imagination. Here the words of novelist and activist Arundhati Roy are especially useful:

The first step towards re-imagining a world gone terribly wrong would be to stop the annihilation of those who have a different imagination—an imagination that is outside of capitalism as well as communism. An imagination which has an altogether different understanding of what constitutes happiness and fulfillment. To gain this philosophical space, it is necessary to concede some physical space for the survival of those who may look like the keepers of our past but who may really be the guides to our future. To do this, we have to ask our rulers: can you leave the water in the rivers, the trees in the forest? Can you leave the bauxite in the mountain? If they say they cannot, then perhaps they should stop preaching morality to the victims of their wars.[3]

This passage has a very specific context and message: Roy is speaking about the peoples who live in the forests of India's Chhattisgarh State, and their struggle to gain rights outside the machinations of both the capitalist and communist political parties. Although the Indian government has labeled them Maoist radicals, Roy uses a more precise set of terms. For her, these are people "engaged in a whole spectrum of struggles all over the country—the landless, the homeless, Dalits, workers, peasants, weavers. They're pitted against a juggernaut of injustices, including policies that allow a wholesale corporate takeover of people's lands and resources."[4] Along with a message to develop and nurture an imagination that comes from within and is negotiated in conjunction with others, I want to emphasize Roy's very direct demand that people need to control the physical places they inhabit, ones that nourish and support them.

To make a place for voice, it is necessary to disencumber ourselves of the notion that some peoples are mere relics of the past. We need to recognize that others' relationships to the planet may be informed by values entirely different from both the extractive mandates of capitalism, and from the distributive models of both capitalism and Communism. Ultimately, their conception of the relation of humans to other forms of life and to the planet is life-affirming, reciprocal, nurturing, and sustainable. Today we are presented with a final reckoning with our exploitative and extractive practices, practices that have largely been made possible by the relegation of whole groups of people into hierarchic categories, through their assignment of places of relative worth or value, the appropriation of their labor and lands, and the deadening, foreclosure, and destruction of their imaginaries of other ways of living together. And one of the most powerful and fundamental devices that has been used to segment and hierarchize people and places is maps.

Maps as Tools of Power

As environmental scholar Rob Nixon points out in his important book *Slow Violence: The Environmentalism of the Poor*, maps have routinely been used to erase the human symbolic content and habitation of space, wiping out all notions of place as home, and the territorial claims of the people who live and work there:

> A vernacular landscape is shaped by affective, historically textured maps the communities have devised over generations, maps replete with names and routes, maps alive to significant ecological features. A vernacular landscape, although neither monolithic nor undisputed, is integral to the socio-environmental dynamics of a community. By contrast, an official landscape—whether governmental, NGO, corporate, or some combination of those—is typically oblivious to such earlier maps; instead, it writes land in a bureaucratic, externalizing, and extraction-driven manner that is often pitilessly instrumental.[5]

Moreover, the very discipline of cartography has been riddled with ideology from the start. Legal scholar Sarah Keenan puts it this way:

> The legal conception of space as blank and inert fits with the mentality of imperialist explorers who would "command views" over the "natural" landscape and assess its suitability for the imposition of a particular socio-legal regime; and with the proprietal mentality of "undeveloped land" where the relationship of society nature is akin to the relationship of consumer to consumable.[6]

Likewise, cartographer Denis Cosgrove's discussion of this point brings in the ideas of voice, place, and rights that we have employed throughout this study: "In projecting ideas and belief forged in one locale across global space, the liberal mission of universal redemption is inescapably ethnocentric and imperial, able to admit 'other' voices only if they speak and are spoken by the language of the (self-denying) center. Desire for perfect, universal language has been a persistent companion of western globalism."[7] As a final example of scholarship on this issue, consider this statement from J. B. Harley, which ties imperialism into the destruction of Indigenous social organization, culture, and belief systems:

> In the 19th century, as maps became further institutionalized and linked to the growth of geography as a discipline, their power effects are again manifest in the continuing tide of European imperialism. The scramble for Africa, in which the European powers fragmented

the identity of indigenous territorial organization, has become almost a textbook example of these effects. . . .

Maps impinged invisibly on the daily lives of ordinary people. Just as the clock, as a graphic symbol of centralized political authority, brought "time discipline" into the rhythms of industrial workers, so to the lines on maps, dictators of a new agrarian topography, introduced a dimension of "space discipline." . . . Maps entered the law, were attached to ordinances, acquired an aureole of science, and helped create an ethic and virtue of ever more precise definition. Tracing on maps excluded as much as they enclosed. They fixed territorial relativities according to the lottery of birth, the accidence of discovery, or, increasingly, the mechanism of the world market.[8]

It's important to consider actual cases of these things happening, so we can understand the ramifications of these practices on people's lives, their communities, their histories, and their homes. I start with Palestine, where we see each and every one of the elements of these critiques of "map practices" in the case of Israel's mappings of Palestine. Alexandre Kedar, a legal scholar at the University of Haifa, has pointed out how maps and laws have worked together to dispossess Palestinians of their lands, and to silence their voices and any claim to rights:

While the legal system often plays a crucial role in facilitating the transfer of land from native populations to the control of the settlers, it simultaneously conceals the dispossession and legitimates the new land regime. Settlers' law and courts attribute to the new land system an aura of necessity and naturalness that protects the new status quo and prevents future redistribution. . . . Intricate legal tools and conventions serve as central instruments in defining and altering laws concerning native's rights. These rules, saturated with a heavy dose of professional, technical, and seemingly scientific language and methods, conceal the violent restructuring with an image of inevitability and neutrality.[9]

Indeed, the linchpin of Israel's project of annexation is its claim that the land in question was never actually inhabited by Palestinians. Here is where maps play a critical role both in the legitimation of Israel's settler-colonial practices and in the presentation to the world of a false image of the land in question.

In 2017, I became involved in a protest about the disappearance of Palestinian villages from both Google Maps and Apple Maps. Both show Israeli settlements and outposts, which are illegal under international law and violate official US policy, while erroneously depicting an empty countryside that in reality contains hundreds of Palestinian villages.[10] In an August 2015 letter to Senator Dianne Feinstein, Israeli prime minister Benjamin Netanyahu claimed that "[c]ontrary to Palestinian claims that the area has been inhabited for decades, only a handful of structures continued to expand their illegal construction by exploiting a cease and desist order that temporarily prohibited Israel from demolishing these structures."[11] In stark contrast to this assertion, according to the Israeli human rights group B'Tselem, "the Palestinian village of Khirbet Susiya has existed for at least a century. It appears on maps as far back as 1917—decades before Israel began occupying the West Bank. Aerial photographs from 1980 show cultivated farmland and livestock pens, indicating the presence of an active community there."[12]

In October 2016, a group of Palestinians working with the Rebuilding Alliance of Burlingame, California, delivered letters to the Silicon Valley headquarters of Google and Apple, requesting that they both update their maps with data that had been missing; they presented the media giants with accurate and detailed reconstructed maps showing the villages. Donna Baranski-Walker, founder and executive director of the alliance, said that "on Apple Maps, at least 550 villages were invisible to the world. Google Maps miss about 220 villages." Nava Sheer, a GIS mapping expert at Bimkom—Planners for Planning Rights similarly claimed: "Thousands of children and families in Area C of the West Bank can't locate their homes on Apple or Google maps, or on Waze (Google's subsidiary). . . . They are real locations—however, in the virtual mapped world of the Web, they simply can't be found. In today's online society, that's as good as saying you don't exist." When I interviewed Rabbi Arik Ascherman, director of the Israeli human rights organization Torat, he told me: "These people have been moved and displaced time after time after time. The psychological toll on people is devastating. People end up in therapy and children . . . are traumatized for life. People need to understand (a) that it is not a benign or neutral process; it's a very intensively political process. And (b) that it's not about security. . . . This is part of an intentional, political effort to displace Palestinians to allow for the expansion of settlements."[13]

What we are talking about is the erasure of a people and a culture, all premised on the lie that they simply do not exist. This is being done to install in their place illegal settlements and to populate the land as part of a long-standing settler-colonial project. In a "post-truth" world, where facts and reality itself are too often simply the products of the powerful who want to place even more of the world under their control, the actions undertaken by the Rebuilding Alliance and others are strong examples of how people can fight back and resist falsification and erasure, both on maps and in the world itself. We continue to fact-check the Silicon Valley companies' maps, aided by teams of experts in cartography, history, and aerial photography. We speak a different voice, from a place of resistance.

I want to draw attention to this instance because it shows how people can defy official and corporate forms of knowledge, and use their resources and their voices to change the world's sense of place—and, in turn, to allow those living in or exiled from those erased landscapes and places to speak as properly located and identified groups. They can legitimize not only their existence under the names they rightfully possess, but also their right to land and territory. Of course, to simply make this claim does not guarantee success, but such acts are necessary corrections that form new foundations for activism, and for a growing solidarity. The spirit behind this is not unlike the restoration of personal names to the migrant workers lost at Los Gatos canyon that we saw in the last chapter; it is a spirit that refuses to acquiesce to the designations of anonymity and nonexistence foisted upon peoples by those in power.

Indigenous Worldviews and Extractive Capitalism

The effort to write from a very different "place" is exactly what we see in struggles for environmental justice. Understanding not only the planet, but also one's relation to the planet and to others is a basic act of re-placing, producing space, and inventing a new voice through which to speak. But, as more and more activists have come to realize, this "different place" has to incorporate Indigenous voices and worldviews. As critical as mainstream environmental justice activism is, Indigenous scholars and their allies have insisted that only where such activism is informed by Indigenous senses of environmental justice, and is rigorously anti-capitalist, is it worth pursuing. Making the connection between extractive capitalism and the destruction of the planet means that we cannot settle for a justice that is arrived at simply by a more even distribution of things. The very relationship between people and "resources" has to be rethought from the bottom up.

This crucial point has been made numerously, and from different angles. For example, journalists Jason W. Moore and Raj Patel's book *A History of the World in Seven Cheap Things: A Guide to Capitalism, Nature, and the Future of the Planet* is concerned with how the modern world, from Columbus on, has been premised on "cheap nature" and the logic of cheapening—"and that doesn't mean just something low in price, but means to cheapen, to treat with less dignity, to degrade, or to disrespect the work and life of women, nature, colonies, Indigenous Peoples, Africans, and many others around the world who were not part of this narrow band of the 1% in Western Europe in the sixteenth and seventeenth centuries."[14] Just as Moore and Patel draw attention to the fact that peoples, lands, and beliefs are cheapened because they fall outside the value system of capitalism, interdisciplinary scholar Candice Fujikane says that, conversely, capitalism has a false sense of "abundance." In her inspiring book *Mapping Abundance for a Planetary Future*, Fujikane ties together the issues of cartography and capitalism:

> Capital produces a human alienation from land and from the elemental forms that constitutes a foundational loss. Humans compulsively try to fill this emptiness through an imaginary plenitude that commodifies land. In what I refer to as the settler colonial mathematics of subdivision, cartographies of capital commodify and diminish the vitality of land by drawing boundary lines around successively smaller, isolated pieces of land that capital proclaims are no longer "culturally significant" or "agriculturally feasible," often portraying abundant lands as wastelands incapable of sustaining life. . . .
>
> The struggle for a planetary future calls for a profound epistemological shift. Indigenous ancestral knowledges are now providing a foundation for our work against climate change, one based on what I refer to as Indigenous economies of abundance—as opposed to capitalist economies of scarcity. Rather than seeing climate change as apocalyptic, we can see that climate change is bringing about the demise of capital, making way for Indigenous lifeways that center familial relationships with the earth and elemental forms.[15]

Fujikane powerfully repudiates capitalism's idea of abundance as one that is necessarily exploitative and destructive, replacing it with a concept of abundance that is constantly replenished by respectful reciprocity between people, planet, and all forms of life.

In *As Long as the Grass Grows*, Indigenous scholar Dina Gilio-Whitaker emphasizes a closely connected point: that besides naming capitalism's representation of a worldview that mandates extraction and exploitation, Gilio-Whitaker argues that capitalism is also part of a larger belief system that subscribes to the idea that justice means redistribution, but that fails to acknowledge or fix historical structures that perpetuate inequality. In this model, it is thus inevitable that the "redistributed" resources flow unevenly. Gilio-Whitaker argues that without understanding the fundamental differences between liberal notions of environmental justice and Indigenous ones, we can never understand how the former remain trapped in the destructive logic of capitalism:

> The underlying assumptions of environmental injustice as it is commonly understood and deployed are grounded in racial and economic terms and defined by norms of distributive justice within a capitalist framework. Indigenous peoples' pursuit of environmental justice (EJ) requires the use of a different lens, one with a scope that can accommodate the full weight of the history of settler colonialism, on one hand, and embrace differences in the ways Indigenous peoples view land and nature, on the other. . . . Overall, a differentiated environmental justice framework—we could call this an "Indigenized environmental justice"—must acknowledge the political existence of Native nations and be capable of explicitly respecting principles Indigenous nationhood and self-determination.[16]

In sum, by leaving structures of domination in place, the liberal notion of environmental justice retains the basic capitalistic stance toward natural resources, which is one of extraction for the sole benefit of capital, with residual benefits disbursed at its will. As one example of this, consider that through its use of the slogan "Water Is Life," the 2016–17 #NoDAPL movement against the Dakota Access Pipeline made clear that Native resistance is "inextricably bound to worldviews that center not only the obvious life sustaining forces of the natural world but also the respect accorded the natural world and relationships of reciprocity based on responsibility toward those life forms."[17]

Another weakness in the liberal model of environmental justice is that it rejects worldviews that lie outside its compass. Gilio-Whitaker gives the example of the United States' refusal to abide by the UN's 2007 Declaration on the Rights of Indigenous Peoples (UNDRIP) during the initial bureaucratic struggle over the Dakota Access Pipeline, "had the United States Army Corps of Engineers taken seriously the United States' commitment to the UN declaration, in which the Standing Rock Sioux tribe would have been given the opportunity to exercise their institutional ability to speak for themselves, one can imagine a different outcome in the Dakota Access Pipeline controversy."[18] Basically, as Gilio-Whitaker argues, "[f]or a conception of environmental justice to be relevant to a group of people, it must fit within conceptual boundaries or [be] meaningful to them."[19] I have addressed this basic concept of voice and justice throughout this book, especially in the chapter on human rights and discussions of refugee protest camps. Here, the point is the same: a capacious sense of "voice" is one that steps outside the confines of what has been predetermined to be acceptable. This is not just a matter of "civility"; it is also one of worldviews and conceptions of social and planetary life.

When it comes to things as momentous as climate change, the struggle to give voice more often than not takes place within radically disrupted mappings of space and time. It is immensely frustrating to environmental activists that so many people simply do not register what is happening to the planet. So when my co-instructor María Gloria Robalino and I teach our course "Why Is Climate Change Unbelievable?," we use the 1986 nuclear meltdown at Chernobyl as a case study of how people reacted to the effects of catastrophe in every aspect of their lives. We ask students to read Svetlana Alexievich's 1997 *Chernobyl Prayer: A Chronicle of the Future*, a study more than ten years in the making, which compiles interviews with dozens of victims of the disaster and their families. I believe Alexievich uses "A Chronicle of the Future" as a subtitle because Chernobyl marked a radical break with the past; and indeed, the future looks exceedingly dim if we do not learn from the many mistakes made that caused that event. By "mistakes," I do not simply mean technological or scientific ones. More than those, I am talking about political and economic corruption, and the abandonment of the social contract between the state and the people they supposedly served. For Alexievich, Chernobyl represented the destruction of everyday assumptions, including one very basic one: the relationship of the human body to what lies outside it.

And yet, to call into doubt all prior points of reference and belief can also have immense benefits. It can dislodge us from bad habits and bad ways of thinking that root us in the status quo and dull our imaginations, bringing about a radically new understanding of what we are and what we can be. And, crucially, Alexievich claims that this new understanding involves a recognition of our relation to things outside of ourselves:

> The knowledge that results from recognition, then, is not of the same kind as the discovery of something new: it arises rather from a renewed reckoning with a potentiality that lies within oneself . . . when inflamed lungs and sinuses prove once again that there is no difference between the without and the within; between using and being used. These too are moments of recognition, in which it dawns on us that the energy that surrounds us, flowing under our feet and through wires in our walls, animating our vehicles and illuminating our rooms, is an all-encompassing presence that may have its own purposes about which we know nothing.[20]

Chernobyl has shown that something more massive and powerful has to be confronted: "What has become clear is that, besides the challenges of Communism, nationalism, and nascent religion where we are living with and dealing with, other challenges lie ahead: challenges more fiendish and all-embracing, although still hidden from view."[21] Climate change is chief among them—a force that industrial society has unleashed on the world and for which we refuse to take responsibility. We are shackled to the extractive logic that sees the planet as a resource, not a home.

Robalino and I draw on Alexievich's book because it shows our new planetary historical case, and it does so through the voices of those who have not only felt the devastation of Chernobyl, but also carry it in their bodies, in their genetic codes, and in their air, water, and soil. One of the most absurd and morbid scenes that people refer to over and over again in the book is troops deployed to bury contaminated earth, or farmers forced to milk their cows and then pour the contaminated milk into the soil.

After the catastrophe, people in Chernobyl were forced to adopt a completely new understanding of their "place." No longer an out-of-the-way town, they have become looped into the global not through economics but because of a human-made disaster. As Alexievich observes: "We're still using the old concepts of 'near and far,' 'them and us.' But what do 'near' and 'far' actually mean after Chernobyl, when, by day four, the fallout clouds were drifting above Africa and China? The earth suddenly became so small, no longer the land of Columbus' age."[22] In the same ways as people began to recognize anew the relation between what was inside their bodies and what was outside, they now realize how small the planet actually is. Planetary thinking therefore takes place in an immensely expansive manner—starting with our bodies and stretching to everything else. Because of the calamity, Alexievich says, all the people in Chernobyl "became philosophers." One person tells her, "With fresh eyes, I look at the world all around me. A little ant is crawling on the ground, and now it is closer to me. Our bird flies in the sky. And too closer. The distance between us shrinks. The previous chasm is gone."[23]

Climate, Place, and Home

If we accept Chernobyl as an analogy for climate change, we can say that we are at a similarly pivotal moment in history, when to survive at all we need to recognize the reality of climate change and its causes, and at the same time rethink our ideas of "globalization." I argue that it is high time we replace that economically saturated term with an alternative formulation: the "planetary." And we need to reimagine the planetary with the aid of Indigenous and other voices that can help us remove the blinders of capitalism. Writer and activist Rebecca Solnit argues for just such a need to see "isolation" and "connectedness" outside the discourse of nation-state politics or the global economy:

> [T]he very idea of climate change is offensive to isolationists because it tells us more powerfully and urgently than anything ever has that everything is connected, that nothing exists in isolation. What comes out of your tailpipe or your smokestack or your leaky fracking site contributes to the changing mix of the atmosphere, where increasing quantities of carbon dioxide and other greenhouse gases cause the earth to retain more of the heat that comes from the sun, which doesn't just result in what we used to call global warming but will lead to climate chaos.[24]

One very important consequence of such "climate chaos" is the violent and radical destruction of place. The planet and all of the rootedness it provides all its inhabitants—in terms of its seasonal rhythms, a sense of locatedness, and confidence in a planetary past, present, and future—are being eroded. It is not an exaggeration to state that, like the senses of the victims of Chernobyl, our very senses of time and space are being torn up at the roots. The checks and balances of the world in which all forms of life play a part have been thrown off-kilter.

And with the global pandemic that began in early 2020, we have seen an omen of the fate that may await us if we fail to take dramatic, immediate action to avert climate change. Here I return to a statement quoted earlier, from Jane Goodall, that "[i]t is our disregard for nature and our disrespect of the animals we should share the planet with that has caused this pandemic, that was predicted long ago." As Goodall reminds us, the ever-increasing proximity of animals and humans has led to a marked rise in the likelihood that a given pathogen will jump the species barrier.[25] What, exactly, is happening to the world? We have discovered that the destruction of any home or habitat has a ripple effect—socially, and environmentally, at one scale or another.

At the National Oceanography Centre, Liverpool, researcher Svetlana Jevrejeva claims that by 2100, sea level rises will deluge Pacific and Indian Ocean island states and displace millions from Miami, Guangzhou, Mumbai, and other low-lying cities. Furthermore, Jevrejeva says, "[t]hey will continue to climb for centuries even after greenhouse-gas levels have been stabilised. We could experience the highest-ever global sea-level rise in the history of human civilisation."[26] Climate change will create more and more environmental refugees, as homes and shelters are either submerged or engulfed by the proliferation of wildfires. Writer and activist Ben Ehrenreich observes that millions will become refugees due to rising sea levels, mega-storms, and other climate-driven events, "By conservative estimates, climate change will displace a quarter of a billion people over the next 31 years. Most will not be wealthy, and most will not be white."[27]

Again, here it is crucial to identify a continuity with a concept discussed in chapter 3: the capitalist production of space, which, facilitated by settler colonialism and racism, gradually but steadily remapped the planet, bending the inhabitants to its logic. What we see in the above quote is in tune with what we noted in our discussions of housing rights, displacement, gentrification, colonization, and the creation of "blighted communities" and refugee populations—but on a planetary scale and carrying the very real threat of complete extinction. Those at the top of the chain will be complacent for as long as possible, believing themselves secure and safe against the ravages of the destruction they have unleashed upon the world for their own profit. But they are gravely mistaken to ignore what is happening to the planet. Because what has been unleashed respects no border, wall, or enclosure. The entire environment is contaminated, and the links of interdependence between people, and between people and the planet, are being broken, with terrible effects.

In its July 2019 report *Climate Change and Poverty*, the United Nations Human Rights Council noted: "Climate change will have devastating consequences for people in poverty. Even under the best-case scenario, hundreds of millions will face food insecurity, forced migration, disease, and death. Climate change threatens the future of human rights. . . . Governments, and too many in the human rights community, have failed to seriously address climate change for decades."[28] While the UN report hits many of the right notes, especially in illuminating the disproportionately heavy burden that the poor will face, it fails in its reproduction of the idea that the global economy must be protected and that divestment from fossil fuel industries is an adequate solution. It does not admit that fossil fuel companies are deeply embedded in the global economy in a myriad of ways, and the capitalist-based global economy is itself part of the problem.

The coupling of the logic of capitalist extraction and exploitation to the value system of neoliberalism has led to the creation of a deadly pair—a dynamic that has been held up, promoted, and advanced by capitalist societies. Both tap into the same ideology of human dominance over others and over nature, and of individualism over and against interdependence; those who acknowledge their debt to others are, under the logic of neoliberalism, weak and dependent. This book argues exactly the opposite: that the recognition of and promotion of interdependence is not a moral failing but a moral victory. Moreover, to recognize the value of interdependence is simply to recognize how things really work. We depend on others and depend on nature. But each and every bit of the capitalist ideological system replaces notions of communal and natural reciprocity with the cold calculations of transaction and self-interest. These calculations are, to adapt Fujikane's critique of "abundance," deeply impoverished. They cannot begin to imagine human interaction in the world outside the logic of economic behavioralism. This tremendously narrow vision of the world makes it impossible for its adherents to think of noneconomic, nontransactional behavior. That is to say, generosity and empathy are marked, in the words of Donald Trump, as for "suckers." But the endgame of capitalism is being played out at lightning speed. There is, in reality, little of substance to sustain it.

Cleavage to the narrow and sterile logic of the market is, as I noted above, aided by nation-states that buy into that logic and instrumentalize hatred and bigotry; by pitting people against each other and against the planet, they advance their own warped idea of "survival." As historian Mark Bray explains:

> Fascist and far-right forces promote notions of ultra-nationalism and xenophobia that block the essential task of putting the interests of the planet and all of its inhabitants over those of any single group. Nationalism has fueled not only opposition to the European Union but also a rejection of the Paris Agreement and widespread climate denial among European far-right parties like [the UK Independence Party], [the French] Front National and the Sweden Democrats. The threat of the climate catastrophe is far more imminent and egregious in the global south, and white supremacy clearly discourages caring about most of the world. There are "ecofacists" who coopt the concept of bio-regionalism to advance their genocidal politics, but their views do not have significant sway in actual far-right policy and their "environmental" solution is not worthy of reasoned engagement. A capitalist system that prioritizes profit and perpetual growth over all else is the mortal enemy of global aspirations for a sustainable economy that satisfies needs rather than stock portfolios.[29]

Finally, within states themselves, mainstream political parties are too entranced with "party unity" and power to prioritize democratic debate about the most pressing issue of our time. Thank the Democratic National Committee for its refusal to host a climate change–focused debate during its 2020 national convention. As one journalist reported: "The vote came at a time when world leaders are ringing the alarm over massive fires in the Amazon rainforest—a disaster pointed to repeatedly by activists to stress the dire threat climate change poses. 'If an asteroid was coming to earth, there would be no question about having a debate about it,' argued Chris Reeves, a DNC member from Kansas. 'But with this existential crisis facing the world, we all sit and wring our hands.'"[30]

Clearly, faced with this failure at both the international and national levels, Ehrenreich is correct to say that "[i]f we are to survive as a species, we must know that no boat can save us except the one we build together. . . . Borders can offer no 'security,' only a plan for murder-suicide, a delusion that gets more deadly with each passing day."[31] *Guardian* columnist George Monbiot echoes the same sentiment in slightly different language: "Those who govern the nation and shape public discourse cannot be trusted with the preservation of life on Earth. There is no benign authority preserving us from harm. No one is coming to save us. None of us can justifiably avoid the call to come together to save ourselves."[32] I hope it's clear that I heartily agree with both these claims—this book was in fact written as a tool for activists and others to learn to think and act together in ways that tap into values and beliefs that elude pundits, experts, and government and industry personnel.

As I argued in the previous chapter with regard to borders, in today's neoliberal cycles of global exploitation, the only way to the fight effectively is to act in the broadest forms of global solidarity possible. To evoke national "protectionism" is to simply cash in on jingoistic nationalism in order to play workers in each country against each other for the economic and political benefit of the corporate state. Borders are, as we saw, simply there to manage the ebb and flow of labor and commodities. But the effects of climate change subordinate everyone and everything, albeit unevenly. The fight to save the planet will necessarily involve an engagement with Indigenous ways of thinking about the earth and the planetary community, and a radical reshaping of our ways of interacting. And, as I have argued from the very beginning of this book, this will necessarily require us to disentangle ourselves from the habits of mind that cause us to unreflexively defer to "authority," "experts," "pundits," and "leaders," and to distrust ourselves. As our home, the planet, is being so violently thrown off course, we need to authorize ourselves—starting with each individual, and also by acting together—to develop our voices and to use them, in both permissible and impermissible ways. And it is no wonder at all that among the very loudest and powerful voices we find today are those of younger people—people who have not yet absorbed the stultifying "lessons" of what the influential Brazilian teacher and philosopher Paulo Freire called the "banking model of education."

September 2019 saw the spread of a global climate strike, drawing seven million people from nearly two hundred countries and led by young people.[33] The organizers' comments displayed an immense intelligence, passion, and sense of responsibility. Brianna Fruean, a 20-year-old from Samoa, said something that has remarkable resonance with this volume's chapter on education: "It's great to see young people being passionate and not backing down to older people saying: 'You should be in school.' Real education sometimes happens outside the classroom. I think the school climate strikes have proved that. I learned about hope and solidarity outside the classroom." And teenagers Lovina and Delema Janvier from Alberta, Canada gave these reasons for attending the protest: "We must think of the future generations: what we do today, tomorrow and the next day will impact the next seven generations. We must change our ways from burning natural resources, from releasing so much carbon, from poisoning what we need to live. We cannot survive by drinking oil."[34]

Unlike older people, the young know that not only will they spend most of their lives under the conditions that runaway climate change will impose; the following generations will, as well. The title of an article by writer and filmmaker Astra Taylor on the subject says it all: "Bad Ancestors: Does the Climate Crisis Violate the Rights of Those Yet to Be Born?"[35] It is also a tragedy that we older people have been "bad ancestors" in the sense that many of us enjoyed a youth that was not forced to confront, with such immediacy, the horrible situation of the environment. Many of us used that time to draw attention to environmental causes, but many others simply ignored those pleas. Those who did organize around such issues faced the wrath and menace of polluting corporations, and the state that supported them. Given that tremendous asymmetry, it is not surprising that many movements failed in the short run. But it cannot be denied that they planted seeds that we see growing today.

Home Defenders

In their informative anthology of news stories on the environment and environmental activism, *The Big Heat: Earth on the Brink*, Jeffrey St. Clair and Joshua Frank include an entry on what many have referred to as the "Green Scare"—a term that harks back to the 1920s Red Scare discussed in chapter 2: "Similar to the movement disruption exemplified by COINTELPRO against Martin Luther King Jr., the Black Panthers and the American Indian Movement, the FBI's crackdown on EarthFirst! in the late 1980s had many alarming parallels to the agency of old." In an interview with the authors, Dave Foreman, cofounder of the environmental direct action group EarthFirst!, argues, "Essentially what we need to understand is that the Federal Bureau of Investigation, which was formed during the Palmer Raids in 1921, which was set up from the very beginning to inhibit internal political dissent."[36] Deploying many of the same tactics as they did against Black militants, union organizers, and other dissidents, the FBI infiltrated environmental activist groups, used informants and undercover agents, tapped phones, and depicted them as terrorists who posed a danger to national security. Doing this allowed them to even more freely break constitutional restraints, aided by warrants from sympathetic judges. "The big lie," Foreman writes, "that the FBI pushed at their press conference the day after the arrests was that [EarthFirst! was] a bunch of terrorists conspiring to cut power lines between Palo Verde and Diablo Canyon nuclear facilities in order to cause a nuclear meltdown and threaten public health and safety."[37]

As the decades have passed, and the list of bad actors behind environmental destruction and climate change as grown, so has the resistance. Naomi Klein tells the history of what she calls "Blockadia," a new constellation of activists, tactics, and strategies:

> Blockadia is not a specific location on a map but rather a roving transnational conflict zone that is cropping up with increasing frequency and intensity. . . . What unites Blockadia is the fact the people at the forefront—packing local council meetings, marching in capital cities, being hauled off in police vans, even putting their bodies between the earth-movers and the earth—do not look much like your typical activists, nor do the people in one Blockadia site resemble those in another. Rather, they each look like the places where they live, and they look like everyone: the local shop owners, the university professors, the high school students, the grandmothers.[38]

For the purposes of this book, the most germane comment Klein makes about Blockadia is this: "[T]he scope of many new extraction and transportation projects has created opportunities for people whose voices are traditionally shut out of the dominant conversation to form alliances with those

who have significantly more social power."[39] This blending of voices—of
those with relatively less social power and those endowed with it—leads to
powerful occupations and remappings of place, and the production of different sorts of spaces, as people contribute different kinds of histories and voices to reterritorialize public spaces. Klein describes one moving instance in
which the possibilities introduced by such a reconfiguration became clear:

> It was in the context of this gradual shift in awareness that Idle No
> More burst onto the political scene in Canada at the end of 2012 and
> then spread quickly south of the border. North American shopping
> centers—from the enormous West Edmonton Mall to Minnesota's
> Mall of America—were suddenly alive with the sounds of hand drums
> and jingle dresses as Indigenous people held flash mob round dances
> across the continent at the peak of the Christmas shopping season. In
> Canada, Native leaders went on hunger strikes, and youths embarked
> on months-long spiritual walks and blockaded roads and railways.[40]

These protesters disrupted the seasonal rhythms of consumerism, super-
imposing the trajectories of spiritual walks upon commuter paths. Each
of these tactics exemplifies the reinvention of place and voice, and shows
that life can and should take on different ways of being, of interacting,
and of growing. Near the end of Klein's book, she beautifully illustrates
the difference between the state-corporate version of her classic notion
of the "shock doctrine" and what she calls the "people's inversion of the
shock doctrine." In her 2007 book *The Shock Doctrine*, Klein showed how
corporations opportunistically exploit the disorder and instability that
follows natural and economic disasters in order to advance their agendas.
In *This Changes Everything*, written seven years later, she shows how progressives can turn the tables:

> [Activists] are also learning in a kind of people's inversion of the shock
> doctrine that one of the most opportune times to build that next econ-
> omy maybe in the aftermath of disasters, particularly climate related
> disasters. . . . Responding to disaster with this kind of soul searching is
> profoundly different from the top down model of the shock doctrine—
> these are attempts not to exploit crisis, but to harness it to actually solve
> the underlying problems at their root, and ways that expand democrat-
> ic participation rather than the opposite.[41]

At precisely this point, I want us to think back upon that key moment
on the Aventine Hill, when the plebians turned the tables on the state.

In taking over space and using it to hold their own forum, for their own political speech, they pointed to a radical expansion of democratic participation. Furthermore, they placed the Aventine Hill on the map of history in an insurgent manner; its name is to this day inseparable from their act of rebellion. My argument throughout this book has been that we need to reclaim place, to mark it with a new set of meanings and values and use that place as a platform for a more just vision of the future—one that takes into account the health and the well-being of all on earth.

Of course, to take up the reimaging of the planet as home requires concrete plans, methods, and strategies for addressing both climate change and housing, along with a clear understanding of the structures that perpetuate both crises. The various versions of a "Green New Deal" that go far beyond conventional understandings of climate and housing justice bear this in mind. Indigenous scholar and activist Nick Estes remarks on the urgency that alliances among activists must draw on Indigenous voices and worldviews. These comments resonate forcefully with the key arguments of this book: instead of accepting, and submitting to, the "places" and "voices" that those in power assign us, progressive activists must create our own senses of place and voice, and do so in ways that involve us all in determining our values and the actions needed to make the world and the planet habitable and sustainable, and social life imaginative, creative, and just. In this respect, Estes' words are especially noteworthy:

> The Green New Deal (GND), which looks and sounds like eco-socialism, offers a real chance at galvanizing popular support for both [Indigenous movements and decolonization]. While anti-capitalist in spirit and paying lip service to decolonization, it must go further—and so too must the movements that support it. That's why the Red Nation, a Native resistance organization I helped cofound in 2014, recently drafted a skeleton outline of what we're calling the Red Deal, focusing on Indigenous treaty rights, land restoration, sovereignty, self-determination, decolonization, and liberation. We don't envision it as a counter program to the GND but rather going beyond it—"Red" because it prioritizes Indigenous liberation, on one hand, and a revolutionary left position on the other. . . .
>
> Prison abolition and an end to border imperialism are key aspects of the Red Deal, for good reason. The GND calls for the creation of millions of "green" jobs. In the United States today, however, about 70 million people—nearly one-third of adults—have some kind of

criminal conviction, whether or not they've served time, that prevents them from holding certain kinds of jobs. If we add this number of people to the approximately 8 million undocumented migrants, the sum is about half the US workforce, two-thirds of whom are not white. Half of the workforce faces employment discrimination because of mass criminalization and incarceration. . . .

The terrorization of black, Indigenous, Latino, migrant, and poor communities by border enforcement agencies and the police drives down wages and disciplines poor people, whether or not they are working, by keeping them in a state of perpetual uncertainty and precariousness. As extreme weather and imperialist interventions continue to fuel migration, especially from Central America, the policies of punishment—such as walls, detention camps, and increased border security—continue to feed capital with cheap, throwaway lives. The question of citizenship— what right does a colonizing settler nation have to say who does and doesn't belong?—is something that will have to be thoroughly challenged as a "legal" privilege to life chances. Equitable access to employment and social care must break down imperial borders, not reproduce them. . . .

A new, green economy—one that will be, if Indigenous peoples have anything to say about it, a "caretaking economy"—is the antithesis to a militarized extractive economy, what we Lakotas call "owasicu owe," the fat-taker, the colonizer, the capitalist economy; or what White Earth activist Winona LaDuke calls the "Weitiko"—a cannibal economy. If prisons, police, and the military are the caretakers of violence, then educators, health-care workers, counselors, Water Protectors, and Land Defenders are caretakers of human and non-human relations. Compare the pay gaps between carceral and military workers (mostly men) to that of care workers (mostly women), and you'll see the values of this current society.[42]

In *A Planet to Win*, Kate Aronoff, Alyssa Battistoni, Daniel Aldana Cohen, and Thea Riofrancos similarly propose a radical Green New Deal that refuses to subscribe to liberal versions of environmental justice that remain tethered to capitalist worldviews and policies. They, like the other authors I have cited in this chapter, argue that piecemeal adjustments to both climate change and the housing crisis will do nothing to prevent the resurgence of injustice: "A radical Green New Deal has to go even further, leaving the energy experts' comfort zone, where the housing market's structural inequalities are taken for granted. The real estate industry might disagree, but we see decent housing as a human right. And housing and carbon are tightly knotted. A Green New Deal for housing would drive decarbonization by guaranteeing homes for everyone."[43]

In the previous chapter I argued against seeing space and place as merely empty and anonymous things to be filled in. Similarly, we should not think of "homes" as merely neutral, empty structures whose construction or removal means the same thing to all people. Aronoff and her coauthors define homes as, among other things, "the private shelters where we sleep, eat, make love, and keep safe from the elements." Our houses and apartments are a critical resource that orients us, grounds us, and places us in communion with others. Nevertheless, it is rarer and rarer that everyday people can afford them, no matter how hard they work. Aronoff et al. draw attention to a startling and depressing fact: "[T]here isn't a single state in the country where someone working a full-time minimum wage job can afford a modest two-bedroom apartment."[44] The devastating division between who our political system serves, and who it does not, is revealed in this fact: despite this national crisis, a proposal by the think tank People's Policy Project that we build ten million public mixed-income, zero-carbon homes over the next ten years, or even the Clintonite Center for American Progress's much more modest proposal for one million new public homes in five years, have not been taken up by the US government. All of this in spite of the fact, as Aronoff et al. point out, that "10,000,000 units of social housing would cost less than the [2017] Trump tax cut."[45]

In order to move beyond the metric of a singular nation, as we must if we are talking about a "planetary home," we must recognize that while there is no absolute consensus, the figure for worldwide homelessness is about one hundred million. Above we saw how this number may be expected to rise exponentially as masses of people are transformed into climate refugees. In all of these cases, this has been brought about by the attempt to think in isolation—that is, without considering the deep connections between neoliberal capital's brutalization of people, on one hand, and planet, on the other. Its rapacious attitude toward both natural and human "resources" obliterates any consideration of the interconnectedness of life and the planet, and the well-being of both. Public subsidies for private corporations supposedly "too big to fail" and "austerity" (meaning refusal of anything but the bare minimum of security and sustenance) for the expendable rest, are habitual projects of the elites.

In February 2020, the UN Economic and Social Council issued a "Draft Resolution on Affordable Housing and Social Protection Systems." The title of the document points to precisely the ways the issue of housing extends beyond access to shelter:

> [H]omelessness is not merely a lack of physical housing, but is often interrelated with poverty, lack of productive employment and access to infrastructure, as well as other social issues that may constitute a loss of family, community and a sense of belonging, and, depending on national context, can be described as a condition where a person or household lacks habitable space, which may compromise their ability to enjoy social relations, and includes people living on the streets, in other open spaces or in buildings not intended for human habitation, people living in temporary accommodation or shelters for the homeless, and, in accordance with national legislation, may include, among others, people living in severely inadequate accommodation without security of tenure and access to basic services.[46]

In other words, the fight for the "right to the city" is not unlike that for a "right to the planet": in both cases we are talking about the right of all peoples to have a voice and a shaping hand in their place and space in the world, their right to form a community and to live together democratically, unsubordinated to economic oligarchy. In this sense, I agree with Aronoff et al. when they declare, "We stand on the precipice of yet another energy revolution and at a fork in the road: solar powered capitalism with a whole new set of opportunities for profit and pillage; or an internationalist Green New Deal, a historic opportunity to remake global power structures and our relationship to the natural world."[47]

Tales of Two Futures

In the remaining pages of this final chapter, I return to the work of Jacques Rancière to argue for the political value of literary texts; for as acts of social imagination, they are invaluable to our efforts both to critique existing structures of oppression and to puzzle out modes of resistance, and of living otherwise. Rancière asks us to think of literature "neither as the art of writing in general nor as a specific state of the language, but as a historical mode of visibility of writing, a specific link between a system of meeting of words and a system of visibility of things."[48] In other words, he is asking us to think of literature as a way to make visible and open for debate and discussion things that have been erased, suppressed, ignored, or deemed inconceivable. In this sense, literature is political. This conception of literature complements our discussion of voice in the sense that certain voices have been similarly erased through their relegation to the status of "out of place."

This volume has argued that to reinvigorate our notion of political voice, we must broaden of our sense of imagination, from any source we find useful. The customary boundaries between expert and amateur, participant and organizer, need to be tested. And, as several examples in these pages have made clear, I am devoted to testing the boundaries between scholar and activist. All of this requires not only acts of translation between these heretofore separate realms, but also acts of good faith. We all must be willing to suspend our comfort and wander with others in places, and in ways of thinking, that we have avoided, or too easily discounted.

In this sense, I am arguing for an activist version of the humanities, and of intellectual life itself. To bring about such a radical reimagination is to change the way we see the world and its possibilities. This requires precisely that we speak out of place, reinventing a place of our own. These actions are not so distant at all from what Rancière means by the "literary": "The modern political animal is first a literary animal, caught in the circuit of a literariness that *undoes the relationships between the order of words and the order of bodies that determine the place of each.*"[49] In his work, Rancière calls the forces that keep bodies in place and words in order the "police." By keeping things segmented and silenced, the police make politics impossible. I have argued that we cannot and should not accept this state of things, that we cannot accept being "placed." Throughout this book, I have shown examples not only of how people can shift their designated places, but also how they might aid others in doing the same.

In Rancière's conception, the literary involves us in a radical reimagining of who belongs where, and what values count. In "undoing" preexisting and predetermining arrangements, and giving us the time and the space to imagine differently, literature can help us break free from the station in life to which we have been assigned and too often accept as inevitable, to intrude into the world of privilege, of political equality. Like the plebs on the Aventine Hill, we can act not *as if* we were equal, but *as* equals, and in so doing ridicule the idea that speech is the exclusive right of the privileged. By taking on the guise of patricians, the plebs asked to be recognized not as "themselves" but what they aspire to be—that is, equal.

Nevertheless, as author Amitav Ghosh has written in a powerful essay, to represent the complexities of climate change will require a radical extension of literature's conventional capacities:

> Are the currents of global warming too wild to be navigated in the accustomed barques of narration? But the truth, as is now widely acknowledged, is that we have entered a time when the wild has become the norm: if certain literary forms are unable to negotiate these torrents, then they will have failed—and their failures will have to be counted as an aspect of the broader imaginative and cultural failure that lies at the heart of the climate crisis.[50]

Ghosh's point is that, like the residents of Chernobyl, we have been thrown into the wild—the profound effects of the unforgiving forces we have unleashed upon the planet. We did not want to imagine just how wrong we had been, and those same habits of mind make it nearly impossible for us to truly recognize the realities of climate change. Ghosh makes the point that science, fiction, and even science fiction no longer have the capacity to give a true picture of what is unfolding all around us.

These habits of mind can lead us to look for familiar solutions to unprecedented problems, which often rely heavily on notions invented by Western rationality, bureaucracy, and capitalism. In his brilliant *Science in the Capital* trilogy of novels, published from 2004 to 2007, Kim Stanley Robinson critiques each and every one of these notions from the perspective of near-future Washington, DC. And he takes his examples from familiar daily routines, to show us just how habitual these ways of viewing life on earth have become. For example, one of the basic understandings of rationality, and rational economic behavior, is that of self-interest. The concept presumes that human beings are guided by the urge to preserve and improve their own material conditions, and that even seemingly cooperative actions are, at base, not about helping others, but about protecting one's self-interest. Looking out at the Southern California traffic, his protagonist wonders how the drivers all seem to survive—he watches as each driver seems to stay in their lane, adjusting to changes in the speed and direction of traffic flows. Is this purposeful cooperation or simply instance after instance of self-preservation? He then thinks that human

existence might be reducible to this riddle: "In traffic, at work, in relationships of every kind—social life was nothing but a series of prisoners'
dilemmas. Compute or cooperate? Be selfish or generous? It would be best
if you could always trust other players to cooperate, and safely practice always generous; but in real life people did not turn out to earn that trust."[51]

In terms of climate change, would it not make sense to think that
everyone's self-interest would be in the mitigation of its destructive effects, given that such damage spares no one? Clearly, the very fact that we
are waging this battle means that for far too many powerful people, their
interests are separate from those of the bulk of humankind. In this, as
Robinson's narrator explains, the capitalist structure holds steady:

> Humanity is exceeding the planet's carrying capacity for our species,
> badly damaging the biosphere. Neoliberal economics cannot cope with
> this situation, and indeed, with its falsely exteriorized costs, was de-
> signed in part to disguise it. If the Earth were to suffer a catastrophic
> anthropogenic extinction event over the next twenty years, which
> it will, American business would continue to focus on its quarterly
> profit and loss. There was no economic mechanism for dealing with
> catastrophe. And yet government and the scientific community are
> not tackling this situation either, indeed both have consented to be run
> by neoliberal economics, an obvious pseudoscience. We might as well
> agree to be governed by astrologers.[52]

The neoliberal emphasis on "independence," and the capitalist emphasis
on extraction and exploitation, not only rob us of any sense of interdependence (and therefore the strength, resilience, and collective imaginative power that working together provides); they also detach us from
every other single life form on earth. In stark contrast to those forms of
social and planetary alienation, consider Robinson's beautiful passage:

> Robot submarines cruise the depth, doing oceanography. Finally ocean-
> ographers have almost as much data as meteorologists. Among other
> things they monitor a deep layer of relatively warm water that flows
> from the Atlantic into the Arctic (ALTEX, the Atlantic Layer Tracking
> Experiment). But they are not as good at it as the whales. White beluga
> whales, living their lives in the open ocean, have been fitted with sen-
> sors for recording temperature, salinity, and nitrate content, matched
> with a GPS record and a depth meter. Up and down in the blue world
> they sport, diving deep into the black realm below, coming back up for
> air, recording data all the while. Casper the Friendly Ghost, Whitey

Ford, The Woman in White, Moby Dick, all the rest: they swim to their own desires, up and down endlessly within their immense territories, fast and supple, continuous and thorough, capable of great depths, pale flickers in the blackest blue, the bluest black. Then back up for air. Our cousins. White whales help us to know this world. The data they are collecting make it clear that the Atlantic's deep warm layer is attenuating. And so the Gulf Stream is slowing down.[53]

In Robinson's novels, the idea of the planet as home requires us to think beyond it being simply, or predominantly, a human habitat. Clearly it is home to flora, fauna, and more. Thus, it is the epitome of human arrogance to think that humans can solve the problem we produced in the first place.

In Richard Powers's 2018 novel The Overstory, we see a similar emphasis on looking to other life-forms for guidance. In this case, it is trees. The book takes its name from the term used to describe the highest layer of foliage in a forest canopy. Powers also uses it to reference the big picture, the metastory that fuses the strands of his many protagonists' stories. In yet another sense, "overstory" works like the word "theory"—the highest level of abstraction, and a hypothesis of all that is below. Consider the theory of evolution or the theory of relativity. How to explain a complex and massive phenomena from the highest viewpoint? In this case, Powers is asking his readers to join him as he thinks through the key problems facing environmental activism.

For me, there are three basic and urgent questions that Powers examines, and they are all linked. First, what connects people to each other? Second, what connects people to nature? And third, how can people work together to forestall the greatest danger to the planet, our home? To both name and puzzle out each of these questions, Powers gives us a set of protagonists, letting each spin their own story. Eventually, they all become connected in an attempt to save the planet from climate change. For my purposes, I will focus only on the protagonists who are, from the very beginning, introduced as a couple, Ray and Dorothy.

Ray works as a patent lawyer; Dorothy is a stenographer. They first meet as players in amateur theater. They fall in love, and eventually marry. Each of the two is strongly individualistic, and their marriage faces many challenges. One of the key issues in their relationship is that of possessiveness, which Powers uses to connect to larger issues of ownership:

Who can own an idea? Who can own another person? Who can own nature? What does the idea of ownership even mean? And what responsibilities come with it? The obsession with owning has the result that people can only see things that they can own, sell, or buy, or else that things they regard as dangerous. Powers expresses this in a passage that resonates with points discussed earlier in this chapter regarding extractive and exploitative capitalism, and especially in the quote from Lefebvre that we saw at the beginning of this chapter: "The fact is that natural space will soon be lost from view." A journal left behind by a climate activist reads: "No one sees trees. We see fruit, we see nuts, we see wood, we see shade. We see ornaments or pretty fall foliage. Obstacles blocking the road or wrecking the ski slope. Dark, threatening places that must be cleared. We see branches about to crush our roof. We see a cash crop. But trees—trees are invisible."[54]

Like all the other characters in *The Overstory*, Ray and Dorothy become entirely committed to saving trees—their home and its gardens are transformed into a sanctuary for threatened species of trees. In the last struggle of his lifetime, Ray hits upon one way to use his expertise and training to defend his home and help other environmental activists. At this point in the narrative, he has been incapacitated by a stroke, and Dorothy has been caring for him. He believes he has found a legal principle with which to win his case, but he cannot present the case due to his debilitating stroke, so he must train Dorothy:

> In silence, he walks his lifelong partner through old and central principles of jurisprudence come one syllable at a time. Stand your ground. The Castle doctrine. Self-help. If you could save yourself, your wife, your child, or even a stranger by burning something down, the law allows you. If someone breaks into your home and starts destroying it, you may stop them however you need to. . . . Our home has been broken into. Our lives are being endangered. The law allows for all necessary force against unlawful and imminent harm.[55]

Of course, this defense fails. The very concept is wasted on the courts, who are unable to see any connection between the planet and the idea that it is our collective home.

To its credit, *The Overstory* ends with neither a hopeful nor a pessimistic note, but with a challenge of its own. It asks us all to both unlearn what we have been taught about living as individuals and as members of society—about the value of place, about our abilities to fill space with our own symbols, values, and purposes—and to learn a new way of living, together and in collaboration. Powers begins with the smallest social unit—Ray and Dorothy: "A page or two may take them a day. Everything they thought their backyard was is wrong, and it takes some time to grow new beliefs to replace the ones that fall. . . . Every leaf out there connects, underground."[56] This new learning helps them understand that "[t]here are brains down there, ones our own brains aren't shaped to see. Root plasticity, solving problems and making decisions. Fungal synapses. What else do you want to call it? Linking enough trees together and a forest grows *aware*."[57] From there, the learning spreads to dozens, hundreds, and thousands of others, who pass on their information and their learning to others: "Other learners, born yesterday, study every button Judith Hanson clicks. They follow her to the gargantuan film archive, where thirteen more years of new video have sprouted so far today. Learners have already watched billions of these clips and begin to make their inferences."[58] As a final example of this theme, which takes over as the novel's ending message, here we have Neelay, a disabled computer wizard and fabulously wealthy videogame entrepreneur in Palo Alto. A person imprisoned in his own body, Neelay is nonetheless able to connect his knowledge to millions, and to join them in answering one basic question:

> While the prisoner thinks, innovations surge over his head, across the flyover from Portland and Seattle to Boston and New York and back again. . . . They split and replicate, these master algorithms that Neelay lofts into the air. They're just starting out, like simplest cells back in the Earth's morning. But already they've learned, in a short few decades, what it took molecules a billion years to learn to do. Now they need only learn what life wants from humans. It's the big question for sure. Too big for people alone. But people aren't alone, and they never have been.[59]

This is a big question, and the one that we have wrestled with in different shapes and forms throughout this study—not only in terms of "the human race," but also in terms of people as individuals. I have argued that the forces that seek to divide us and perpetuate that division in order to profit from it—the wretched market individualism of neoliberalism and extractive, exploitative capitalism—cannot be sustained. The planet will not allow it. We, on the other hand, have a say in how things end.

Something has to give. Hence, I close with excerpts from three texts that leave us with that fatal question.

First, I use the following two citations as a kind of dyad—they present diametrically different images of human's relations to nature. The first is from Ben Ehrenreich's 2020 *Desert Notebooks: A Road Map for the End of Time*. It is hard to know what to call this text, for it is part memoir, part journalism, part fiction, part fantasy, part mythology. His central question is: Will we survive climate change? In that sense, the subtitle of Ehrenreich's book reflects both his optimism and his pessimism. There are many positive, and indeed encouraging, moments in the book, but also many depressing ones as well. Ehrenreich informs his readers:

> In late July, a young couple had gone missing [at Joshua Tree]. They were kids from the suburbs, but even if you know the desert it isn't hard to lose your bearings. Canyons fork and twist. The landscape plays tricks on your eyes. The light shifts and familiar terrain becomes suddenly alien. . . . Search parties in helicopters scoured the area for weeks. . . . In mid-October, searchers found them a couple of miles from my house, and maybe a mile from the wash in which my friends and I were hiking. The young woman's father led the group that found them. The corpses, the newspapers did not neglect to report, were intertwined, embracing even in death. A few days later the authorities revealed that they had found a pistol at the scene: the young man had shot the young woman before turning the gun on himself. The police didn't believe there was any malice in it. The pair appeared to have gotten lost, and having run out of food and water, chose to avoid a slower death.[60]

It is the image of the couple embraced in death on which I want to focus, for it shows two lovers dying at odds with the environment. As much as they clearly loved nature, for them it, and the thought of meeting others there, posed such a threat that they chose to carry a gun. Ehrenreich notes this fact as well, "The fact that they had brought a handgun on the day hike was apparently so normal that few of the news reports considered it worth highlighting."[61] While the couple's death has a tragic and romantic tonality, I interpret Ehrenreich's use of the story as an analogy for of our current situation: we feel that there is no way out but suicide. But there are other ways of viewing our place in the world; in *The Overstory*, Powers draws from mythology to give us a very different image of a couple, and their deaths:

> The Greeks had a word, *xenia*—guest friendship—a command to take care of traveling strangers, to open your door to whoever is out there,

because anything passing by, far from home, might be God. Ovid tells the story of two immortals who came to earth in disguise to cleanse the sickened world. No one would let them in but one old couple, Baucis and Philemon. And their reward for opening their door to strangers was to live on after death as trees—an oak and a linden—huge and gracious and intertwined. What we care for, we will grow to resemble. And what we resemble will hold us, when we are us no longer.[62]

In contrast to the couple in *Desert Notebooks*, who arm themselves against nature and strangers, Ovid's couple open their home to traveling strangers, and their selfless hospitality earns them an eternal life in and through nature. The question this raises is an important one: How and why have we reached a point in our existence with others and with nature that we are determined to maintain our role as antagonists, isolated even at the cost of our own demise? To end this chapter, I want to call on one more text that links the two stories of death we just read.

Octavia Butler's dystopian, futuristic novel *Parable of the Sower* was written in 1993 and takes place in 2024. We enter a world already in chaos and anarchy. Entire economic and political systems are barely functional; people fight and kill neighbors for food. The novel's main events center on moments of hope, and of despair, as people struggle for a semblance of peace, calm, and stability. Butler chooses to bookend her narrative with essentially the same message as Ehrenreich's: the way toward justice has never been radically altered, nor has it been achieved.

The novel is narrated by a young Black teenager, Lauren Oya Olamina, who attempts to build a community around a specific project, called Prodigy. Lauren begins recording her observations and budding belief system as a way to guide others. The document becomes known as *Earthseed: Books of the Living*. Here is the entry that serves as the epigraph for *Parable of the Sower*: "Prodigy is, at its essence, adaptability and persistent, positive obsession. Without persistence, what remains is an enthusiasm of the moment. Without adaptability, what remains may be channeled into destructive fanaticism. Without positive obsession, there is nothing at all."[63] In many ways this could be taken as a message of guidance, directed toward any activists who face an enormous task; people can take to the streets in the "enthusiasm of the moment," and then disappear when that enthusiasm subsides. But simply relying on that same enthusiasm, without understanding the need to adapt and move beyond the initial moment that gave rise to the movement, risks resulting in unswerving, brittle, and doctrinaire fanaticism. The "positive obsession" the text recommends has at is root commitment, and an ability to learn and to grow. And tales of learning and growing, as well as of seeing the dangers of both momentary enthusiasm and destructive fanaticism, are what fill the novel to its end.

Lauren's group starts off on an unlikely and arduous march from Southern California to the far north, where they hope to build a community in some land one of their members is supposed to have. When they finally reach it, here is the scene they encounter: "There is no house. There are no buildings. There was almost nothing. A broad black smear on the hillside; a few charred planks sticking up from the rubble; some leaning against others; and a tall brick chimney, standing black and solitary like a tombstone in a picture of an old-style graveyard. A tombstone amid bones and ashes."[64] The final chapter, which immediately follows, begins with this poem:

> Create no images of God.
> Accept the images
> That God has provided.
> They are everywhere,
> In everything.
> God is Change—
> Seed to tree.
> Tree to forest,
> Rain to river.
> River to sea;
> Grubs to bees,
> Bees to swarm.
> From one, many;
> From many, one;
> Forever uniting, growing, dissolving—
> Forever Changing.
> The universe
> Is God's self-portrait.[65]

The poem is yet another illustration of the message of the present chapter, and of this book. Instead of seeking value and validation from some external source, I have urged us to look for those things in ourselves, by cultivating our connections to each other and to all the planet. And these relationships are precisely what Lauren honors at the end of the novel: "So today we remembered the friends and the family members we've lost. We spoke our individual memories and quoted Bible passages, Earthseed verses, and bits of songs and poems that were favorites of the living or the dead. Then we buried our dead and planted oak trees. Afterward, we sat together and talked and ate a meal and decided to call this place Acorn."[66] It is hard to miss the fact that Lauren and her friends have christened this new place with a collective act of voicing, and giving voice. Their history as a loose community has become solidified by re-voicing those lost and marking their continued presence with the seeds Lauren and others plant. They are marking this their place. This outcome would have been impossible without the persistence, adaptability, and positive obsession that compelled them to this place. And it is those things, and the lessons they have learned along the way, that enable them to work past and through death and devastation.

Desert Notebooks, *The Overstory*, and *Parable of the Sower* each in their own way send us the same message: defeat is the norm, but not necessarily the end. A positive obsession with justice, entailing a willingness to learn, together, to speak a new language and redefine place, is the only option we have.

AFTERWORD

On January 6, 2021, the day a joint session of Congress convened to ratify Joe Biden's election as president of the United States, thousands of Trump supporters gathered at Washington, DC's Ellipse Park to hear Trump declare that the elections were a fraud and urge his supporters to rise up in protest. Many of them did exactly as he wished: they invaded and occupied the Capitol for hours, destroying offices and hunting down lawmakers. Declaring their intent to find and hang Vice President Mike Pence, who had refused to go along with Trump's idea that he had lost the election, protesters set up a scaffold and a noose. Only after seemingly interminable hours of rioting, which left five people dead, did Trump take to Twitter to ask people to stop what became known as "the insurrection." Yet he did so while maintaining that their actions were based on a legitimate cause: "These are the things and events that happen when a sacred landslide election victory is so unceremoniously and viciously stripped away from great patriots who have been badly and unfairly treated for so long," he tweeted.[1]

Trump's version of the election clashed with all the established facts. By December 14, 2020, Trump's claim that he had won the election had been soundly repudiated—on which date journalist Sonam Sheth summed up the situation: "In addition to being on track to lose the Electoral College, Trump has lost the national popular vote; multiple state recounts; nearly 40 lawsuits from his campaign and key Republican officials and 86 lawsuits overall; and a Supreme Court case."[2] Nevertheless, and even after the January insurrection, in April 2021, a *Reuters* poll found that six in ten Republicans still believed Trump won the election, and thought that he should run again in 2024—which the accompanying article called "a dangerous spin on reality."[3] After the election, Republicans lost no time in taking a legislative sledgehammer to democracy. At least 250 new laws were proposed in forty-three states to restrict mail-in ballots and early in-person and Election Day voting.[4]

Why are all these events important to the arguments I have been making in this book? It is because the Capitol insurrection, and all that led up to it and followed, presents a perversely distorted and dangerous instance in which people used their "voice" to "take place." That is to say, it should be regarded as a vivid and disturbing symbol of what progressive, prodemocracy and anti-fascist, anti-racist activists are up against. The insurrection, by defying the facts and instead following the orders of an irrational and self-serving racist, appropriated the mantle of rebellious democratic spirit for the sole purpose of enforcing authoritarianism, championing white supremacy, and in fact destroying democracy. It formed a terrible bookend to the incident cited at the opening of this book, when Trump supporters willingly and enthusiastically allowed Trump to be their voice. It is clear that even if Trump does not run again, his toxic worldview is already being carried on by another TV personality—Tucker Carlson—who has openly supported such hallmarks of white supremacy as "replacement theory"—the notion that the white race is being "replaced" by Jews and other racial and ethnic groups.[5] Carlson has a huge following on *Fox News*, in part because he feeds white racists a slew of rationalizations that legitimize their rage and hatred. The Capitol insurrection thus consolidated nearly everything this book is against. We must repudiate this false image of "democratic" "patriotism" to see what it actually promotes: white supremacy.

The fight will be fierce and long-lasting, but there is hope to be found in the fact that more and more people understand—with greater clarity—the urgent need for a radically different relationship to politics, just as James and Grace Lee Boggs urged us to recognize decades ago. And our numbers are swelling. As labor organizer Mindy Isser noted, by the time of the 2020 election, the Democratic Socialists of America boasted eighty thousand members, and a tremendous record of wins for the candidates and ballot measures it had endorsed. Twenty of the twenty-nine candidates it backed won election, and eight of the eleven ballot measures it endorsed passed. There are now democratic socialist caucuses in fifteen statehouses. All the members of the progressive block in Congress (representatives Rashida Tlaib, Ilhan Omar, Alexandria Ocasio-Cortez, and Ayanna Pressley) won reelection, despite being targeted by massive Republican efforts.[6] At the end of October 2020, Ocasio-Cortez's Republican opponent had raised 9.6 million dollars, while Ocasio-Cortez had raised nearly twice as much—17.3 million.[7] Three of the major issues that define democratic socialist candidates, over and against both Republicans and Democrats, are defunding the police and dismantling the country's systems of mass incarceration; support for Palestinian rights and the Boycott, Divestment, and Sanctions movement; and the establishment of a Green New Deal. There is massive organizing behind each of these goals.

Another sign of a groundswell in these directions is seen in the results of a survey by the Center for Information and Research on Civic Learning and Engagement (CIRCLE):

> While young voters overall were vital to Joe Biden's electoral victory, young people of color played an especially critical role. While white youth voted for Biden by a slim margin (51% to 45%), youth of color gave him overwhelming support, ranging from 73% among Latino youth to 87% among Black youth. In key states: 90% of Black youth supported Biden in Georgia, 85% of young voters of color backed Biden in Pennsylvania (33 points higher than white youth), and 77% of young voters of color in Michigan (19 points higher than white youth). In fact, in states like Georgia and Arizona, Black and Latino youth may have single-handedly made Biden competitive.[8]

There is a clear demographic trend toward a more racially diverse population, and if these young people hold onto their political values, such statistics offer a strong reason for hope. Many of them were compelled to the polls precisely in opposition to Trump and his policies and practices.

Biden's victory came in spite of the fact that election forecasters were off by a wide margin in their prediction of a Democratic landslide.[9] In part, he may owe his win to the organizing and activism on the parts of young people and others, who showed their political savvy as well as a healthy skepticism toward pundits and experts. They knew the cost of defeat would be a loss for pro-environmental, anti-racist, pro-science, pro-democratic causes. Moreover, what all this signals is that, as we move into this new political and historical era, we must build on this momentum by taking a shaping role in our futures. The fact that the right wing is not only still alive, but alive in a nakedly violent, racist, and anti-democratic manner, means that we have to recognize both the threats we face and the strength we truly have.

We need to look at the world, and ourselves, with new eyes. What do we see when we look at a place, or our own reflection? What potential do we see to transform seemingly neutral or forbidden places into spaces for real democracy to flourish? We need to learn to speak in multiple, passionate, committed, and just ways with others, and to do so both for ourselves and for the planet that is our place of home. My hope is that the book you just read can help us.

ACKNOWLEDGMENTS

I am glad to have this opportunity to thank all the people with whom I have had the pleasure of organizing over the years, and others who have sustained and inspired me. First, I wish to thank my editor, Anthony Arnove, for believing in this project and for his infinite patience, my elegant and discerning copyeditor Sam Smith, and everyone else at Haymarket Books. I also thank the people I have worked with in these venues: at *Truthout*, Maya Schenwar, Alana Price, and Leslie Thatcher; at *The Nation*, Roane Carey and Lizzy Ratner; at *Jacobin*, Sebastian Budgen, Micah Uetricht, and Bhaskar Sunkara; at *In These Times*, Sarah Lazare; and at (the old) *Salon*, Dave Daley and Ruth Henrich.

I want to acknowledge the essential work of the following organizations and urge people to support them: the Institute for Middle East Understanding, Jewish Voice for Peace, Students for Justice in Palestine, Palestine Legal, the US Campaign for the Academic and Cultural Boycott of Israel, the Campus Antifascist Network, and the organizing committee of Palestine Writes Literature Festival.

And much gratitude to these comrades in various causes: Ahmed Abbes, Rabab Abdulhadi, Susan Abulhawa, Ali Abunimah, Anthony Alessandrini, Samer Ali, Dina Al-Kassim, Samirah Alkassim, Diana Allan, Lori Allen, Maximillian Alvarez, Arturo Arias, Bill Ayers, Paola Bacchetta, Kristian Davis Bailey, Ian Balfour, Étienne Balibar, Omar Barghouti, Khalil Barhoum, Hatem Bazian, Joel and Miriam Beinin, Yael Ben-zvi Morad, Jacqueline Berry, Homi Bhabha, Tithi Bhattacharya, George Bisharat, Houria Bouteldja, Mark Bray, Neil Brenner, Haim Bresheeth, Shane Burley, Judith Butler, Diana Buttu, Darren Byler, Joy Castro, James Cavallero, Jeff Chang, Eric Cheyfitz, Ebony Coletu, Kathleen Coll, Elliott Colla, Rebecca Comay, Craig and Cindy Corrie, Ayça Çubukçu, Susan

Muaddi Darraj, Angela Davis, Chandler Davis, Natalie Zemon Davis, Colin Dayan, Stephanie DeGooyer, Lucy Diavolo, Veena Dubal, Lisa Duggan, Ben Ehrenreich, Nada Elia, Elsadig Elsheikh, Noura Erakat, Nick Estes, Richard Falk, Mireille Fanon-Mendès-France, Éric Fassin, Margaret Ferguson, Jackie Fielder, Candace Fujikane, Meleiza Figueroa, Katherine Franke, Cynthia Franklin, H. Bruce Franklin, Nora Barrows Friedman, Jess Ghannam, Amitav Ghosh, Henry Giroux, Ariel Gold, Neve Gordon, Kelly Grotke, Nacira Guénif-Souilamas, Ayten Gündoğdu, Estella Habal, Lisa Hajjar, Sondra Hale, dream hampton, Lenora Hanson, Alan Harvey, Salah Hassan, Chris Hazou, Doug Henwood, Jack Herrera, Andrew Herscher, Neil Hertz, Anita Hill, Liz Jackson, Aaron Jaffe, Pranav Jani, David Johnson, Gaye Theresa Johnson, Fady Joudah, Remi Kanazi, Azeezah Kanji, Persis Karim, Charlotte Kates, J. Kēhaulani Kauanui, Robin D. G. Kelley, Laleh Khalili, Lara Kiswani, Nancy Kricorian, Scott Kurashige, Laila Lalami, Layo Olaoluwakitan Laniyan, Silyane Larcher, Mary Layoun, Alana Lentin, Ronit Lentin, Michael Letwin, Mark Levine, David Lloyd, Ania Loomba, Alex Lubin, Colleen Lye, Sunaina Maira, Saree Makdisi, Catherine Malabou, Curtis Marez, Sophia McClennen, Rima Najjar Merriman, Blanca Missé, Koritha Mitchell, W. J. T. Mitchell, Adam Miyashiro, Freida Lee Mock, Dan Moshenberg, Bill Mullen, Nadine Naber, Christopher Newfield, Lynda Ng, Viet Thanh Nguyen, Rob Nixon, Hilton Obenzinger, Michael Omi, Ruth Ozeki, A. Naomi Paik, Ilan Pappé, Nicola Perugini, Khury Peterson-Smith, Vijay Prashad, Jasbir Puar, Linda Quiquivix, Timothy Reiss, Jerome Reyes, Russell Rickford, Alex Rivera, Bruce Robbins, Lisa Rofel, Ninotchka Rosca, Jordy Rosenberg, Andrew Ross, Steven Salaita, Saskia Sassen, Daniel Saver, Daniel A. Segal, James Schamus, Omar Shakir, Anton Shammas, C. Heike Schotten, Malini Schueller, Sarah Schulman, Sherene Seikaly, Rinku Sen, Anton Shammas, Simona Sharoni, Gayatri Chakravorty Spivak, Rajini Srikanth, Penn Szittya, Neferti Tadiar, Astra Taylor, Keeanga-Yamahtta Taylor, Françoise Vergès, Christopher Vials, Suchitra Vijayan, Kamala Visweswaran, Alan Wald, Ling-chi Wang, Robert Warrior, Cornel West, Howard Winant, Jessica Winegar, Karen Tei Yamashita, Louisa Yousef, Maung Zarni, Oded Zipory, and Stephen Zunes; and to anyone I have missed—thank you.

At Stanford, these people have made an often-unbearable place far less so; though some have moved on to other places, they remain part of our community, and all have buoyed me up with their energy and commitment: Cécile Alduy, Patricia Alessandrini, H. Samy Alim, anthony antonio, Jan Barker-Alexander, Jason Beckman, Terry Berlier, Jen Brody, Geoff Browning, Eamonn Callan, Al Camarillo, Clayborne Carson, Prudence Carter, Gordon Chang, Truman Chen, Calvin Cheung-Miaw, Elena Dancu, Adrian Daub, Michele Dauber, Todd Davies, Shane Denson, Adrienne Emory, Tania Flores, Richard Ford, Zephyr Frank, Jessica Femenias, Jennifer Freyd, Theresa Gao, Thomas Blom Hansen, Alan Harvey, Linda Hess, Allyson Hobbs, Shanta Katipamula, Diana Khong, Dharshani Lakmali Jayasinghe, Heejoo Ko, Jeffrey Koseff, Marci Kwon, Elis Imboden, Usha Iyer, Branislav Jakovljević, Alexander Key, Maryam Khalil, Joshua Landy, Emily Lemmerman, Cole Manley, Carol McKibben, Jisha Menon, Stephen Monismith, Daniel Murray, Monica Moore, Tom Mullaney, Umniya Najaer, Juliana Nalerio, Nikolaj Nielsen, Cindy Ng, Natasha Patel, Sid Patel, Rush Rehm, John Rickford, Gloria Robalino, Jonathan Rosa, Ramzi Salti, David Spiegel, Steven Stedman, Sharika Thiranagama, Elaine Treharne, Jeanne Tsai, Emma Tsurkov, Ge Wang, Mai Wang, Tom Wasow, Em Wilder, Mikael Wolfe, and Sylvia Yanagisako.

Also essential to my well-being and state of mind have been these friends who have been with me through times bad and good. Many thanks to my fantastic trainer, Briana Antes, and to Elix Colón, Monika Greenleaf, Ashley Kinseth, Karen Kuo, David Mahler, Nirvana Tanoukhi, Les Zwiebel, and with the most profound gratitude possible to the late Leta Zwiebel.

Finally and most importantly, my family has been through the processes of me struggling to write every single one of my books, and of course a great deal more, educating me over all these years in ways that go beyond words—tremendous thanks to my wife, Sylvie Palumbo-Liu, and our son, Fabrice Palumbo-Liu.

NOTES

Introduction

1. James Boggs and Grace Lee Boggs, *Revolution and Evolution in the Twentieth Century* (New York: Monthly Review Press, 1974), 203.
2. Keeanga-Yamahtta Taylor, "Reality Has Endorsed Bernie Sanders," *The New Yorker*, March 30, 2020.
3. Nancy Fraser, *The Old Is Dying and the New Cannot Be Born: From Progressive Neoliberalism to Trump and Beyond* (London and New York: Verso, 2019), 29–30.
4. Bhaskar Sunkara, *The Socialist Manifesto: The Case for Radical Politics in an Era of Extreme Inequality* (New York: Basic Books, 2019), 218.
5. Bhaskar Sunkara, "How Wide Is Bernie Sanders' Appeal?," *Guardian*, April 16, 2019.
6. Mohamed Younis, "Four in 10 Americans Embrace Some Form of Socialism," *Gallup News*, May 20, 2019.
7. See Astra Taylor, "Bernie Sanders' Exit Is an Indictment of Our Broken System," *In These Times*, April 9, 2020.
8. Bill McCarthy, "CNBC's Joe McKernan Wrong about US Per Capita COVID-19 Deaths," *Politifact*, May 20, 2020.
9. Ryan Cooper, "The World Is Putting America in Quarantine," *The Week*, June 25, 2020.
10. Aimee Picchi, "Trump Adviser Says America's 'Human Capital Stock' Ready to Return to Work," *CBS News*, May 26, 2020.
11. Yasmin Abutaleb et al., "US Was Beset by Denial and Dysfunction as the Coronavirus Raged," *Washington Post*, April 4, 2020.
12. "Jane Goodall Says 'Disrespect for Animals' Caused the Pandemic," AFP, November 4, 2020.
13. Robinson Meyer, "Zombie Diseases of Climate Change," *The Atlantic*, November 6, 2017.
14. Margaret Levi, "Frances Perkins Was Ready!," *Social Science Space*, March 2020.
15. Quoted in Elaine Godfrey, "Thousands of Americans Have Become Socialists Since March," *The Atlantic*, May 14, 2020.
16. Nicholas Quah and Laura Davis, "Here's a Timeline of Unarmed Black People Killed by Police over the Past Year," *Buzzfeed News*, May 1, 2015.
17. "In Harm's Way," *New York Times*, August 1, 2020.
18. ArLuther Lee, "Trump Accuses 75-Year-Old Shoved by Police of Being Antifa 'Provocateur,'" *Atlanta Journal-Constitution*, June 9, 2020.

19. See, for instance, Robert O. Paxton, *The Anatomy of Fascism* (New York: Vintage, 2004).

20. Umberto Eco, "Ur-Fascism," *New York Review of Books*, June 22, 1995.

21. Christina Zhao, "'Article 2' Trends after Trump Falsely Claims It Gives Him Unlimited Powers as President: I Can 'Do Whatever I Want,'" *Newsweek*, July 23, 2019.

22. Victor Garcia, "McConnell Says 'Zero Chance' Trump Will Be Removed," *Fox News*, December 12, 2019.

23. See Ryan Bort, "This Is What a White Nationalist Administration Looks Like," *Rolling Stone*, November 12, 2019.

24. Alexandra Minna Stern, "It's Come to This: White Nationalism Is Inciting Mass Murder in America," *Newsweek*, August 5, 2019.

25. Jennifer Hansler, "Human Rights Organizations File Suit over Pompeo's 'Unalienable Rights' Commission," *CNN*, March 6, 2020.

26. Tom McCarthy, "'I Am the Chosen One': With Boasts and Insults, Trump Sets New Benchmark for Incoherence," *Guardian*, August 21, 2019.

27. Commission on Unalienable Rights, *Draft Report of the Commission on Unalienable Rights*, July 2020.

28. Michael Warren, "Trump Risks Potential Backlash from Evangelicals with 'Tone-Deaf' Bible Photo-Op," *CNN*, June 3, 2020.

29. Paul LeBlanc, "Bishop at DC Church Outraged by Trump Visit: 'I Just Can't Believe What My Eyes Have Seen,'" *CNN*, June 2, 2020.

30. Ed Pilkington, "'These Are His People': Inside the Elite Border Patrol Unit Trump Sent to Portland," *Guardian*, July 27, 2020.

31. Leblanc, "Bishop Outraged."

32. Harvey J. Kaye, *Take Hold of Our History: Make America Radical Again* (Winchester, UK, and Washington, DC: Zero Books, 2020), 113.

33. Eric Fassin, "The Neo-fascist Moment of Neoliberalism," *OpenDemocracy*, August 10, 2018.

34. Bertholt Brecht, "Fascism Is the True Face of Capitalism," *OffGuardian*, December 1, 2018.

35. Jake Johnson, "Fed Up with Constant Attacks and Insults, Ocasio-Cortez Slams Pelosi as 'Outright Disrespectful' for Singling Out Progressives," *Common Dreams*, July 11, 2019.

36. Hannah Arendt, "The Decline of the Nation-State and the End of the Rights of Man," in *The Origins of Totalitarianism* (New York: Harcourt, Brace & Co., 1973), 267–302.

37. Arendt, "Decline of the Nation-State," 275.

38. Arendt, "Decline of the Nation-State," 298.

39. Arendt, "Decline of the Nation-State," 296.

40. Hannah Arendt, *The Human Condition*, 2nd ed (Chicago: University of Chicago Press, 1998), 27.

41. Jacques Rancière, *Disagreement*, Julie Rose, trans (Minneapolis: University of Minnesota Press, 1999), 30.

42. Rancière, *Disagreement*, 23.

43. Rancière, *Disagreement*, 24.

44. Mark Engler and Paul Engler, *This Is an Uprising: How Nonviolent Revolt Is Shaping the Twenty-First Century* (New York: Nation Books, 2016), 114.

45. "Popularity of Black Lives Matter Jumps to 62%," *Rasmussen Reports*, June 20, 2020.

46. Jacques Rancière, *Dissensus: On Politics and Aesthetics*, Steven Corcoran, trans. (London: Bloomsbury Academic, 2015; repr.), 152.

47. Rancière, *Dissensus*, 157, my emphasis.

48. Wendy Brown, *Undoing the Demos: Neoliberalism's Stealth Revolution* (New York: Zone Books, 2015), 202.

49. John Nichols, *The "S" Word: A Short History of an American Tradition—Socialism* (London and New York: Verso, 2015), 227.

50. Astra Taylor, *Democracy May Not Exist, but We'll Miss It when It's Gone* (New York: Metropolitan, 2019), 90.

51. Caitlin Oprysko, "'Our President Gave Us So Much Hope': MyPillow CEO Goes Off Script at Coronavirus Briefing," *Politico*, March 30, 2020.

52. Veronica Stracqualursi, "'Plaid Shirt Guy' Thinks He Was Removed from Trump Rally for 'Not Being Enthusiastic Enough,'" *CNN*, September 8, 2018.

53. Alex Kack, "#GreenShirtGuy: How I Went Viral," *CNN*, August 19, 2019.

54. Bobby Allyn, "'Lock Him Up': Trump Greeted with Boos and Jeers at World Series Game 5," *NPR*, October 28, 2019.

55. Mari Uyehara, "Blacklist Every Last One of Them," *GQ*, June 26, 2018.

56. Engler and Engler, *This Is an Uprising,* 67–68.

Chapter 1

1. Tricontinental Institute for Social Research, "The World Oscillates between Crises and Protests," January 7, 2020.

2. Ben Ehrenreich, "Welcome to the Global Rebellion against Neoliberalism," *The Nation*, November 25, 2019.

3. As of autumn 2020, the four richest entities in the world were Jeff Bezos ($166.3 billion), Bill Gates ($109.9 billion), Bernard Arnault and family ($106.8 billion), and Mark Zuckerberg (a paltry $85.4 billion): "The World's Billionaires," *Forbes*, March 8, 2020. See Josh Barro, "The Companies That Stand to Profit from the Pandemic," *The New Yorker*, April 14, 2020; Kenya Evelyn, "Amazon CEO Jeff Bezos Grows Fortune by $24bn amid Coronavirus Pandemic," *Guardian*, April 15, 2020.

4. Jack Kelly, "The 1% Owns Almost as Much Wealth as the Middle Class: Will the Rich Keep Getting Richer?," *Forbes*, November 12, 2019.

5. Annie Palmer, "Senators Ask Jeff Bezos for Answers on Fired Amazon Whistleblowers," *CNBC*, May 7, 2020.

6. Veena Dubal, personal communication.

7. Ben Golliver, "LeBron James: NFL Owners Are 'Old White Men' with 'Slave Mentality' toward Players," *Washington Post*, December 21, 2018.

8. See Johnny Smith's excellent account in "Jackie Robinson Was Asked to Denounce Paul Robeson. Instead, He Went After Jim Crow," *The Undefeated*, April 15, 2019.

9. Robert Lipstye, "Evidence Ties Olympic Taint to 1936 Games," *New York Times*, February 21, 1999.

10. Lipstye, "Olympic Taint."

11. John Carlos with Dave Zirin, *The John Carlos Story* (Chicago: Haymarket, 2011), 79.

12. Carlos and Zirin, *John Carlos Story*, 107.

13. Carlos and Zirin, *John Carlos Story*, 111.

14. Carlos and Zirin, *John Carlos Story*, 123.

15. Philip Barker, "Black Lives Matter Movement Brings Ex–IOC President Brundage under New Scrutiny," *Inside the Games*, June 28, 2020.

16. Dave Zirin, "After Forty-Four Years, It's Time Brent Musburger Apologized to John Carlos and Tommie Smith," *The Nation*, June 4, 2012.

17. Tom Lutz, "Donald Trump Aims Tweets at NFL over Protests to Reopen Anthem Debate," *Guardian*, June 8, 2020.

18. Carlos and Zirin, *John Carlos Story*, 118.

19. Kelly Moffitt, "Meet St. Louis Native Harry Edwards, the Man behind the Black Power Protest at the '68 Olympics," *St Louis Public Radio*, February 24, 2017.

20. Adam Kilgore, "For Decades, the NFL Wrapped Itself in the Flag. Now, That's Made Business Uneasy," *Washington Post*, September 6, 2018.

21. Quoted in Kilgore, "NFL."

22. J. J. Gallagher, "US Soccer Star Joins Kaepernick in National Anthem Protest," *ABC News*, September 4, 2016.

23. Julie Turkewitz, "Protest Started by Colin Kaepernick Spreads to High School Students," *New York Times*, October 4, 2016; Associated Press, "German Soccer Team Kneels in Solidarity with N.F.L. Players' Protests," *New York Times*, October 14, 2017.

24. Kim Reynolds, "Learners Take a Knee during Israeli National Anthem," *GroundUp*, November 14, 2018.

25. Dave Zirin, "Why Michael Bennett Walked Away from the NFL's Israel Delegation," *The Nation*, February 13, 2017.

26. Natalie Weiner, "A Softball Team's Tweet to Trump Leads Players to Quit Mid-series," *New York Times*, June 24, 2020.

27. Carlos and Zirin, *John Carlos Story*, 177.

28. Quoted in Carlos and Zirin, *John Carlos Story*, 176.

29. Dave Zirin, "DeMaurice Smith: In an NFL Lockdown and Inspiration from Egypt," *The Nation*, February 14, 2011.

30. Jake Johnson, "US President Greeted with Thunderous Boos and 'Impeach Trump' Banner at World Series," *Common Dreams*, October 28, 2019.

31. Jason Gay, "America Is Raging. Listen to What's Being Said," *Wall Street Journal*, May 31, 2020; Kareem Abdul-Jabbar, "Don't Understand the Protests? What You're Seeing Is People Pushed to the Edge," *Los Angeles Times*, May 30, 2020.

32. Jalen Rose, "I Wish America Loved Black People as much as They Love Black Culture," *TMZ Sports*, May 29, 2020.

33. See Elliott Johnston, "Back Up the Truck," *Boulder Weekly*, August 21–27, 2008. I thank Sam Smith for this reference.

34. Quoted in Gavin Brown et al., eds., *Protest Camps in International Context: Spaces, Infrastructures and Media of Resistance* (Chicago and Bristol, UK: Policy Press, 2018), 4.

35. Brown, *Protest Camps*, 4.

36. Carlos and Zirin, *John Carlos Story*, 188.

37. Henri Lefebvre, *The Production of Space* (Oxford: Blackwell, 1991).

38. Anastasia Kavada and Orsalia Dimitriou, "Protest Spaces Online and Offline: The Indignant Movement in Syntagma Square," in Brown, *Protest Camps*, 76.

39. Harvey J. Kaye, *Take Hold of Our History: Make America Radical Again* (Winchester, UK, and Washington, DC: Zero Books, 2020), 24–25.

40. Mark Engler and Paul Engler, *This Is an Uprising: How Nonviolent Revolt Is Shaping the Twenty-First Century* (New York: Nation Books, 2016), 163–65.

41. Dalzell, Tom, and Liam O'Donoghue, "'If It Takes a Bloodbath, Let's Get It Over With': When Ronald Reagan Sent Troops into Berkeley," *East Bay Yesterday*, May 8, 2019.

42. Sam Whiting, "People's Park at 50: A Recap of the Berkeley Struggle That Continues," *San Francisco Chronicle*, May 12, 2019.

43. June Jordan, "Civil Wars," in *Civil Wars* (New York: Simon & Schuster, 1995), 182–83.

44. Jordan, "Civil Wars," 188. At the 2019 Socialism Conference in Chicago, I had the opportunity to ask Francis Fox Piven about this episode, and she remembered every detail.

45. Frances Fox Piven, *Challenging Authority: How Ordinary People Change America* (Lanham, MD: Rowman & Littlefield, 2006), 1.

46. Sarah Jaffe, *Necessary Trouble: Americans in Revolt* (New York: Nation Books, 2017; repr.), 284.

47. Aristide Zolberg, "Moments of Madness," *Politics and Society* 2 (1972), 183.

48. Elizabeth Findell and Valerie Bauerlein, "Protests Spread beyond Big Cities, from Raleigh to Santa Rosa," *Wall Street Journal*, June 2, 2020; Elie Mystal, "The Bravery of Marching for Black Lives in the Middle of a Pandemic," *The Nation*, June 10, 2020.

49. Damien Cave et al., "Huge Crowds around the Globe March in Solidarity against Police Brutality," *New York Times*, June 9, 2020.

50. Amanda Taub and Max Fisher, "A Rush to the Street as Protesters Worldwide See Democracies Backsliding," *New York Times*, June 25, 2019; Yumna Patel, "Palestinians Hold Vigil for George Floyd and Eyad al-Halaq," *Mondoweiss*, June 4, 2020.

51. Tricontinental Institute for Social Research, "There's Something That's Ours on Those Streets and We Are Going to Take it Back," October 2019.

52. John Berger, "The Nature of Mass Demonstrations," *Socialist Worker*, August 16, 2013.

53. Étienne Balibar, *Violence and Civility: On the Limits of Political Philosophy* (New York: Columbia University Press, 2015), 97–99.

54. Balibar, *Violence and Civility*, 99.

55. James and Grace Lee Boggs, *Revolution and Evolution in the Twentieth Century* (New York: Monthly Review Press, 1974), 208.

56. Rebecca Sprang, "The Revolution Is Under Way Already," *The Atlantic*, April 5, 2020.

57. Palumbo-Liu, "As Violence Consumes Dhaka, Young Protesters Struggle to Get Their Story Out," *Truthout*, August 9, 2018.

58. "Mass Protests over Traffic Deaths Paralyze Dhaka for 5 Days," *US News and World Report*, August 3, 2018.

59. Maria Abi-Habib, "Violence Intensifies as Student Protests Spread in Bangladesh," *New York Times*, August 6, 2018.

60. "The Bangladesh Government Is at War with Its Children," *Muktiforum*, August 5, 2018.

61. Julfikar Ali Manik. "Undeterred by Violence, Students Close Dhaka's Roads to Demand Justice," *Sydney Morning Herald*, August 6, 2018.

62. Özge Yaka and Serhat Karakayali, "Emergent Infrastructures: Solidarity, Spontaneity and Encounter at Istanbul's Gezi Park Uprising," in Brown, *Protest Camps*, 59–60.

Chapter 2

1. David Harvey, *Rebel Cities: From the Right to the City to the Urban Revolution* (London and New York: Verso, 2012), xvii–xiii.
2. Blue Telusma, "Black and White Witnesses Agree: McKinney Pool Party Fight Started when White Mother Slapped a Black Teen," *The Grio*, June 8, 2015.
3. Cameron McWhirter, *Red Summer: The Summer of 1919 and the Awakening of Black America*, 1st ed. (New York: Henry Holt & Co., 2011), 56.
4. McWhirter, *Red Summer*, 56.
5. McWhirter, *Red Summer*, 185.
6. McWhirter, *Red Summer*, 184.
7. Much of this discussion comes from my article "America Is Still a Segregationist State: The Brutal Lessons of McKinney," *Salon*, June 12, 2015.
8. See George Lipsitz, *How Racism Takes Place* (Philadelphia: Temple University Press, 2011).
9. Henri Lefebvre, "The Right to the City," in *Writings on Cities*, Eleonore Kofman and Elizabeth Lebas, eds., 1st ed. (Cambridge, MA: Wiley-Blackwell, 1996), 147–48.
10. Lefebvre, "Right to the City," 158.
11. Harvey, *Rebel Cities*, xvii.
12. Henri Lefebvre, *The Production of Space* (Oxford: Blackwell, 1991), ·33–35, my emphasis.
13. Harvey, *Rebel Cities*, xi–xii.
14. Right to the City Alliance official website, https://righttothecity.org/.
15. My discussion here is indebted to Jon Liss, "The Right to the City: From Theory to Grassroots Alliance," in Neil Brenner, Peter Marcuse, and Margit Mayer, eds., *Cities for People, Not Profit: Critical Urban Theory and the Right to the City* (London: Routledge, 2012).
16. Mayer, "The 'Right to the City' in Urban Social Movements," in Brenner et al., *Cities for People*, 63.
17. Sarah Keenan, *Subversive Property: Law and the Production of Spaces of Belonging* (London: Routledge, 2015), 6, 13, my emphasis.
18. John Locke, *The Second Treatise of Government and A Letter Concerning Toleration* (Mineola, NY: Dover, 2002), 123.
19. Jeff Cox, "CEOs See Pay Grow 1000% in the Last 40 Years, Now Make 278 Times theAverage Worker," *CNBC*, August 16, 2019.
20. Harvey, *Rebel Cities*, 137
21. Hannah Arendt, *Essays in Understanding* (New York: Schocken, 2005), 208.
22. For instance, see Sydney Combs, "Want to Visualize Inequality? View Cities from Above," *Culture*, March 22, 2019.
23. Roger Friedland, Frances Fox Piven, and Robert R. Alford, "Political Conflict, Urban Structure, and Fiscal Crisis," in Douglas E. Ashford, ed., *Comparing Public Policies: New Concepts and Methods* (Beverly Hills: Sage, 1978), 198, 201.

24. Andrew Herscher, ."Black and Blight," in Irene Cheng, Charles L. Davis, and Mabel O. Wilson, eds., *Race and Modern Architecture: A Critical History from the Enlightenment to the Present* (Pittsburgh: University of Pittsburgh Press, 2020), 303.

25. Herscher, "Black and Blight," 293.

26. Herscher, "Black and Blight," 296–97.

27. Herscher, "Black and Blight," 297, citing Stanley McMichael and Robert F. Bingham, *City Growth Essentials* (Cleveland: Stanley McMichael, 1928), 343.

28. Herscher, "Black and Blight," 293.

29. Norman Fainstein and Susan Fainstein, "Regime Strategies, Communal Resistance, and Economic Forces," in Susan Fainstein, Norman Fainstein, Richard Child Hill et al., eds., *Restructuring the City: The Political Economy of Urban Redevelopment* (New York: Longman, 1983), 252.

30. Herbert Gans, "The Balanced Community: Homogeneity or Heterogeneity in Residential Areas?," in Jon Pynoos, Robert Schafer, and Chester Hartman, eds., *Housing Urban America*, 2nd ed. (New York: Aldine, 1980), 141.

31. See "Why Did Pruitt-Igoe Fail?," *PD&R Edge*, HUD User official website.

32. Marc V. Levine, "The Politics of Partnership: Urban Redevelopment Since 1945," in Gregory Squires, ed., *Unequal Partnerships: The Political Economy of Urban Redevelopment in Postwar America* (New Brunswick: Rutgers University Press, 1989), 20.

33. Gregory Squires, "Public-Private Partnerships: Who Gets What and Why," in Squires, ed., *Unequal Partnerships*, 3.

34. Levine, "Politics of Partnership," 25. See Michael E. Stone's classic essay on housing, financing, wages, and capitalism for a discussion on how these terms come into contradiction: "Housing and the Dynamics of US Capitalism," in Rachel Bratt et al., eds., *Critical Perspectives on Housing*, 41–67.

35. Keenga-Yamahtta Taylor, *Race for Profit: How Banks and the Real Estate Industry Undermined Black Homeownership* (Chapel Hill: University of North Carolina Press, 2019), 3–7.

36. Gaye Theresa Johnson, *Spaces of Conflict, Sounds of Solidarity: Music, Race, and Spatial Entitlement in Los Angeles* (Berkeley: University of California Press, 2013), 176. Note, as well, that "[f]rom 2007 to 2012, US banks also foreclosed on 3.6 million American homes. Despite decades of 'color-blind' policies intended to ignore racial inequality, the impacts of the recession were also undeniably racialized. . . . The recession cost white families 16% of their household wealth, while Hispanic families saw 66% drop and Black families lost 53%." Dawson Barrett, *The Defiant: Protest Movements in Post-Liberal America* (New York: New York University Press, 2018), 139.

37. David Harvey and David Wachsmuth, "What Is to Be Done? And Who the Hell Is Going to Do It?," in Brenner et al., *Cities for People*, 266.

38. Quoted in Tom Slater, "Missing Marcuse: On Gentrification and Displacement," in Brenner et al., eds., *Cities for People*, 171–97.

39. Jeff Chang, *We Gon' Be Alright: Notes on Race and Resegregation* (New York: Picador, 2016), 72.

40. George Lipsitz, *How Racism Takes Place* (Philadelphia: Temple University Press, 2011), 75.

41. Lipsitz, *How Racism Takes Place*, 81.

42. Chang, *We Gon' Be Alright*, 66.

43. Chang, *We Gon' Be Alright*, 72–73. The 2019 film *The Last Black Man in San Francisco*, directed by Joe Talbot, is a wrenching and beautiful statement on everything we have been talking about.

44. Lipsitz, *How Racism Takes Place*, 5.

45. Keenan, *Subversive Property*, 7.

46. Matthew Desmond, *Evicted: Poverty and Profit in the American City* (New York: Crown, 2017), 298.

47. Alicia Adamczyk, "Minimum Wage Workers Cannot Afford Rent in Any U.S. City," *CNBC*, July 14, 2020; Low Income Housing Coalition, *Out of Reach: The High Cost of Housing*.

48. David Palumbo-Liu and Tony Roshan Samara, "The Battle for Fair Housing in the Bay Area," *Truthout*, June 6, 2016.

49. Lacino Hamilton, "The Gentrification to Prison Pipeline," *Truthout*, April 30, 2017.

50. St. Clair Drake and Horace Cayton, *Black Metropolis: A Study of Negro Life in a Northern City* (Chicago: University of Chicago Press, 1945), 206. My discussion is based on Andrew Herscher's "Black and Blight."

51. Anne C. Bailey, "The Day I Met James Baldwin at Harvard," *Anne C. Bailey* (blog), June 6, 2020.

52. Johnson, *Spaces of Conflict*, 48.

53. Johnson, *Spaces of Conflict*, 48.

54. Johnson, *Spaces of Conflict*, 65

55. Johnson, *Spaces of Conflict*, 57, 50–51.

56. Frank Viviano and Alton Chinn, "The Hong Kong Connection," *San Francisco Magazine*, February 1982, 54.

57. Estella Habal, *San Francisco's International Hotel: Mobilizing the Filipino American Community in the Anti-eviction Movement* (Philadelphia: Temple University Press, 2008), 3.

58. The exhibition *Until Today: Spectres of the International Hotel* has received critical acclaim. See Michele Carlson, "Jerome Reyes," *ARTnews.com* (blog), September 16, 2010.

59. Carlson, "Jerome Reyes."

60. Zoie Matthew, "Caltrans Owns 163 Empty Homes around Pasadena. Homeless Families Want to Live in Them," *Curbed LA*, March 16, 2020.

61. Akela Lacy, "Philadelphia Activists on Verge of Historic Win for Public Housing," *The Intercept*, September 20, 2020.

62. Pat Ralph, "Philly Homeless Encampment Leaders Claim Victory," *PhillyVoice*, September 27, 2020.

63. Derek Hawkins, "Protesters Holed Up in DC Home Overnight," *Washington Post*, June 2, 2020.

Chapter 3

1. Neil Smith, "New Globalism, New Urbanism: Gentrification as Global Urban Strategy," *Antipode*, December 16, 2002, 431.

2. Smith, "New Globalism," 428.

3. Smith, "New Globalism," 429–30.

4. Smith, "New Globalism," 435, my emphasis.

5. Smith, "New Globalism," 441–42.

6. Frank Jacobs, "'The West' Is, in Fact, the World's Biggest Gated Community," *Big Think*, October 12, 2019.

7. Atossa Araxia Abrahamian, "The Real Wall Isn't at the Border," *New York Times*, January 26, 2019.

8. Saskia Sassen, *Losing Control? Sovereignty in an Age of Globalization* (New York: Columbia University Press, 1996), 38–39.

9. Sassen, *Losing Control?*, 63.

10. Angela Nagle, "The Left Case against Open Borders," *American Affairs Journal*, November 20, 2018.

11. See, for example, Cas Mudde, "Why Copying the Populist Right Isn't Going to Save the Left," *Guardian*, May 14, 2019; Briana Rennix and Nathan Robinson, "Responding to 'The Left Case against Open Borders,'" *Current Affairs*, November 29, 2018.

12. "The Border Crossing Us," *Viewpoint Magazine*, November 7, 2018.

13. While the US Border Patrol was "officially" established in 1924, as early as 1915 the US had set up "mounted guards" to prevent the entry of Chinese laborers from Mexico.

14. Juliana Hing, "Trump Admits That His Deportation Agenda Is a 'Military Operation,'" *The Nation*, February 24, 2017.

15. Tanya Maria Golash-Boza, *Deported: Immigrant Policing, Disposable Labor and Global Capitalism* (New York: New York University Press, 2015), 8.

16. Niall McCarthy, "How Much Tax Do America's Undocumented Immigrants Actually Pay?," *Forbes*, October 6, 2016.

17. Julian Borger, "Fleeing a Hell the US Helped Create: Why Central Americans Journey North," *Guardian*, December 19, 2018.

18. Golash-Boza, *Deported*, 259.

19. Golash-Boza, *Deported*, 2–3.

20. Golash-Boza, *Deported*, 5.

21. Rubén Martínez, *Crossing Over: A Mexican Family on the Migrant Trail* (New York: Picador, 2013), 35–36.

22. Woody Guthrie, "Plane Wreck at Los Gatos—Deportee," lyrics from Woody Guthrie official website.

23. Malia Wollan, "65 Years Later, a Memorial Gives Names to Crash Victims," *The New York Times*, September 3, 2013.

24. Jack Holmes, "Expert on Concentration Camps Says That's Exactly What the US Is Running at the Border," *Esquire*, June 13, 2019.

25. Liisa Malkki, "Speechless Emissaries: Refugees, Humanitarianism, and Dehistoricization," *Cultural Anthropology* 11:3 (1996), 386.

26. Cited in Ayten Gündogdu, *Rightlessness in an Age of Rights: Hannah Arendt and the Contemporary Struggles of Migrants* (New York: Oxford University Press, 2015), 140–41.

27. Gündogdu, *Rightlessness*, 126–27.

28. Gündogdu, *Rightlessness*, 141, my emphasis.

29. Gündogdu, *Rightlessness*, 145.

30. Loren B. Landau, "Urban Refugees and IDPs," in Elena Fiddian-Qasmiyeh, Gil Loescher, Katy Long et al., eds., *The Oxford Handbook of Refugee and Forced Migration Studies* (New York: Oxford University Press, 2014), 147.

31. Andrew Herscher, *Displacements* (Berlin: Sternberg Press, 2017), 29.

32. Katy Long, "When Refugees Stopped Being Migrants: Movement, Labor, and Humanitarian Protection," *Migration Studies* 1, no. 1 (March 2013): 10.

33. Herscher, *Displacements*, 119

34. Herscher, *Displacements*, 124–25.

35. Catherine Schiochet, "Judge on Trump Deportation Policies: 'Even the Good Hombres Are Not Safe,'" *CNN*, May 30, 2020.

36. United States Court of Appeals for the Ninth Circuit, *Andrews Magana Ortiz v. Jefferson B. Sessions III*, May 8, 2017.

37. What follows is based on my "Contending with the Trump Regime's New Immigration Policies," *Truthout*, June 25, 2017.

38. "2017–19," California Legislative Information official website.

39. Ezra Marcus, "In the Autonomous Zones," *New York Times*, July 1, 2020.

40. Fenit Nirappil, "What Is the Black House Autonomous Zone?," *Washington Post*, June 23, 2020.

41. Matt Perez, "Trump Praises US Marshalls," *Forbes*, October 15, 2020.

42. Ed Pilkington, "The Day Police Bombed a City Street: Can Scars of 1985 MOVE Atrocity Be Healed?," *Guardian*, May 10, 2020.

43. Maggie Blackhawk, "The Indian Law That Helps Build Walls," *New York Times*, May 26, 2019.

44. Trevor Timm, "Camouflaged Federal Agents Have Descended on Portland: Trump's DHS Is out of Control," *Guardian*, July 18, 2020.

45. See Richard Winton, Maura Dolan, and Anita Chabria, "Far-Right 'Boogaloo Boys' Linked to Killing of California Police Officers and Other Violence," *Los Angeles Times*, June 17, 2020.

46. Brett Samuels, "Trump Claims 75-Year-Old Man Shoved by Buffalo Police Could Be Part of a 'Set Up,'" *The Hill*, June 6, 2020.

47. Kevin Schaul and Samuel Granados, "5 Challenges Trump May Face Building a Border Wall," *Washington Post*, January 25, 2017.

48. Martínez, *Crossing Over*, 109.

49. Michael Dear, "Why Walls Won't Work," in Ronald Rael, ed., *Borderwall as Architecture: A Manifesto for the U.S.-Mexico Border* (Berkeley: University of California Press, 2017), 160.

50. Ronald Rael, *"Recuerdos / Souvenirs: A Nuevo Grand Tour,"* in Rael, ed., *Borderwall as Architecture*, 31–32.

51. Rael, *"Recuerdos / Souvenirs,"* 44.

52. Rael, *"Recuerdos / Souvenirs,"* 38–39.

53. Elisa Pascucci, "From 'Refugee Population' to Political Community: The Mustapha Mahmoud Refugee Protest Camp," in Gavin Brown et al., eds., *Protest Camps in International Context: Spaces, Infrastructures and Media of Resistance* (Chicago and Bristol, UK: Policy Press, 2018), 289.

54. Marcella Arruda, "The Marconi Occupation in São Paolo, Brazil: A Social Laboratory of Common Life," in Brown et al., eds., *Protest Camps*, 309.

55. Carolina Moulin and Peter Nyers, "We Live in a Country of UNHRC—Refuge Protests and Global Political Society," *International Political Sociology* 1, no. 4 (November 2007): 356–72.

56. Moulin and Nyers, "Country of UNHRC," 200.

57. Adam J. Barker and Russell Myers Ross, "Reoccupation and Resurgence: Indigenous Protest Camps in Canada," in Brown et al., eds., *Protest Camps*, 207.

58. Gavin Brown, Anna Feigenbaum, Fabian Frenzel et al., "Introduction," in Brown et al., eds., *Protest Camps in International Context*, 5.

59. Diana Flores Ruíz, "By Radical Means Necessary: Interview with Alex Rivera and Cristine Ibarra," *Film Quarterly*, September 10, 2019.

60. Ruíz, "By Radical Means Necessary."

61. Ruíz, "By Radical Means Necessary."

62. Ryan Devereaux, "Humanitarian Volunteer Scott Warren Reflects on the Borderlands and Two Years of Government Persecution," *The Intercept*, November 23, 2019.

63. Will Morrow, "'We Are All Equal!' Captain Who Saved Refugees Refuses Award from Paris Mayor," *Countercurrents*, August 24, 2019.

Chapter 4

1. Naomi Klein, *This Changes Everything: Capitalism vs. the Climate* (New York: Simon & Schuster, 2015), 165.

2. Henri Lefebvre, *The Production of Space* (Oxford: Blackwell, 1991), 31.

3. Arundhati Roy, *Walking with the Comrades* (New York: Penguin), 214.

4. Roy, *Walking with the Comrades*, 3.

5. Rob Nixon, *Slow Violence: The Environmentalism of the Poor* (Cambridge, MA: Harvard University Press, 2013), 17.

6. Sarah Keenan, *Subversive Property: Law and the Production of Spaces of Belonging* (London: Routledge, 2015), 25. Again, "Legal judgments, executive powers, legislation and legal commentaries tend to treat space as something to be planned over, built on, cultivated, bought, sold and or protected; a blank canvas or platform to be smoothly acted upon . . . law is underpinned by notions of universality and neutrality—notions such as the 'reasonable person' (who has no class, gender, race or sexuality) and this standard of objectivity deployed in both civil and criminal law" (21).

7. Denis Cosgrove, *Apollo's Eye: A Cartographic Genealogy of the Earth in the Western Imagination* (Baltimore: Johns Hopkins University Press, 2001), 265–55.

8. J. B. Harley, *The New Nature of Maps: Essays in the History of Cartography*, Paul Laxton, ed., 1st ed. (Baltimore: Johns Hopkins University Press, 2002), 59, 62.

9. Alexandre Kedar, "On the Legal Geography of Ethnocratic Settler States," *Current Legal Issues 5* (2003), 414–15.

10. The following discussion is adopted from my article "By Making Palestinian Villages Invisible, Google Maps and Apple Maps Facilitate Their Demolition," *Truthout*, December 21, 2016.

11. Benjamin Netanyahu to Senator Diane Feinstein, August 11, 2015.

12. "A Chronicle of Dispossession," B'Tselem: Israel Information Center for Human Rights in the Occupied Territories, July 19, 2015.

13. For the latest news on this effort, see the website of the Rebuilding Alliance: https://www.rebuildingalliance.org/maps/.

14. Stepha Velednitsky, "Jason W. Moore Calls for Ecological Reparations in the Wake of Capitalism," *Edge Effects*, October 31, 2017.

15. Candace Fujikane, *Mapping Abundance for a Planetary Future: Kanaka Maoli and Critical Settler Geographies in Hawai'i* (Durham, NC: Duke University Press, 2021), 3, 4.

16. Dina Gilio-Whitaker, *As Long as the Grass Grows: The Indigenous Fight for Environmental Justice, from Colonization to Standing Rock* (New York: Beacon, 2020; repr.), 12.
17. Gilio-Whitaker, *As Long as the Grass Grows*, 13.
18. Gilio-Whitaker, *As Long as the Grass Grows*, 23.
19. Gilio-Whitaker, *As Long as the Grass Grows*, 25–26.
20. Svetlana Alexievich, *Chernobyl Prayer: A Chronicle of the Future* (London: Penguin Classics, 2017; repr.), 5.
21. Alexievich, *Chernobyl Prayer*, 25.
22. Alexievich, *Chernobyl Prayer*, 49.
23. Alexievich, *Chernobyl Prayer*, 31.
24. Rebecca Solnit, *Call Them by Their True Names: American Crises (and Essays)* (Chicago: Haymarket, 2018), 49.
25. "Jane Goodall Says 'Disrespect for Animals' Caused the Pandemic," AFP, April 11, 2020.
26. Robin McKie, "Portrait of a Planet on the Verge of Climate Catastrophe," *Guardian*, December 2, 2018.
27. Ehrenreich, "To Those Who Think We Can Reform Our Way Out of the Climate Crisis." *The Nation*, January 15, 2019.
28. UN Human Rights Council, *Climate Change and Poverty*, July 2019.
29. Mark Bray, "How Capitalism Stokes the Far Right and Climate Change," *Truthout*, October 30, 2018.
30. Casey Tolan, "DNC Votes against Climate Change Debate," *Mercury News*, August 24, 2019.
31. Ben Ehrenreich, "Open Borders Must Be Part of Any Response to Climate Change," *The Nation*, June 6, 2019.
32. George Monbiot, "Only Rebellion Will Prevent an Ecological Apocalypse," *Guardian*, April 15, 2019.
33. See *New York Times*, "Pictures from Youth Climate Strikes around the World," *New York Times*, March 15, 2019.
34. Brianna Fruean et al., "Young Climate Activists around the world: Why I Am Striking Today," *Guardian*, March 15, 2019.
35. Astra Taylor, "Bad Ancestors: Does the Climate Crisis Violate the Rights of Those yet to Be Born?," *Guardian*, October 1, 2019.
36. Dave Foreman, quoted in Jeffrey St. Clair and Joshua Frank, *The Big Heat: Earth on the Brink* (Chico, CA: AK Press, 2018), 272.
37. Foreman, quoted in St. Clair and Frank, *The Big Heat*, 266
38. Klein, *This Changes Everything*, 294–95.
39. Klein, *This Changes Everything*, 315.
40. Klein, *This Changes Everything*, 381.
41. Klein, *This Changes Everything*, 405–7.
42. Nick Estes, "A Red Deal," *Jacobin*, August 6, 2019.
43. Kate Aronoff, Alyssa Cohen, Daniel Aldana et al., *A Planet to Win: Why We Need a Green New Deal* (London and New York: Verso, 2019), 118.
44. Aronoff et al., *A Planet to Win*, 118–19.
45. Aronoff et el., *A Planet to Win*, 123.
46. United Nations Economic and Social Council, "Draft Resolution on Affordable Housing and Social Protection Systems," February 2020.
47. Aronoff et al., *A Planet to Win*, 156–57.

48. Jacques Rancière, *Dissensus: On Politics and Aesthetics*, Steven Corcoran, trans. (London: Bloomsbury Academic, 2015; repr.), 155.

49. Rancière, *Dissensus*, 37, my emphasis.

50. Amitav Ghosh, *The Great Derangement: Climate Change and the Unthinkable*, 1st ed. (Chicago: University of Chicago Press, 2017), 8.

51. Kim Stanley Robinson, *Green Earth: Science in the Capital Trilogy* (New York: Del Rey, 2015), 86.

52. Robinson, *Green Earth*, 143.

53. Robinson, *Green Earth*, 137.

54. Richard Powers, *The Overstory* (New York: W. W. Norton & Company, 2019), 423.

55. Powers, *The Overstory*, 497–98.

56. Powers, *The Overstory*, 443.

57. Powers, *The Overstory*, 453.

58. Powers, *The Overstory*, 483.

59. Powers, *The Overstory*, 489.

60. Ben Ehrenreich, *Desert Notebooks: A Road Map for the End of Time* (Berkeley: Counterpoint, 2020), 3–4.

61. Ehrenreich, *Desert Notebooks*, 4.

62. Powers, *The Overstory*, 498–99.

63. Octavia Butler, *Parable of the Sower* (New York: Grand Central, 2019), 1.

64. Butler, *Parable of the Sower*, 314.

65. Butler, *Parable of the Sower*, 315.

66. Butler, *Parable of the Sower*, 328.

Afterword

1. Anne Gearan and Josh Dawsey, "Trump Issued a Call to Arms. Then He Urged His Followers to 'Remember This Day Forever!,'" *Washington Post*, January 6, 2021.

2. Sonam Steth, "Here Are All the Losses Trump's Campaign Has Faced since Election Day," *Business Insider*, December 20, 2020.

3. "Poll: Half of Republicans Believe False Accounts of Deadly US Capitol Riot," *Reuters*, April 5, 2021.

4. Amy Gardner, Kate Rabinowitz, and Harry Stevens, "How GOP-Backed Voting Measures Could Create Hurdles for Tens of Millions of Voters," *Washington Post*, March 11, 2021.

5. See Charles Blow, "Tucker Carlson and White Replacement," *New York Times*, April 11, 2011.

6. Mindy Isser, "What Democrats Should Learn from the Spate of Socialist Wins on Election Day," *In These Times*, November 5, 2020.

7. Jacob Jarvis, "AOC Has Raised Nearly $9m More than Her GOP Opponent in House Race," *Newsweek*, October 25, 2020.

8. "Election Week 2020: Youth Voter Turnout 52%–55%," Center for Information and Research on Civic Learning and Engagement, November 18, 2020.

9. Domenico Montanaro, "Where Polling Went Wrong in the 2020 Presidential Election," *NPR*, November 13, 2020.

BIBLIOGRAPHY

Abdul-Jabbar, Kareem. "Don't Understand the Protests? What You're Seeing Is People Pushed to the Edge." *Los Angeles Times*, May 30, 2020. https://www.latimes.com/opinion/story/2020-05-30/dont-understand-the-protests-what-youre-seeing-is-people-pushed-to-the-edge.

Abi-Habib, Maria. "Violence Intensifies as Student Protests Spread in Bangladesh." *New York Times*, August 6, 2018. https://www.nytimes.com/2018/08/06/world/asia/bangladesh-student-protests.html.

Abrahamian, Atossa Araxia. "The Real Wall Isn't at the Border." *New York Times*, January 26, 2019. https://www.nytimes.com/2019/01/26/opinion/sunday/border-wall-immigration-trump.html.

Abutaleb, Yasmin, Josh Dawsey, Ellen Nakamura, and Greg Miller. "US Was Beset by Denial and Dysfunction as the Coronavirus Raged." *Washington Post*, April 4, 2020. https://www.washingtonpost.com/national-security/2020/04/04/coronavirus-government-dysfunction/?arc404=true.

"ACLU Comment on US Senate Vote on 'Sanctuary' Policies Bill." American Civil Liberties Union, October 20, 2015. https://www.aclu.org/press-releases/aclu-comment-us-senate-vote-sanctuary-policies-bill.

Adamczyk, Alicia. "Minimum Wage Workers Cannot Afford Rent in Any U.S. State." *CNBC*, July 14, 2020. https://www.cnbc.com/2020/07/14/minimum-wage-workers-cannot-afford-rent-in-any-us-state.html.

Agence France-Presse. "Jane Goodall Says 'Disrespect for Animals' Caused Pandemic." November 4, 2020. https://www.france24.com/en/20200411-jane-goodall-says-disrespect-for-animals-caused-pandemic.

Alexievich, Svetlana. *Chernobyl Prayer: A Chronicle of the Future*. London: Penguin Classic, 2017.

Allyn, Bobby. "'Lock Him Up': Trump Greeted with Boos and Jeers at World Series Game 5." *NPR*, October 28, 2019. https://www.npr.org/2019/10/28/774044200/lock-him-up-trump-greeted-with-boos-and-jeers-at-world-series-game.

Arendt, Hannah. *Essays in Understanding*. Reprint, New York: Schocken, 2005.

———. *The Human Condition*. 2nd ed. Chicago and London: University of Chicago Press, 1998.

———. *Origins of Totalitarianism*. New York: Harcourt, Brace, Jovanovich, 1973.

Aronoff, Kate, Alyssa Cohen, Daniel Aldana, and Thea Riofrancos. *A Planet to Win: Why We Need a Green New Deal*. London and New York: Verso, 2019.

Ashford, Douglas E., ed. *Comparing Public Policies: New Concepts and Methods*. Beverly Hills: Sage, 1978.

Associated Press. "German Soccer Team Kneels in Solidarity With N.F.L. Players'
　Protests." *New York Times*, October 14, 2017. https://www.nytimes.com/2017/10/14
　/sports/soccer/german-soccer-team-kneels-in-solidarity-with-nfl-players-protests
　.html.

Bailey, Anne C. "The Day I Met James Baldwin at Harvard." *Anne C. Bailey* (blog), June
　6, 2020. https://annecbailey.net/the-day-i-met-james-baldwin-at-harvard/.

Balibar, Étienne. *Violence and Civility: On the Limits of Political Philosophy*. New York:
　Columbia University Press, 2015.

Barker, Philip. "Black Lives Matter Movement Brings Ex-IOC President Brundage under
　New Scrutiny." *Inside the Games*, June 28, 2020. https://www.insidethegames.biz
　/articles/1095751/big-read-brundage-legacy.

Barrett, Dawson. *The Defiant: Protest Movements in Post-liberal America*. New York: New
　York University Press, 2018.

Barro, Josh. "The Companies That Stand to Profit from the Pandemic." *The New Yorker*,
　April 14, 2020. https://nymag.com/intelligencer/2020/04/the-companies-that-stand
　-to-profit-from-the-coronavirus.html.

Batchelor, Tim. "'Climate Apartheid': Rich People Will Buy Their Way Out of the
　Environmental Crisis while the Poor Suffer, UN Warns." *The Independent*, June 26,
　2019. https://www.independent.co.uk/environment/climate-change-crisis-rich
　-poor-wealth-apartheid-environment-un-report-a8974231.html.

Bates, Karen Grigsby. "Red Summer in Chicago: 100 Years after the Race Riots." *NPR*,
　July 17, 2019. https://www.npr.org/sections/codeswitch/2019/07/27/744130358/red
　-summer-in-chicago-100-years-after-the-race-riots.

Berger, John. "The Nature of Mass Demonstrations." *Socialist Worker*, August 16, 2013.
　https://socialistworker.org/2013/08/16/nature-of-mass-demonstrations.

Blackhawk, Maggie. "The Indian Law That Helps Build Walls." *New York Times*, May 26,
　2019. https://www.nytimes.com/2019/05/26/opinion/american-indian-law-trump
　.html.

Blow, Charles. "Tucker Carlson and White Replacement." *New York Times*, April 11,
　2011. https://www.nytimes.com/2021/04/11/opinion/tucker-carlson-white
　-replacement.html

Boggs, James, and Grace Lee Boggs. *Revolution and Evolution in the Twentieth Century*.
　New York: Monthly Review Press, 1974.

Borger, Julian. "Fleeing a Hell the US Helped Create: Why Central Americans Journey
　North." *Guardian*, December 19, 2018. https://www.theguardian.com/us
　-news/2018/dec/19/central-america-migrants-us-foreign-policy.

Bort, Ryan. "This Is What a White Nationalist Administration Looks Like." *Rolling
　Stone*, November 12, 2019. https://www.rollingstone.com/politics/politics-news
　/stephen-miller-leaked-white-nationalist-emails-911312/.

Bratt, Rachel G., Chester W. Hartman, and Ann Meyerson, eds. *Critical Perspectives on
　Housing*. Philadelphia: Temple University Press, 1986.

Bray, Mark. "How Capitalism Stokes the Far Right and Climate Catastrophe." *Truthout*,
　October 30, 2018. https://truthout.org/articles/how-capitalism-stokes-the-far-right
　-and-climate-catastrophe/.

Brecht, Bertholt. "Fascism Is the True Face of Capitalism." *OffGuardian*, December 1,
　2018. https://off-guardian.org/2018/12/01/fascism-is-the-true-face-of-capitalism/.

Brenner, Neil, Peter Marcuse, and Margit Mayer, eds. *Cities for People, Not for Profit:
　Critical Urban Theory and the Right to the City*. London and New York: Routledge,
　2012.

Brown, Gavin, Anna Feigenbaum, Fabian Frenzel, and Patrick McCurdy, eds. *Protest Camps in International Context: Spaces, Infrastructures and Media of Resistance*. Chicago and Bristol, UK: Polity Press, 2018.

Brown, Wendy. *Undoing the Demos: Neoliberalism's Stealth Revolution*. New York: Zone Books, 2015.

B'Tselem: Israel Information Center for Human Rights in the Occupied Territories. "A Chronicle of Dispossession." July 19, 2015. https://www.btselem.org/south_hebron_hills/201507_facts_on_susiya.

Butler, Chris. *Henri Lefebvre: Spatial Politics, Everyday Life and the Right to the City*. Reprint, Milton Park, Abingdon, Oxon: Routledge-Cavendish, 2014.

Butler, Octavia E. *Parable of the Sower*. New York: Grand Central Publishing, 2019.

California Legislative Information. "2017–19." https://leginfo.legislature.ca.gov/faces/billVotesClient.xhtml?bill_id=201720180SB54.

Carlos, John, with Dave Zirin. *The John Carlos Story*. Chicago: Haymarket Books, 2011.

Carlson, Michele. "Jerome Reyes." *Artnews*, September 16, 2010. https://www.artnews.com/art-in-america/aia-reviews/jerome-reyes-60666/.

Cave, Damien, Livia Albeck-Ripka, and Iliana Magra. "Huge Crowds around the Globe March in Solidarity against Police Brutality." *New York Times*, June 9, 2020. https://www.nytimes.com/2020/06/06/world/george-floyd-global-protests.html?referringSource=articleShare.

Center for Systems Science and Engineering, Johns Hopkins University. "COVID-19 Dashboard." https://gisanddata.maps.arcgis.com/apps/opsdashboard/index.html#/bda7594740fd40299423467b48e9ecf6.

Chang, Jeff. *We Gon' Be Alright: Notes on Race and Resegregation*. New York: Picador, 2016.

Cheng, Irene, Charles L. Davis, and Mabel O. Wilson, eds. *Race and Modern Architecture: A Critical History from the Enlightenment to the Present*. Pittsburgh: University of Pittsburgh Press, 2020.

Center for Information and Research on Civic Learning and Engagement (CIRCLE). "Election Week 2020: Youth Voter Turnout 52%–55%." November 18, 2020. https://circle.tufts.edu/latest-research/election-week-2020.

Combs, Sydney. "Want to Visualize Inequality? View Cities from Above." *National Geographic*, March 22, 2019. https://www.nationalgeographic.com/culture/2019/03/visualize-inequality-by-viewing-cities-from-above/.

Commission on Unalienable Rights. *Draft Report of the Commission on Unalienable Rights*. July 2020. https://www.state.gov/draft-report-of-the-commission-on-unalienable-rights/.

Cooper, Ryan. "The World Is Putting America in Quarantine." *The Week*, June 25, 2020. https://theweek.com/articles/921833/world-putting-america-quarantine.

Cosgrove, Denis. *Apollo's Eye: A Cartographic Genealogy of the Earth in the Western Imagination*. Illustrated edition. Baltimore: Johns Hopkins University Press, 2001.

Cox, Jeff. "CEOs See Pay Grow 1,000% in the Last 40 Years, Now Make 278 Times the Average Worker." *CNBC*, August 16, 2019. https://www.cnbc.com/2019/08/16/ceos-see-pay-grow-1000percent-and-now-make-278-times-the-average-worker.html.

Crawford, James. *The Rights of Peoples*. Oxford: Clarendon Press, 1988.

Dear, Michael, "Why Walls Won't Work" in *Borderwall as Architecture: A Manifesto for the U.S.-Mexico Border*. Ronald Rael ed. Oakland: University of California Press, 2017.

Desmond, Matthew. *Evicted: Poverty and Profit in the American City*. New York: Crown, 2017.

Devereaux, Ryan. "Humanitarian Volunteer Scott Warren Reflects on the Borderlands and Two Years of Government Persecution." *The Intercept*, November 23, 2019. https://theintercept.com/2019/11/23/scott-warren-verdict-immigration-border/.

Dickinson, Robert, Elena Katselli, Colin Murray, and Ole W. Petersen, eds. *Examining Critical Perspectives on Human Rights*. Cambridge, UK: Cambridge University Press, 2012.

DiLeo, Jeffrey R., and Peter Hitchcock, eds. *The New Public Intellectual: Politics, Theory, and the Public Sphere*. London: Palgrave Macmillan, 2016.

Dockrill, Peter. "We're Headed for a Class-Based 'Climate Apartheid,' Warns Chilling New UN Report." *ScienceAlert*, June 26, 2019. https://www.sciencealert.com /hundreds-of-millions-at-risk-of-devastating-climate-apartheid-un-expert-warns.

Drake, St. Clair, and Horace R. Cayton, *Black Metropolis: A Study of Negro Life in a Northern City*. Chicago: University of Chicago Press, 1947.

Dalzell, Tom, and Liam O'Donoghue, "'If It Takes a Bloodbath, Let's Get It Over With': When Ronald Reagan Sent Troops into Berkeley." *East Bay Yesterday* podcast. May 8, 2019. https://eastbayyesterday.com /episodes/if-it-takes-a-bloodbath-lets-get-it-over-with/.

Eco, Umberto. "Ur-Fascism." *New York Review of Books*, June 22, 1995. https://www .nybooks.com/articles/1995/06/22/ur-fascism/.

Ehrenreich, Ben. *Desert Notebooks: A Road Map for the End of Time*. Berkeley: Counterpoint, 2020.

———. "Open Borders Must Be Part of Any Response to the Climate Crisis." *The Nation*, June 6, 2019. https://www.thenation.com/article/archive/climate -change-refugees-open-borders/.

———. "To Those Who Think We Can Reform Our Way Out of the Climate Crisis." *The Nation*, January 15, 2019. https://www.thenation.com/article/archive/climate -change-fossil-fuel-capitalism-divorce/.

———. "Welcome to the Global Rebellion against Neoliberalism." *The Nation*, November 25, 2019. https://www.thenation.com/article/archive/global-rebellions -inequality/.

Engler, Mark, and Paul Engler. *This Is an Uprising: How Nonviolent Revolt Is Shaping the Twenty-First Century*. New York: Nation Books, 2016.

Estes, Nick. "A Red Deal." *Jacobin*. August 6, 2019. https://jacobinmag.com/2019/08 /red-deal-green-new-deal-ecosocialism-decolonization-indigenous-resistance -environment.

Evelyn, Kenya. "Amazon CEO Jeff Bezos Grows Fortune by $24bn amid Coronavirus Pandemic." *Guardian*, April 15, 2020. https://www.theguardian.com/technology /2020/apr/15/amazon-jeff-bezos-gains-24bn-coronavirus-pandemic.

Fainstein, Susan S., Norman I. Fainstein, Richard Child Hill, Dennis Judd, and Michael Peter Smith, eds. *Restructuring the City: The Political Economy of Urban Redevelopment*. New York: Longman, 1983.

Fassin, Éric. "The Neo-Fascist Moment of Neoliberalism." *OpenDemocracy*, August 10, 2018. https://www.opendemocracy.net/en/can-europe-make-it/neo-fascist-moment -of-neoliberalism/.

Fiddian-Qasmiyeh, Elena, Gil Loescher, Katy Long, and Nando Sigona. *The Oxford Handbook of Refugee and Forced Migration Studies*. Oxford: Oxford University Press, 2014.

Findell, Elizabeth, and Valerie Bauerlein. "Protests Spread beyond Big Cities, from Raleigh to Santa Rosa." *Wall Street Journal*, June 2, 2020. https://www.wsj.com /articles/protests-spread-beyond-big-cities-from-raleigh-to-santa-rosa-11591099005.

Findlay, Stephanie, Anna Gross, Stefania Palma, and Andres Schipani. "Global Deforestation Accelerates during Pandemic." *Financial Times*, August 9, 2020. https://www.ft.com/content/b72e3969-522c-4e83-b431-c0b498754b2d.

Foley, Gary and Noura Erakat. "Black Power Australia and Aboriginal-Palestinian Solidarity: An Interview with Dr. Gary Foley." *Status*, July 17, 2019. http://www.statushour.com/en/Interview/2397.

Forbes. "World's Billionaires: 2020's Richest." https://www.forbes.com/billionaires/.

Fraser, Nancy. *The Old Is Dying and the New Cannot Be Born: From Progressive Neoliberalism to Trump and Beyond*. London and New York: Verso, 2019.

Fruean, Brianna, et al. "Young Climate Activists around the World: Why I'm Striking Today. Brianna Fruean and Others." *Guardian*, March 15, 2019. https://www.theguardian.com/commentisfree/2019/mar/15/young-climate-activists-striking-today-campaigners.

Fujikane, Candace. *Mapping Abundance for a Planetary Future: Kanaka Maoli and Critical Settler Geographies in Hawai'i*. Durham, NC: Duke University Press, 2021.

Gallagher, J. J. "US Soccer Star Joins Kaepernick in National Anthem Protest." *ABC News*, September 4, 2016. https://abcnews.go.com/US/us-soccer-star-joins }-kaepernick-kneeling-protest-national/story?id=41866258.

Garcia, Victor. "Hannity Exclusive: McConnell Says 'Zero Chance' Trump Is Removed, 'One or Two Democrats' Could Vote to Acquit." *Fox News*, December 12, 2019. https://www.foxnews.com/media/hannity-exclusive-senate-majority-leader-mcconnell-says-theres-no-chance-president-trump-is-removed.

Gardner, Amy, Kate Rabinowitz, and Harry Stevens. "How GOP-Backed Voting Measures Could Create Hurdles for Tens of Millions of Voters." *Washington Post*, March 11, 2021. https://www.washingtonpost.com/politics/interactive/2021/voting-restrictions-republicans-states/.

Gay, Jason. "America Is Raging. Listen to What's Being Said." *Wall Street Journal*, May 31, 2020. https://www.wsj.com/articles/america-is-raging-listen-to-whats-being-said-11590934708.

Gearan, Anne, and Josh Dawsey. "Trump Issued a Call to Arms. Then He Urged His Followers to 'Remember This Day Forever!'" *Washington Post*, January 6, 2021. https://www.washingtonpost.com/nation/interactive/2021/capitol-insurrection-visual-timeline/.

Ghosh, Amitav. *The Great Derangement: Climate Change and the Unthinkable*. 1st ed. Chicago and London: University of Chicago Press, 2017.

Gilio-Whitaker, Dina. *As Long as Grass Grows: The Indigenous Fight for Environmental Justice, from Colonization to Standing Rock*. Reprint, New York: Beacon Press, 2020.

Godfrey, Elaine. "Thousands of Americans Have Become Socialists since March." *The Atlantic*, May 14, 2020. https://www.theatlantic.com/politics/archive/2020/05/dsa-growing-during-coronavirus/611599/.

Golash-Boza, Tanya Maria. *Deported: Immigrant Policing, Disposable Labor and Global Capitalism*. New York: New York University Press, 2015.

Golliver, Ben. "LeBron James: NFL Owners Are 'Old White Men' with 'Slave Mentality' toward Players." *Washington Post*, December 21, 2018. https://www.washingtonpost.com/sports/2018/12/22/lebron-james-nfl-owners-are-old-white-men-with-slave-mentality-toward-players/.

Goodale, Mark, ed. *Human Rights: An Anthropological Reader*. West Sussex, UK: Wiley-Blackwell, 2009.

Gündogdu, Ayten. *Rightlessness in an Age of Rights: : Hannah Arendt and the Contemporary Struggles of Migrants.* Oxford and New York: Oxford University Press, 2015.

Guthrie, Woody. "Plane Wreck at Los Gatos—Deportee." Woody Guthrie official website. https://www.woodyguthrie.org/publicationsindex.htm.

Habal, Estella. *San Francisco's International Hotel: Mobilizing the Filipino American Community in the Anti-eviction Movement.* Philadelphia: Temple University Press, 2008.

Hamilton, Lacino. "The Gentrification-to-Prison Pipeline." *Truthout*, April 30, 2017. https://truthout.org/articles/the-gentrification-to-prison-pipeline/.

Hansler, Jennifer. "Human Rights Organizations File Suit over Pompeo's 'Unalienable Rights' Commission." *CNN*, March 6, 2020. https://www.cnn.com/2020/03 /06/politics/human-rights-organizations-lawsuit-unalienable-rights-commission /index.html.

Harley, J. B. *The New Nature of Maps: Essays in the History of Cartography.* Edited by Paul Laxton. 1st ed. Baltimore: Johns Hopkins University Press, 2002.

Harney, Stefano, and Fred Moten. *The Undercommons: Fugitive Planning and Black Study.* 1st ed. New York: Autonomedia, 2013.

Harvey, David. *Rebel Cities: From the Right to the City to the Urban Revolution.* London and New York: Verso, 2012.

Hawkins, Derek, "Protesters Holed up in D.C. Home Overnight Emerge after Curfew Lifts." *Washington Post*, June 2, 2020. https://www.washingtonpost.com/local /protesters-holed-up-in-northwest-dc-home-overnight-emerge-after-curfew-lifts /2020/06/02/843bbba8-a4d7-11ea-bb20-ebf0921f3bbd_story.html.

Herscher, Andrew. *Displacements.* Berlin: Sternberg Press, 2017.

Hesson, Kristina Cooke. "What Are 'Sanctuary' Cities and Why Is Trump Targeting Them?" *Reuters*, February 26, 2020. https://www.reuters.com/article/us-usa -immigration-crime-idUSKBN20J25R.

Hing, Julianne. "How Donald Trump Will Make America White Again," *The Nation*, January 4, 2017. https://www.thenation.com/article/archive/how-donald-trump- will-make-america-white-again/.

———. "Trump Admits That His Deportation Agenda Is a 'Military Operation,'" *The Nation*, February 24, 2017. https://www.thenation.com/article/archive/trump -admits-that-his-deportation-agenda-is-a-military-operation/.

Holmes, Jack. "An Expert on Concentration Camps Says That's Exactly What the U.S. Is Running at the Border." *Esquire*, June 13, 2019. https://www.esquire.com/news -politics/a27813648/concentration-camps-southern-border-migrant-detention-facili- ties-trump/.

Institut de Monde Arabe. "For a Museum in Palestine." 2018. https://www.imarabe.org /en/exhibitions/for-a-museum-in-palestine.

Isser, Mindy. "What Democrats Should Learn from the Spate of Socialist Wins on Election Day." *In These Times*, November 5, 2020. https://inthesetimes.com/article /dsa-election-2020-democrats-socialism.

Jackson, Janine. "Housing, Community and Land Are Human Rights." *Truthout*, March 24, 2017. https://truthout.org/audio/housing-community-land-are-human-rights/.

Jacobs, Frank. "'The West' Is, in Fact, the World's Biggest Gated Community." *Big Think*, October 12, 2019. https://bigthink.com/strange-maps/walled-world.

Jaffe, Sarah. *Necessary Trouble: Americans in Revolt.* Reprint, New York: Nation Books, 2017.

Jarvis, Jacob. "AOC Has Raised Nearly $9m More Than Her GOP Opponent in House Race." *Newsweek*, October 25, 2020. https://www.newsweek.com/aoc-alexandria -ocasio-cortez-fundraising-rival-house-race-1541950.

Johnson, Gaye Theresa. *Spaces of Conflict, Sounds of Solidarity: Music, Race, and Spatial Entitlement in Los Angeles*. Berkeley: University of California Press, 2013.

Johnson, Jake. "Fed Up with Constant Attacks and Insults, Ocasio-Cortez Slams Pelosi as 'Outright Disrespectful' for Singling Out Progressives." *Common Dreams*, July 11, 2019. https://www.commondreams.org/news/2019/07/11/fed-constant-attacks-and -insults-ocasio-cortez-slams-pelosi-outright-disrespectful?fbclid= IwAR05R2djUwojTcCpJcNtGPwiA4JV7s4cqTR18n1kV57UXABSIlrmbZza5Ts.

———. "US President Greeted with Thunderous Boos and 'Impeach Trump' Banner at World Series." *Common Dreams*, October 28, 2019. https://www.commondreams .org/news/2019/10/28/us-president-greeted-thunderous-boos-and-impeach-trump -banner-world-series.

Johnston, Elliott. "Back Up the Truck." *Boulder Weekly*, August 21–27, 2008. https://www .boulderweekly.com/archives/20080821/buzz.html.

Jordan, June. *Civil Wars*. New York and London: Simon & Schuster, 1995.

Kack, Alex. "#GreenShirtGuy: How I Went Viral." *CNN*, August 19, 2019. https://www. cnn.com/2019/08/09/opinions/greenshirtguy-how-i-went-viral-kack /index.html.

Kaye, Harvey. *Take Hold of Our History: Make America Radical Again*. Winchester, UK, and Washington, DC: Zero Books, 2020.

Kedar, Alexandre. "On the Legal Geography of Ethnocratic Settler States: Notes toward a Research Agenda." *Current Legal Issues* 5 (2003): 401–41.

Keenan, Sarah. *Subversive Property: Law and the Production of Spaces of Belonging*. New York and London: Routledge, 2015.

Kelly, Jack. "The 1% Owns Almost as Much Wealth as The Middle Class: Will the Rich Keep Getting Richer?" *Forbes*, November 12, 2019. https://www.forbes.com/sites /jackkelly/2019/11/12/the-1-owns-almost-as-much-wealth-as-the-middle-class-will -the-rich-keep-getting-richer/#6f0e53b04323.

Kilgore, Adam. "For Decades, the NFL Wrapped Itself in the Flag. Now, That's Made Business Uneasy." *Washington Post*, September 6, 2018. https://www.washingtonpost .com/sports/for-decades-the-nfl-wrapped-itself-in-the-flag-now-thats-made-business -uneasy/2018/09/06/bc9aab64-b05d-11e8-9a6a-565d92a3585d_story.html?noredirect =on.

Klein, Naomi. *The Shock Doctrine: The Rise of Disaster Capitalism*. 1st ed. New York: Picador, 2007.

———. *This Changes Everything: Capitalism vs. the Climate*. Reprint, New York: Simon & Schuster, 2015.

Lacy, Akela. "Philadelphia Activists on Verge of Historic Win for Public Housing." *The Intercept*, September 20, 2020. https://theintercept.com/2020/09/29/philadelphia -public-housing/.

LeBlanc, Paul. "Bishop at DC Church Outraged by Trump Visit: 'I Just Can't Believe What My Eyes Have Seen,'" *CNN*, June 2, 2020. https://www.cnn.com/2020/06/01 /politics/cnntv-bishop-trump-photo-op/index.html.

Lee, ArLuther. "Trump Accuses 75-Year-Old Shoved by Police of Being Antifa 'Provocateur.'" *Atlanta Journal-Constitution*, June 9, 2020. https://www.ajc.com /news/trump-accuses-year-old-shoved-police-being-antifa-provocateur /d7xstnGVS7y1XO0T4H4oIL/.

Lefebvre, Henri. *The Production of Space*. Oxford: Blackwell, 1991.

———. *State, Space, World*. Edited by Stuart Elden and Neil Brenner. Translated by Gerald Moore. 1st ed. Minneapolis: University of Minnesota Press, 2009.

———. *Writings on Cities*. Edited by Eleonore Kofman and Elizabeth Lebas. 1st ed. Cambridge, MA: Wiley-Blackwell, 1996.

Levi, Margaret. "Frances Perkins Was Ready!" *Social Science Space*, March 2020. https://www.socialsciencespace.com/2020/03/frances-perkins-was-ready/.

Levitt, Peggy, and Sally Engle Merry. "Vernacularization on the Ground: Local Uses of Global Women's Rights in Peru, China, India and the United States." *Global Networks* 9, no. 4 (2009): 441–61.

Lin, Joanne. "A Bill Up for a House Vote Today to Punish 'Sanctuary Cities' Won't Improve Public Safety. It Will Undermine It." American Civil Liberties Union, July 23, 2015. https://www.aclu.org/blog/immigrants-rights/state-and-local-immigration-laws/bill-house-vote-today-punish-sanctuary.

Lipsitz, George. *How Racism Takes Place*. Philadelphia: Temple University Press, 2011.

Lipsyte, Robert. "Evidence Ties Olympic Taint to 1936 Games." *New York Times*, February 21, 1999. https://www.nytimes.com/1999/02/21/sports/olympics-evidence-ties-olympic-taint-to-1936-games.html.

Locke, John. *The Second Treatise of Government and A Letter Concerning Toleration*. Mineola, NY: Dover Publications, 2002.

Long, Katy. "When Refugees Stopped Being Migrants: Movement, Labor, and Humanitarian Protection." *Migration Studies* 1, no. 1 (2013): 4–26.

Low Income Housing Coalition. *Out of Reach: The High Cost of Housing*. 2020. https://reports.nlihc.org/sites/default/files/oor/OOR_BOOK_2020.pdf.

Lutz, Tom. "Donald Trump Aims Tweets at NFL over Protests to Reopen Anthem Debate." *Guardian*, June 8, 2020. https://www.theguardian.com/sport/2020/jun/08/donald-trump-nfl-national-anthem-protests-roger-goodel.

Malik, Nesrine. "Hillary Clinton's Chilling Pragmatism Gives the Far Right a Free Pass." *Guardian*, November 23, 2018. https://www.theguardian.com/commentisfree/2018/nov/23/hillary-clinton-populism-europe-immigration.

Malkki, Liisa H. "'Speechless Emissaries: Refugees, Humanitarianism, and Dehistoricization.'" *Cultural Anthropology* 11, no. 3 (1996): 377–404.

Manik, Julfikar Ali. "Undeterred by Violence, Students Close Dhaka's Roads to Demand Justice." *Sydney Morning Herald*, August 6, 2018. https://www.smh.com.au/world/asia/undeterred-by-violence-students-close-dhaka-s-roads-to-demand-justice-20180806-p4zvrb.html.

Marcus, Ezra. "In the Autonomous Zones." *New York Times*, July 1, 2020. https://www.nytimes.com/2020/07/01/style/autonomous-zone-anarchist-community.html.

Martínez, Rubén. *Crossing Over: A Mexican Family on the Migrant Trail*. 1st ed. New York: Picador, 2013.

Matthew, Zoie. "Caltrans Owns 163 Empty Homes around Pasadena. Homeless Families Want to Live in Them." *Curbed LA*, March 16, 2020. https://la.curbed.com/2020/3/16/21182478/moms-occupy-el-sereno-house-caltrans.

McCarthy, Bill. "CNBC's Joe Kernan Wrong about US Per Capita COVID-19 Deaths." *Politifact*, May 20, 2020. https://www.politifact.com/factchecks/2020/may/28/joe-kernen/cnbcs-joe-kernen-wrong-about-us-capita-covid-19-de/.

McCarthy, Niall. "How Much Tax Do America's Undocumented Immigrants Actually Pay?" *Forbes*, October 6, 2016. https://www.forbes.com/sites/niallmccarthy/2016/10/06/how-much-tax-do-americas-undocumented-immigrants-actually-pay-infographic.

McCarthy, Tom. "'I Am the Chosen One': With Boasts and Insults, Trump Sets New Benchmark for Incoherence." *Guardian*, August 21, 2019. https://www.theguardian.com/us-news/2019/aug/21/trump-press-conference-greenland-jewish-democrats?CMP=Share_iOSApp_Other.

McFarland, Susan. "U.N. Report: With 40M in Poverty, U.S. Most Unequal Developed Nation." UPI, June 22, 2018. https://www.upi.com/Top_News/US/2018/06/22/UN-report-With-40M-in-poverty-US-most-unequal-developed-nation/8671529664548/.

McKay, Tom. "DNC Votes 222–137 against Allowing Candidates to Participate in Climate Debate." *Gizmodo*, August 2019. https://earther.gizmodo.com/dnc-votes-222-137-against-allowing-candidates-to-partic-1837543829.

McKie, Robin. "Portrait of a Planet on the Verge of Climate Catastrophe." *Guardian*, December 2, 2018, https://www.theguardian.com/environment/2018/dec/02/world-verge-climate-catastophe.

McWhirter, Cameron. *Red Summer: The Summer of 1919 and the Awakening of Black America*. 1st ed. New York: Henry Holt & Co, 2011.

Menchú, Rigoberta. *I, Rigoberta Menchí: An Indian Woman in Guatemala*. Edited by Elisabeth Burgos-Debray. Translated by Ann Wright. 2nd ed. London and New York: Verso, 2010.

Meyer, Robinson. "Zombie Diseases of Climate Change." *The Atlantic*, November 6, 2017. https://www.theatlantic.com/science/archive/2017/11/the-zombie-diseases-of-climate-change/544274/.

Moffitt, Kelly. "Meet St. Louis Native Harry Edwards, the Man behind the Black Power Protest at the '68 Olympics." *St Louis Public Radio*, February 24, 2017. https://news.stlpublicradio.org/show/st-louis-on-the-air/2017-02-24/meet-st-louis-native-harry-edwards-the-man-behind-the-black-power-protest-at-the-68-olympics#stream/0.

Monbiot, George. "Only Rebellion Will Prevent an Ecological Apocalypse." *Guardian*, April 15, 2019. https://www.theguardian.com/commentisfree/2019/apr/15/rebellion-prevent-ecological-apocalypse-civil-disobedience.

Montanaro, Domenico. "Where Polling Went Wrong in the 2020 Presidential Election." *NPR*, November 13, 2020. https://www.npr.org/2020/11/13/934459456/where-polling-went-wrong-in-the-2020-presidential-election.

Morrow, Will. "'We Are All Equal!' Captain Who Saved Refugees Refuses Award from Paris Mayor." *Countercurrents*, August 24, 2019. https://countercurrents.org/2019/08/we-are-all-equal-captain-who-saved-refugees-refuses-award-from-paris-mayor/.

Moulin, Carolina, and Peter Nyers. "'We Live in a Country of UNHCR'—Refugee Protests and Global Political Society." *International Political Sociology* 1, no. 4 (November 2007): 356–72.

Mudde, Cas. "Why Copying the Populist Right Isn't Going to Save the Left." *Guardian*, May 14, 2019. https://www.theguardian.com/news/2019/may/14/why-copying-the-populist-right-isnt-going-to-save-the-left.

Muktiforum, "The Bangladesh Government Is at War with Its Children," August 5, 2018.

Mystal, Elie. "The Bravery of Marching for Black Lives in the Middle of a Pandemic." *The Nation*, June 10, 2020. https://www.thenation.com/article/society/protest-coronavirus-justice/.

Nagle, Angela. "The Left Case against Open Borders." *American Affairs*, November 20, 2018. https://americanaffairsjournal.org/2018/11/the-left-case-against-open-borders/.

Netanyahu, Benjamin. Letter to Senator Diane Feinstein. August 11, 2015. https://www.feinstein.senate.gov/public/_cache/files/e/1/e14c8261-2f01-4923-871b

-b15abe84000d/8CB5696D1DFF22CC3E810C7B728EACE3.2015-08-11-netanyahu
-response.pdf.

New York Times. "In Harm's Way." Photo essay, August 1, 2020. https://www.nytimes.
com/interactive
/2020/world/coronavirus-health-care-workers.html.

———. "Pictures from Youth Climate Strikes around the World (Published 2019)."
Photo essay, March 15, 2019. https://www.nytimes.com/2019/03/15/climate/cli-
mate-school-strikes.html.

Nichols, John. *The "S" Word: A Short History of an American Tradition—Socialism.* London
and New York: Verso, 2015.

Nirappil, Fenit. "What Is the 'Black House Autonomous Zone,' and How Is D.C.
Policing It?" *Washington Post,* June 23, 2020. https://www.washingtonpost.com
/dc-md-va/2020/06/23/bhaz-trump-dc-protests-police/.

Nixon, Rob. *Slow Violence and the Environmentalism of the Poor.* Cambridge, MA: Harvard
University Press, 2013.

Oprysko, Caitlin. "'Our President Gave Us so Much Hope': MyPillow CEO Goes off
Script at Coronavirus Briefing." *Politico,* March 30, 2020. https://www.politico.com
/news/2020/03/30/my-pillow-lindell-trump-coronavirus-156335.

Palestine Museum. "A Museum for Palestine: The Palestine Museum Establishes
Partnership with the Institute for the Arab World in Paris." http://www.palmuseum
.org/news-1/-a-museum-for-palestine-.

Palmer, Annie. "Senators Ask Jeff Bezos for Answers on Fired Amazon Whistleblowers."
CNBC, May 7, 2020. https://www.cnbc.com/2020/05/07/senators-ask-jeff-bezos-for
-more-info-on-amazon-firings.html.

Palumbo-Liu, David. "America Is Still a Segregationist State: The Brutal Lessons of
McKinney." *Salon,* June 12, 2015. https://www.salon.com/2015/06/12/when_blacks
_intrude_into_white_space_yes_were_still_living_in_a_world_of_de_facto
_segregation/.

———. "As Violence Consumes Dhaka, Young Protesters Struggle to Get Their Story
Out." *Truthout,* August 9, 2018. https://truthout.org/articles/as-violence-consumes
-dhaka-protesters-struggle-to-get-their-story-out/.

———. "The Battle for Fair Housing in the Bay Area: An Interview with Housing
Activist Tony Roshan Samara." *Truthout,* June 6, 2016. https://truthout.org/articles
/an-interview-with-housing-activist-tony-roshan-samara/.

———. "By Making Palestinian Villages Invisible, Google and Apple Maps Facilitate
Their Demolition." *Truthout,* December 21, 2016. https://truthout.org/articles/by
-making-palestinian-villages-invisible-google-and-apple-maps-facilitate-their
-demolition/.

———. "Contending with the Trump Regime's New Immigration Practices: A Dispatch
from the Trenches." *Truthout,* June 25, 2017. https://truthout.org/articles
/contending-with-the-trump-regime-s-new-immigration-practices-a-dispatch-from
-the-trenches/.

———. "Justice Denied: Rachel Corrie Died Protesting the Demolition of Palestinian
Homes by Israeli Forces. Her Parents Carry on the Fight." *Salon,* December 20, 2015.
https://www.salon.com/2015/12/20/justice_denied_rachel_corrie_died_protesting
_the_demolition_of_palestinian_homes_by_israeli_forces_her_parents_carry_on
_the_fight/.

Patel, Yumna. "Palestinians Hold Vigil for George Floyd and Eyad al-Halaq." *Mondoweiss*, June 4, 2020. https://mondoweiss.net/2020/06/palestinians-hold-vigil-for-george-floyd-and-eyad-al-halaq/.

Paxton, Robert. *The Anatomy of Fascism*. New York: Vintage, 2004.

Perez, Matt. "Trump Praises U.S. Marshals Who Shot and Killed Antifa Activist." *Forbes*, October 15, 2020. https://www.forbes.com/sites/mattperez/2020/10/15/trump-praises-us-marshals-who-shot-and-killed-antifa-activist/.

Picchi, Aimee. "Trump Adviser Says 'America's Human Capital Stock' Is Ready to Return to Work." *CBS News*, May 26, 2020. https://www.cbsnews.com/news/human-capital-stock-kevin-hassett-trump-economic-advisor-back-to-work/.

Pilkington, Ed. "The Day Police Bombed a City Street: Can Scars of 1985 Move Atrocity Be Healed?" *Guardian*, May 10, 2020. https://www.theguardian.com/us-news/2020/may/10/move-1985-bombing-reconciliation-philadelphia.

———. "'These Are His People': Inside the Elite Border Patrol Unit Trump Sent to Portland." *Guardian*, July 27, 2020. https://www.theguardian.com/us-news/2020/jul/27/trump-border-patrol-troops-portland-bortac.

Piven, Frances Fox. *Challenging Authority: How Ordinary People Change America*. Lanham, MD: Rowman & Littlefield Publishers, 2006.

Piven, Frances Fox, and Richard Cloward. *Poor People's Movements: Why They Succeed, How They Fail*. New York: Vintage, 1978.

Powers, Richard. *The Overstory*. Illustrated ed. New York: W. W. Norton & Company, 2019.

Pynoos, Jon, Robert Schafer, and Chester Hartman, eds. *Housing Urban America*. Updated 2nd ed. New York: Aldine, 1980.

Quah, Nicholas, and Laura Davis. "Here's a Timeline of Unarmed Black People Killed by Police over the Past Year." *Buzzfeed News*, May 1, 2015. https://www.buzzfeednews.com/article/nicholasquah/heres-a-timeline-of-unarmed-black-men-killed-by-police-over.

Rael, Ronald. "*Recuerdos*/Souvenirs: A Nuevo Grand Tour" in *Borderwall as Architecture: A Manifesto for the U.S.-Mexico Boundary*. Ronald Rael, ed. Oakland: University of California Press, 2017.

Rajan, Nithya. "What Do Refugees Want? Reading Refugee Lip-Sewing Protests through a Critical Lens." *International Feminist Journal of Politics* 21, no. 4 (2019): 527–43.

Ralph, Pat. "Philly Homeless Encampment Leaders Claim Victory in City Deal for 50 Vacant Homes." *PhillyVoice*, September 27, 2020. https://www.phillyvoice.com/philadelphia-city-homeless-encampments-housing-action-agreement-vacant-homes-protest-camps/.

Rancière, Jacques. *Disagreement*. Translated by Julie Rose. Minneapolis: University of Minnesota Press, 1999.

———. *Dissensus: On Politics and Aesthetics*. Translated by Steven Corcoran. Reprint, London and New York: Bloomsbury Academic, 2015.

Rasmussen Reports. "Popularity of Black Lives Matter Jumps to 62%," June 20, 2020. https://www.rasmussenreports.com/public_content/politics/current_events/social_issues/popularity_of_black_lives_matter_jumps_to_62.

Rennix, Briana, and Nathan J. Robinson. "Responding to 'The Left Case against Open Borders.'" *Current Affairs*, November 29, 2018. https://www.currentaffairs.org/2018/11/responding-to-the-left-case-against-open-borders.

Reuters. "Poll: Half of Republicans Believe False Accounts of Deadly US Capitol Riot." April 5, 2021. https://www.nbcnews.com/politics/donald-trump/poll-half-republicans-believe-false-accounts-deadly-us-capitol-riot-rcna595.

Reynolds, Kim. "Learners Take a Knee during Israeli National Anthem." *GroundUp*, November 14, 2018. https://www.groundup.org.za/article/learners-take-knee-during-israeli-national-anthem/.

Rivera, Alex, dir. *Sleep Dealer*. Film. 2008; New York: Likely Story.

Rivera, Alex, and Cristine Ibarra, dirs. *The Infiltrators*. Film. 2019; 3DMC.

Roberts, Sam. "A Racial Attack That, Years Later, Is Still Being Felt." *City Room*, December 18, 2011. https://cityroom.blogs.nytimes.com/2011/12/18/a-racial-attack-that-years-later-is-still-being-felt/.

Robinson, Kim Stanley. *Green Earth: The Science in the Capital Trilogy*. New York: Del Rey, 2015.

Rogin, Ali. "Members of New Pompeo Task Force Have Previously Praised Human-Rights Abusers." *PBS News Hour*, July 10, 2019. https://www.pbs.org/newshour/world/members-of-new-pompeo-task-force-have-previously-praised-human-rights-abusers.

Rose, Jalen. "I Wish America Loved Black People as Much as They Love Black Culture." *TMZ Sports*, May 29, 2020. https://www.tmz.com/2020/05/29/jalen-rose-black-people-america-culture-george-floyd/.

Roy, Arundhati. *Walking with the Comrades*. 1st ed. New York: Penguin, 2011.

rs21. "Precarious Work, 'Compression' and Class Struggle 'Leaps.'" February 10, 2015. https://rs21.org.uk/2015/02/10/precarious-work-compression-and-class-struggle-leaps/.

Ruíz, Diana Flores. "By Radical Means Necessary: Interview with Cristina Ibarra and Alex Rivera." *Film Quarterly*, September 10, 2019. https://filmquarterly.org/2019/09/10/by-radical-means-necessary-interview-with-cristina-ibarra-and-alex-rivera/.

Said, Edward. "Of Dignity and Solidarity." *Counterpunch*, June 23, 2003. https://www.counterpunch.org/2003/06/23/ofdignityandsolidarity/.

———. *Power, Politics and Culture: Interviews with Edward Said*. New York: Vintage, 2002.

———. *The Question of Palestine*. New York: Vintage, 1992.

Samuels, Brett. "Trump Claims 75-Year-Old Man Shoved by Buffalo Police Could Be Part of a 'Set Up.'" *The Hill*, June 6, 2020. https://thehill.com/homenews/administration/501784-trump-claims-75-year-old-man-shoved-by-buffalo-police-could-be-part.

Sassen, Saskia. *Guests and Aliens*. 1st ed. New York: New Press, 1999.

———. *Losing Control? Sovereignty in an Age of Globalization*. New York: Columbia University Press, 1996.

Schaul, Kevin, and Samuel Granados. "5 Challenges Trump May Face Building a Border Wall." *Washington Post*, January 25, 2017. https://www.washingtonpost.com/graphics/national/challenges-building-border-wall/.

Schiochet, Catherine. "Judge on Trump Deportation Policies: 'Even the Good Hombres Are Not Safe.'" *CNN*, May 30, 2020. https://www.cnn.com/2017/05/30/politics/appeals-court-judge-reinhardt-immigration-opinion/index.html.

Smith, Johnny. "Jackie Robinson Was Asked to Denounce Paul Robeson. Instead, He Went After Jim Crow." *The Undefeated*, April 15, 2019. https://theundefeated.com/features/jackie-robinson-was-asked-to-denounce-paul-robeson-before-huac-instead-he-went-after-jim-crow/.

Smith, Neil. "New Globalism, New Urbanism: Gentrification as Global Urban Strategy." *Antipode*, December 16, 2002. 427–50.

Solnit, Rebecca. *Call Them by Their True Names: American Crises (and Essays)*. Chicago: Haymarket Books, 2018.

Sprang, Rebecca. "The Revolution Is Under Way Already." *The Atlantic*, April 5, 2020. https://www.theatlantic.com/ideas/archive/2020/04/revolution-only-getting -started/609463/.

Squires, Gregory D., ed. *Unequal Partnerships: The Political Economy of Urban Redevelopment in Postwar America*. New Brunswick: Rutgers University Press, 1989.

St. Clair, Jeffrey, and Joshua Frank. *The Big Heat: Earth on the Brink*. Chico, CA: AK Press, 2018.

Stern, Alexandra. "It's Come to This: White Nationalism Is Inciting Mass Murder in America." *Newsweek*, August 5, 2019. https://www.newsweek.com/its-come-this -white-nationalism-inciting-mass-murder-america-opinion-1452563.

Steth, Sonam. "Here Are All the Losses Trump's Campaign Has Faced since Election Day." *Business Insider*, December 20, 2020. https://www.businessinsider.com.au /all-the-ways-trump-lost-2020-presidential-election-list-2020-12.

Stoll, David. *Rigoberta Menchu and the Story of All Poor Guatemalans*. Boulder, CA, and Oxford, UK: Westview Press, 1998.

Stracqualursi, Veronica. "'Plaid Shirt Guy' Thinks He Was Removed from Trump Rally for 'Not Being Enthusiastic Enough.'" *CNN*, September 8, 2018. https://www .cnn.com/2018/09/08/politics/plaid-shirt-guy-trump-montana-rally-cnntv/index.html.

Sunkara, Bhaskar. "How Wide Is Bernie Sanders' Appeal?" *Guardian*, April 16, 2019. https://www.theguardian.com/us-news/commentisfree/2019/apr/16/bernie -sanders-appeal-cheering-fox-news?fbclid= IwAR14r09QIchqPlqNq9MaAx7PfJs79FexTy1UrQoUJtZyvjJtmSfrsDH8zSg.

———. *The Socialist Manifesto: The Case for Radical Politics in an Era of Extreme Inequality*. New York: Basic Books, 2019.

Talbot, Joe, dir. *The Last Black Man in San Francisco*. Film. 2019; Beverly Hills, Plan B Entertainment.

Taub, Amanda, and Max Fisher. "A Rush to the Street as Protesters Worldwide See Democracies Backsliding." *New York Times*, June 25, 2019. https://www.nytimes .com/2019/06/25/world/czech-hong-kong-protests.html?smid=nytcore-ios-share.

Taylor, Astra. "Bad Ancestors: Does the Climate Crisis Violate the Rights of Those yet to Be Born?" *Guardian*, October 1, 2019.

———. "Bernie Sanders' Exit Is an Indictment of Our Broken System—Not His Campaign." *In These Times*, April 9, 2020. https://inthesetimes.com/article/ bernie-sanders-drops-out-broken-system-campaign-voter-suppression-pandemic. https://www.theguardian.com/environment/2019/oct/01/bad-ancestors-climate -crisis-democracy.

———. *Democracy May Not Exist, but We'll Miss It When It's Gone*. New York: Metropolitan Books, 2019.

Taylor, Keeanga-Yamahtta. *Race for Profit: How Banks and the Real Estate Industry Undermined Black Homeownership*. Chapel Hill: University of North Carolina Press, 2019.

———. "Reality Has Endorsed Bernie Sanders." *The New Yorker*, March 30, 2020. https:// www.newyorker.com/news/our-columnists/reality-has-endorsed-bernie -sanders.

Telusma, Blue. "Black and White Witnesses Agree: McKinney Pool Party Fight Started When White Mother Slapped a Black Teen." *The Grio*, June 8, 2015. https://thegrio .com/2015/06/08/black-and-white-witnesses-agree-mckinney-pool-party-fight -started-when-white-mother-slapped-a-black-teen/.

"The Undefeated." Facebook page. https://www.facebook.com/theundefeatedsite /videos/241870890453377/.

Timm, Trevor. "Camouflaged Federal Agents Have Descended on Portland. Trump's DHS Is out of Control." *Guardian*, July 18, 2020. https://www.theguardian.com /commentisfree/2020/jul/18/portland-oregon-federal-officers-trump-department -homeland-security.

Tolan, Casey. "DNC Votes against Climate Change Debate." *San Jose Mercury News*, August 24, 2019. https://www.mercurynews.com/2019/08/24/dnc-vote-climate -debate-san-francisco-meeting/.

Tricontinental Institute for Social Research. "There's Something That's Ours on Those Streets and We Are Going to Take It Back." October 24, 2019. https://www .thetricontinental.org/newsletterissue/theres-something-thats-ours-on-those -streets-and-were-going-to-take-it-back-the-forty-third-newsletter-2019/.

———. "The World Oscillates between Crises and Protests." January 7, 2020. https:// www.thetricontinental.org/wp-content/uploads/2020/01/20200105_Dossier-24 _EN_Web.pdf.

Turkewitz, Julie. "Protest Started by Colin Kaepernick Spreads to High School Students." *New York Times*, October 4, 2016. https://www.nytimes.com/2016/10/04 /us/national-anthem-protests-high-schools.html.

United Nations Economic and Social Council. "Draft Resolution on Affordable Housing and Social Protection Systems." 2020. https://undocs.org/E/CN.5/2020/L.5.

United Nations Human Rights Council. "Climate Change and Poverty." July 2019. https://www.ohchr.org/EN/HRBodies/HRC/RegularSessions/Session41 /Documents/A_HRC_41_39.docx.

United States Court of Appeals for the Ninth Circuit. *Andres Magana Ortiz v. Jefferson B. Sessions III*. May 8, 2017.

United States Housing and Urban Development. "Why Did Pruitt-Igoe Fail?" *HUD User*. https://www.huduser.gov/portal/pdredge/pdr_edge_featd_article_110314.html.

US News and World Report. "Mass Protests over Traffic Deaths Paralyze Dhaka for 5 Days." August 3, 2018. https://www.usnews.com/news/world/articles/2018-08-03 /mass-protests-over-traffic-deaths-paralyze-dhaka-for-5-days?src=usn_fl.

Uyehara, Mari. "Blacklist Every Last One of Them." *GQ*, June 26, 2018. https://www .gq.com/story/trump-administration-blacklist-them-all.

Varela, Amarela. "Migrant Struggles for the Right to Have Rights: Three Examples of Social Movements Powered by Migrants in New York, Paris and Barcelona." *Transfer: European Review of Labour and Research* 14, no. 4 (2008): 677–94.

Velednitsky, Stepha. "Jason W. Moore Calls for Ecological Reparations in the Wake of Capitalism." *Edge Effects*, October 31, 2017. https://edgeeffects.net/jason-w-moore/.

Viewpoint Magazine. "The Border Crossing Us." November 7, 2018. https://www .viewpointmag.com/2018/11/07/from-what-shore-does-socialism-arrive/.

Villagra, Hector. "Opinion: ICE vs. the Constitution." *Los Angeles Times*, July 13, 2015. https://www.latimes.com/opinion/op-ed/la-oe-villagra-detainers-arent -constitutional-20150713-story.html.

Viviano, Frank, and Alton Chinn, "The Hong Kong Connection." *San Francisco Magazine*, February 1982, 54–60.

Wagoner, James. "On Opening Day, a Rarity for M.L.B.: Support for Black Lives Matter." *New York Times*, July 23, 2020. https://www.nytimes.com/2020/07/23 /sports/baseball/mlb-black-lives-matter.html.

Warren, Michael. "Trump Risks Potential Backlash from Evangelicals with 'Tone-Deaf' Bible Photo-Op." *CNN*, June 3, 2020. https://www.cnn.com/2020/06/03 /politics/trump-evangelicals-church-protests/index.html.

Weiner, Natalie. "A Softball Team's Tweet to Trump Leads Players to Quit Mid-series." *New York Times*, June 24, 2020. https://www.nytimes.com/2020/06/24/sports /scrap-yard-softball-anthem-tweet.html.

Whiting, Sam. "People's Park at 50: A Recap of the Berkeley Struggle That Continues." *San Francisco Chronicle*, May 12, 2019. https://www.sfchronicle.com/bayarea/article /People-s-Park-at-50-A-recap-of-the-Berkeley-13838786.php.

Winton, Roger, Maura Dolan, Anita Chabria. "Far-Right 'Boogaloo Boys' Linked to Killing of California Police Officers and Other Violence." *Los Angeles Times*, June 17, 2020. https://www.latimes.com/california/story/2020-06-17/far-right -boogaloo-boys-linked-to-killing-of-california-lawmen-other-violence.

Wollan, Malia. "65 Years Later, a Memorial Gives Names to Crash Victims." *New York Times*, September 3, 2013. https://www.nytimes.com/2013/09/04/us/california -memorial-names-crashs-forgotten-victims.html.

Yamashita, Karen Tei. *I Hotel*. Coffee House Press, 2010.

———. *Through the Arc of the Rain Forest*. Coffee House Press, 1990.

———. *Tropic of Orange*. Coffee House Press, 1997.

Younis, Mohamed. "Four in 10 Americans Embrace Some Form of Socialism." *Gallup News*, May 20, 2019. https://news.gallup.com/poll/257639/four-americans -embrace-form-socialism.aspx.

Yuhas, Alan. "Philadelphia's Osage Avenue Police Bombing, 30 Years On: 'This Story Is a Parable.'" *Guardian*, May 13, 2015. https://www.theguardian.com/us-news/2015 /may/13/osage-avenue-bombing-philadelphia-30-years.

Zhao, Christina. "'Article 2' Trends after Trump Falsely Claims It Grants Him Unlimited Powers as President: I Can 'Do Whatever I Want.'" *Newsweek*, July 23, 2019. https://www.newsweek.com/article-2-trends-after-trump-falsely-claims-it -grants-him-unlimited-powers-president-i-can-do-1450798.

Zirin, Dave. "After Forty-Four Years, It's Time Brent Musburger Apologized to John Carlos and Tommie Smith," *The Nation*, June 4, 2012. https://www.thenation.com /article/archive/after-forty-four-years-its-time-brent-musburger-apologized-john -carlos-and-tommie-smith/.

———. "DeMaurice Smith: In an NFL Lockdown and Inspiration from Egypt." *The Nation*, February 14, 2011. https://www.thenation.com/article/archive /demaurice-smith-nfl-lockout-and-inspiration-egypt/.

———. "Why Michael Bennett Walked Away from the NFL's Israel Delegation." *The Nation*, February 13, 2017. https://www.thenation.com/article/archive/why -michael-bennett-walked-away-from-the-nfls-israel-delegation/.

Zolberg, Aristide. "Moments of Madness." *Politics and Society* 2, no. 2 (1972): 183–207.

INDEX

ABOUT THE AUTHOR

David Palumbo-Liu is the Louise Hewlett Nixon Professor, and Professor of Comparative Literature, at Stanford University. He is also the founding editor of *Occasion: Interdisciplinary Studies in the Humanities*, and writes for *Truthout*'s Public Intellectual Project. His work has also appeared in the *Washington Post*, the *Nation*, the *Guardian*, *Jacobin*, *Salon*, *Al Jazeera*, *The Hill*, *Buzzfeed*, *Vox*, and other venues.

ABOUT HAYMARKET BOOKS

Haymarket Books is a radical, independent, nonprofit book publisher based in Chicago.

Our mission is to publish books that contribute to struggles for social and economic justice. We strive to make our books a vibrant and organic part of social movements and the education and development of a critical, engaged, international left.

We take inspiration and courage from our namesakes, the Haymarket martyrs, who gave their lives fighting for a better world. Their 1886 struggle for the eight-hour day—which gave us May Day, the international workers' holiday—reminds workers around the world that ordinary people can organize and struggle for their own liberation. These struggles continue today across the globe—struggles against oppression, exploitation, poverty, and war.

Since our founding in 2001, Haymarket Books has published more than five hundred titles. Radically independent, we seek to drive a wedge into the risk-averse world of corporate book publishing. Our authors include Noam Chomsky, Arundhati Roy, Rebecca Solnit, Angela Y. Davis, Howard Zinn, Amy Goodman, Wallace Shawn, Mike Davis, Winona LaDuke, Ilan Pappé, Richard Wolff, Dave Zirin, Keeanga-Yamahtta Taylor, Nick Turse, Dahr Jamail, David Barsamian, Elizabeth Laird, Amira Hass, Mark Steel, Avi Lewis, Naomi Klein, and Neil Davidson. We are also the trade publishers of the acclaimed Historical Materialism Book Series and of Dispatch Books.